AF709755

The Wisdom of Henry Hazlitt

The Foundation for Economic Education, Inc.
Irvington-on-Hudson, New York 10533

Published March 1993
ISBN 910614-83-0
Copyright © by
The Foundation for Economic Education, Inc.

TABLE OF CONTENTS

INTRODUCTION

Introduction

It was in 1954 that I first met Henry Hazlitt. I was a young instructor at Iona College in New Rochelle, New York, lecturing on the principles of economics and conducting a seminar in German conversation. In both my assignments I relied heavily on FEE publications which I distributed in large quantities to my students, such as *Clipping of Note* and small pamphlets called *In Brief.* In my language colloquium I spoke of German philosophers and economists and frequently referred to Ludwig von Mises' *Omnipotent Government,* which FEE made available at bargain prices. When, upon Leonard Read's invitation, I attended the fall Board meeting and reported about my use of FEE material, Henry Hazlitt questioned me with great interest and insight. He was a senior member of the Board having participated in the very inception of FEE. In the world of the written word he was the renowned associate of *Newsweek* and the columnist of "Business Tides."

I watched with awe and admiration how Henry Hazlitt, in the years that followed, never failed to find eloquent words and lucid composition to dwell upon economic subjects. He, more than any other English writer I knew, wrote as the common people speak, but thought as wise men do. Proper writing, to Mr. Hazlitt, was but a different name for lucid conversation. His guide was truth which made him write powerfully, naturally, and convincingly. He wrote until he was four-score-and-ten because he liked to write and liked himself better when he did.

The spoken word soon perishes; the written word remains; it may survive for many decades or even centuries. Henry Hazlitt's writing may point the way for generations to come. Of all that he wrote, he wrote most candidly and forcefully for *The Freeman.* After all, he was instrumental in the rebirth of the journal after World War II. He had read it with great interest ever since it made its first appearance in 1920, edited by Albert Jay Nock, the great libertarian journalist. It had folded, as most new periodicals do, a few years later; re-emerged under the editorship of Suzanne LaFollette in 1929, and perished again during the Great Depression in 1931; reappeared in 1938 and folded again during World War II. In 1950, Henry Hazlitt together with Suzanne LaFollette and John Chamberlain revived *The Freeman* again like the Phoenix of Egyptian mythology, lifting it renewed from the ashes to start another long life. When it again ran into economic turbulence, they steered it to Leonard Read's Foundation which became its sole owner in 1954 and its publisher in 1956. With FEE as the permanent base, *The Freeman* was to soar to new heights.

Henry Hazlitt's name is forever carved in the annals of *The Freeman*. He served it as co-editor and then editor-in-chief from 1950 to 1954; when it joined the Foundation, he became its most illustrious and industrious contributor. He penned sixty major essays and articles as well as dozens of book reviews. All along, he wrote immortal books which are the full-length mirrors of his active mind.

He was still an editorial writer for the *New York Times* when he wrote his most popular and influential book, *Economics in One Lesson*. Since its first printing in 1946 it sold more than one million copies in numerous editions and continues to sell at a rate of several thousand a year. It is probably the best "little book" on the fallacies of popular economic notions and policies ever written.

One source of the numerous fallacies which haunt economics, according to Hazlitt, is the endless pleadings of self-interest. Every economic group has interests which are antagonistic to those of all other groups. Many of these groups argue plausibly and persistently for special policies which benefit them at the expense of all other groups. They either convince the public that the special policies are sound, or so befuddle it that confusion prevails.

Another source of the countless fallacies which plague economics more than any other field of knowledge is the persistent tendency to see only the immediate, short-run effects of a policy and ignore its long-run effects. Henry Hazlitt was convinced that this inclination is an important difference between good economics and bad.

Economics in One Lesson explodes both fallacies. From automation and unemployment to rent control and price fixing, it confronts and refutes them all. Based on classical economic principles, the book was hailed around the world as the best "lesson" in economics for anyone who seeks truthful answers to the burning economic issues of our time.

Despite the popularity of *Economics in One Lesson* the search for economic truth was becoming increasingly difficult because two important groups, professional economists and economic policymakers, were falling under the influence of John Maynard Keynes. The politicians were persuaded by his simple explanation of the Great Depression, laying all blame on businessmen, in particular their "failure to invest." Many economists were dazzled with a whole new holistic, nationalistic vocabulary: "aggregate demand," "national income," "gross national product," etc. His counsel was as easy to understand by economists as it was enticing to policymakers: proceed with the most pleasant of all political activities, government spending, and run budgetary deficits as long as there is stagnation and unemployment.

Henry Hazlitt demolished the whole Keynesian structure in his *The Failure of the "New Economics": An Analysis of the Keynesian Fallacies* (1959) and his *The Critics of Keynesian Economics* (1960). He exploded one pillar after another, cutting the ground from under all its notions and doctrines. Above all, he laid bare the autocratic nature of Keynes, his ominous call for political force and coercion. Lord Keynes, according to Hazlitt, was the Karl Marx of the twentieth century, a demagogue who sought popularity by pleasing the holders of political power and denouncing the money lenders. In the Keynesian system, the money lender replaced the capitalist of the Marxian system as the villain.

Faulty economic doctrines may give rise to erroneous moral condemnation. Although morality is of a fixed nature, eternal and immutable, popular notions of morals may differ from the given principles carried to dubious conclusions and misguided by popular economic doctrines. Where the Marxian doctrine of labor exploitation holds sway, the capitalist is not only an exploiter of labor but also a wretched evil-hearted monster who feasts on the sweat and blood of innocent victims. In countries where Keynesian thought is taught on every level of education, the consumer is a great social benefactor, the saver and investor a greedy egotist deserving public censure and rejection.

Henry Hazlitt saw the urgent need of a thorough discussion of systems of ethics resting on faulty economic doctrines. In 1964, at the age of 70, he wrote *The Foundations of Morality,* building on the foundation laid by David Hume, Jeremy Bentham, Immanuel Kant, George Santayana, and his good friend, Ludwig von Mises. In the Hazlitt system of refined utilitarianism, benevolence, social cooperation, egoism, and altruism create a viable community. Hazlitt is at his best when he discusses the ethics of a capitalist country. His conclusion is a powerful brief in defense of the private property order.

The system of capitalism, according to Hazlitt, assures freedom, justice, and productivity. In all these respects it is infinitely superior to socialism, communism, and fascism. But these three virtues are inseparable. Each builds on the other. Only when men are free can they choose between right and wrong. Only when they are free to earn and keep the fruits of their labor do they feel treated justly. When they understand that their reward depends on their own activity they have greater incentive to maximize their efforts, and all have an incentive to cooperate in helping each other. Justice builds on the freedom it insures; economic productivity grows out of the justice of the rewards it provides.

Freedom, justice, and productivity differ diametrically from the principles which guide the welfare state. Mr. Hazlitt explained and elucidated the difference in his 1970 book, *Man vs. The Welfare State,* which is a masterly study of the absurdity of transfer policies. He is at his best when he punctures the welfare pretensions with a single telling thrust. What politicians like to call "the public sector," to Henry Hazlitt actually is the "coercive sector"; to him, the private sector is the "voluntary sector." In the welfare-transfer state, nobody pays for his or her education, medical care, retirement, etc.; but everybody is forced to pay for everyone else's education, medical care, and retirement. Everyone has to live at the expense of everyone else; the effect of such a system on individual incentives is obvious.

Henry Hazlitt was 90 years old when he, together with his wife Frances, published a small collection of passages from the great writings of the Roman Stoics. It undoubtedly sheds some light on the Hazlitt thought and conduct at their particular stage of life. Old age has a great sense of calm and riches. But it also brings aches and pains, and every little illness is thought to be the beginning of the end. Yet, a man of 90 is a great comfort to all his elderly friends for he is the vanguard in front of the line. His friends of 60 and 70 are convinced that the enemy must reach him first before he will reach their lines.

At the age of 90, many an individual finds his way to Stoic answers to the calamities of life. Suffering bodily frailties and ailments and encountering misfortune, they seek consolation in natural austerity and divine power. They convince themselves that suffering is merely a divine instrument of training designed to strengthen their power and stress the unimportance of the external conditions. It is this idea of virtue by experience and exercise which is distinctly Stoic.

The Wisdom of the Stoics (Lanham, Md.: University Press of America, Inc., 1984) presents selections from the Roman philosophers Seneca, Epictetus, and Marcus Aurelius. The Hazlitt introduction as well as the selection itself point at the Hazlitt philosophy which is both critical and laudatory of the Stoic position. Appealing to the noblest among the ancients, and holding that appeal for more than two thousand years, it is one of the permanent philosophies of life. In fact, the Hazlitts were convinced that it is still an indispensable element in any rational philosophy. For all men must eventually die; and before that we are bound to experience the loss of loved ones. And no matter how prudently or wisely we try to manage our lives, we at some time suffer disappointment, hardship, accident, defeat, ingratitude, rejection, affronts, humiliation, pain, and even periods of agony. We need patience—the companion of wisdom, endurance—for what can't be cured must be endured, and fortitude—which conquers all things. These are the great virtues that the Stoic philosophy teaches and inculcates. When the Hazlitts needed these virtues most, they liked to turn to the calm wisdom of Seneca, the stern admonishments of Epictetus, or the lofty serenity of Marcus Aurelius to renew their own courage and strength.

Stoicism bore abundant fruit in the lives and teachings of many Romans. The earnestness of the national character during the Roman republic was receptive to the Stoic doctrine which became the philosophy of many great men. But it did not become the creed of Frances and Henry Hazlitt who were too knowledgeable of the history of philosophy to be swayed by the Stoic world of thought. To them, Stoicism gives far too grim an impression of the bulk of the writings of the Stoics whose advice on the conduct of life does not differ widely from that given to this day by many non-Stoic philosophers. Henry Hazlitt is keenly aware of a glaring contradiction in the Stoic system: if it is true that happiness as ordinarily understood is not necessary, and pain is no evil, what is the point in morality or in any human striving whatever?

To Henry Hazlitt, happiness is to be desired and pain is in itself an evil. The end of human action, indeed, the only right and proper and universally desirable end, is the greatest happiness of all. Human life is a wonderful mystery in which he loved to lose himself, a mystery of infinite space and infinite time. But these mysteries do not obscure the validity and truth of the inexorable principles by which man is destined to live.

—Hans F. Sennholz

TRIBUTES

1

A Man for Many Seasons

Bettina Bien Greaves

Henry Hazlitt, author, journalist, editor, reviewer, economist, has written or edited 18 books and countless articles, columns, editorials, and book reviews. He has gained renown in at least three areas: as a popularizer of sound economic thinking, as a critic of John Maynard Keynes, and as a contributor to moral philosophy. His *Economics in One Lesson* (1946), a long-time best seller, is one of the finest introductions there is to sound economics. His critique of Keynes, *The Failure of the "New Economics"* (1959), and his explanation of moral philosophy, *The Foundations of Morality* (1964), are valuable contributions to knowledge and understanding, to economic theory and the principles of social cooperation. Henry Hazlitt is a man for many seasons. His writings will live for generations.

Early Childhood and Youth

Henry Stuart Hazlitt was born in Philadelphia on November 28, 1894, the son of Stuart Clark Hazlitt and Bertha (Zauner) Hazlitt. His father died when Henry was a baby. His first years in school were spent at Girard College, a school in Philadelphia for poor, fatherless boys.

When Henry was 9, his mother remarried and their fortunes revived. The family moved to Brooklyn, New York, and it was there, at Public School 11 and Boys' High School, that Henry received most of his formal education.

Henry has apparently always had a gift for writing. His high school English teacher recognized his talent and appointed him "chief critic" of his fellow students' test papers. This was "not an entirely

November 28, 1992 marked the 98th birthday of the noted author and economist Henry Hazlitt who has served with great distinction as a Trustee of The Foundation for Economic Education since FEE was founded in 1946, and whose personal papers and library are now housed at FEE. To mark his 95th birthday in 1989, Bettina Bien Greaves, a member of the Senior Staff of FEE and long-time admirer of Hazlitt, wrote this essay.

gratifying distinction,"* Henry wrote later, for it did not endear him to his classmates.

When Henry finished high school, he entered New York City's free-tuition City College of New York (CCNY), but was forced to drop out after a few months. His stepfather had died and he had to support his widowed mother.

An inexperienced high school graduate wasn't worth much on the job market. The only work for which Henry was then qualified was as an office boy at $5 a week. He was fired from his first job after only two days. But that didn't faze him. He simply went out and got another job.

At that time there were no legal obstacles to hiring and firing—no minimum wage with which an employer had to comply, no Social Security or unemployment taxes to pay, no income taxes to withhold, no restrictions on hours or working conditions. Any would-be employer could hire anyone who wanted to work. If the arrangement didn't work out, the employer could let the employee go without penalty. Or the employee could leave, confident that he could easily find other employment.

Henry had a succession of jobs at $5 per week. When he learned that secretaries could earn $15 per week, he determined to learn shorthand and typing. For several weeks he attended a secretarial school. With his newly acquired skills, he could command $10 to $12 per week. But again none of his jobs lasted very long—he hadn't yet found his niche. Finally he decided he wanted to be a newspaper reporter. He applied for a job and was hired by *The Wall Street Journal.*

The Journal at that time was much smaller than it is now, and it reported primarily Wall Street news. Hazlitt's bosses at *The Journal* dictated editorials to him on the typewriter and reporters called in their stories to him over the phone. Gradually he learned through on-the-job training.

Although he still knew very little about economics or the market, he was assigned to be the reporter in charge of following a half dozen small companies. When he attended one annual meeting, he learned how very little he knew. The management voted unexpectedly to "pass" its dividend, that is to pass over or to omit it. Hazlitt assumed

*Phrases within quotation marks attributed to Hazlitt are taken either from his autobiographical notes or from transcripts of interviews with him.

"passing" a dividend meant "approving" the dividend. Fortunately for him, however, when he turned in his report he used their term; he said the dividend had been "passed." His on-the-job training proceeded apace; he promptly learned the investment definition of that word, and no one was the wiser.

The Journal at that time had a "By-the-Way" column, composed of brief quips about current events. Members of the staff were encouraged to submit entries anonymously. To collect payment if an entry was used (75 cents per published entry), the author turned in the carbon copy of his entry. With Henry's gift for expression, he soon became a persistent contributor and in time almost doubled his income with what he received for his short, clever "By-the-Way" paragraphs.

Hazlitt's Do-It-Yourself Education

Henry Hazlitt was energetic, ambitious, and industrious. On-the-job training wasn't enough for him. He was determined to get the education he had missed when he had to drop out of college. So he started his own reading program. He read about Shakespeare and the Marlowe controversy. He learned about evolution and the role of the state by reading Herbert Spencer. He began to read about economics and the stock market. In time, the depth and breadth of his reading gave him a broad liberal arts education. A book titled *The Work of Wall Street* made him realize the importance of economics and philosophical reasoning. From then on he read with a purpose—concentrating on economics. He read a couple of college texts. Although he lacked sophistication in economics, his natural good sense warned him to be on guard against socialist ideas.

One book he ran across while browsing in a library, *The Common Sense of Political Economy* (1910) by Philip H. Wicksteed, a British Unitarian minister, had a profound influence on him. Wicksteed had become acquainted with the Austrian School of Economics, the first school of economics to recognize that "value" is subjective and that market prices stem from the subjective values of individuals. This insight helped to shape Hazlitt's intellectual development and led him to a firm understanding of market operations and the marginal utility theory of economics.

In addition to reading, young Henry also devoted some time every day to writing. He set out to write a book on a very ambitious subject, *Thinking as a Science,* and before many months had passed, it was finished. He submitted the book to five publishers, received five rejections, and got discouraged. Then a friend urged him to send it out once more. He did—and this time it was accepted by the well-known firm of E. P. Dutton & Co. In 1916, at the age of 22, Henry Hazlitt became a published author.

In 1916, Hazlitt left *The Wall Street Journal* and moved to the *New York Evening Post,* where he put his Wall Street experience to use writing "Wall Street Paragraphs." He was working at the *Post* in 1917 when the United States entered World War I.

World War I

Henry wanted to volunteer, as some of his friends were doing, but he couldn't afford to do so. The Army paid only $30 per month, not enough for him to support his mother. Then the Air Force announced that it was offering enlistees $100 per month. Henry volunteered, only to discover that, in spite of their published offer, the Air Force paid enlistees no more than the Army did. But once in the Air Force, he couldn't get out. Henry's mother had a rough time financially while he was away.

The Air Force sent Henry to Texas, to Princeton for ground school studies, and then back to Texas for flying instruction; he didn't get overseas. Hazlitt was still in Texas when the war ended.

A few days after the Armistice was signed, the *New York Evening Post* wired Hazlitt that his successor in writing "Wall Street Paragraphs" was leaving. He could have his old job back if he could be there in five days. Hazlitt took off almost immediately for New York by train, went directly to the office, suitcase in hand, and worked in uniform his first day back on the job.

Hazlitt soon returned to his old regimen of reading and writing for his own education and edification. Before long he had written a second book, *The Way to Will Power,* published in 1922. At that time, *Who's Who* had a policy of automatically listing any author who had had two books published by reputable firms. So at 28, Henry was a two-time author and his name appeared in *Who's Who.*

Benjamin M. Anderson

After Hazlitt returned from the Air Force, he continued his pursuit of economic understanding. Among other books on monetary theory, he read Benjamin M. Anderson's *The Value of Money* (1917). Hazlitt considered that book "profound and original" and he learned a great deal from it. Anderson, then teaching at Harvard, later became economist with the Bank of Commerce and then with the Chase National Bank. When Hazlitt was financial editor for the *New York Evening Mail* (1921–1923), he occasionally interviewed Anderson in connection with articles he was writing, and the two men soon became friends. Hazlitt wrote the foreword to Anderson's important work, *Economics and the Public Welfare: Financial and Economic History of the United States, 1914–1946* (1949).

In *The Value of Money,* Anderson had reviewed a large number of writers, American and foreign, most of them rather critically, on the subject of money. But when he came to the Austrian economist Ludwig von Mises, he wrote that he found in his work "very noteworthy clarity and power. His *Theorie des Geldes und der Umlaufsmittel* [later translated into English as *The Theory of Money and Credit*] is an exceptionally excellent book." This was the first time Hazlitt had heard of Mises, but he remembered his name and Anderson's comment. Years later when Mises' works became available in English, Hazlitt made it a point to read them.

A Career of Reading and Writing

Throughout his life, Henry Hazlitt has spent most of his time at the typewriter and with books. From age 20, he wrote something almost every day—news items, editorials, reviews, articles, columns. By his 70th birthday, he figured he must have written "in total some 10,000 editorials, articles, and columns; some 10,000,000 words! And in print! The verbal equivalent of about 150 average-length books." Hazlitt has also written or edited 17 books. (See the list at the end of this article.) His early works were literary and philosophical, his later books largely economic.

After leaving *The Wall Street Journal,* Hazlitt worked in various capacities—as economic commentator, financial editor, book reviewer, editorial writer, literary editor, columnist, and editor—for five different newspapers including *The New York Times* (1934–1946), a monthly financial letter, and three magazines, including *Newsweek* (1946–1966) for which he wrote the "Business Tides" column. In 1950, while still writing for *Newsweek,* Hazlitt and John Chamberlain became editors of the newly founded biweekly magazine, *The Freeman,* predecessor of this journal. (See the note at the end of this article for a list of the publications with which Hazlitt has been associated.) After he left *Newsweek* in 1966, he became an internationally syndicated columnist.

Hazlitt's reading and studying over the years to satisfy his own intellectual curiosity spanned a broad spectrum of subjects. His vast reading, especially when he was a literary editor and book reviewer, is evident in *The Anatomy of Criticism* (1933), in which he discussed the critic's role, the influence of the critic on the public, and the influence of the times on the critic. Hazlitt's prodigious reading and prolific writing throughout these years were preparing him for the important contributions he was to make to the understanding of economic theory and social cooperation.

As a result of Hazlitt's various assignments writing about financial and stock market news, his interests had been gradually directed toward business and economics. He read many books on economics, and he became knowledgeable as an economist. But he did not write a book on the subject until 1946.

The New York Times

As a patriotic gesture, *The New York Times* had made a promise not to fire anyone during the Depression. This proved a very costly promise to keep. It meant for one thing that *The Times* did no hiring for a couple of years. By 1934 they were in dire need of someone who knew economics. Thus, in the midst of the Depression, Hazlitt was hired by *The Times* as an editorial writer.

The Times was then being run by Arthur Sulzberger, son-in-law of the fairly "conservative" publisher and controlling owner, Adolph S. Ochs. Management seldom interfered with Hazlitt's editorials, although Ochs' daughter, Mrs. Sulzberger, would occasionally call Hazlitt and suggest some "leftist" idea. Hazlitt would explain, "The trouble with that, Mrs. Sulzberger, is . . ." She would reply, "Well, you know best." Thus, *The Times* pretty much published what Hazlitt wrote—at least until 1944. More about this later.

Mises and Hayek

Hazlitt is proud of his role in helping to introduce two economic giants to readers in this country—Ludwig von Mises, leading spokesman for the Austrian school of economics for many years, and Friedrich A. Hayek, also an Austrian economist, Mises' protegé, and Nobel Prize Laureate in 1974.

As mentioned above, Hazlitt first heard of Mises through Benjamin Anderson's *The Value of Money*. Years later when Hazlitt came across Mises' *Socialism,* he reviewed it in *The New York Times*. His review appeared in the January 9, 1938, Book Review Section: "[T]his book must rank as the most devastating analysis of socialism yet penned. Doubtless even some anti-Socialist readers will feel that he occasionally overstates his case. On the other hand, even confirmed Socialists will not be able to withhold admiration from the masterly fashion in which he conducts his argument. He has written an economic classic in our time."

Mises was then living and teaching in Switzerland. As a courtesy, Hazlitt mailed a copy of his review to the author and the two men exchanged a couple of brief letters. Two years later Mises came to the United States to escape the strife of World War II. Hazlitt was one of Mises' few contacts in this country and Mises telephoned him. To Hazlitt, Mises was a "classic," an author from a previous era. Mises' call, Hazlitt recalled later, was almost as much of a surprise as if he had heard from such a legendary economic figure as Adam Smith or John Stuart Mill.

In 1944, Hazlitt reviewed F. A. Hayek's *The Road to Serfdom* in *The New York Times*. As a young man in his native Austria, Hayek had come to know Nazism firsthand. In England where he was living and teaching just before the start of World War II, he observed the same interventionist trends that he had seen on the Continent. In 1944, in a devastating critique of Nazism, *The Road to Serfdom,* he warned the British that they were heading down the same path.

The book stunned academia and the political world. Hazlitt's review, featured on page one of *The Times*' Book Review Section (September 24, 1944), compared Hayek's *The Road to Serfdom* to John Stuart Mill's *On Liberty*. Hazlitt described it as "one of the most important books of our generation." The University of Chicago Press had printed only 3,000 copies, and when the book made the best-seller list the publisher's stock was soon exhausted, and they had to begin reprinting right away.

Bretton Woods

When John Maynard Keynes' scheme for the International Monetary Fund and the International Bank for Reconstruction and Development (World Bank) was under discussion in Bretton Woods, New Hampshire, *The Times* offered to send Hazlitt to the conference. But Hazlitt saw no reason to go. He was opposed to the discussions. He said he could learn more by reading about them than he could by going there and talking with participants. Besides, if he stayed in New York he could also write editorials on other subjects. So he didn't go.

While editorial opinion across the nation was largely favorable to the Bretton Woods discussions, Hazlitt was criticizing them. His editorials were the only "sour note." When it was announced that 43 governments had signed the "marvelous" Bretton Woods Agreement, Sulzberger called Hazlitt to his office. "Now, Henry, when 43 governments sign an agreement, I don't see how *The Times* can any longer combat this."

"All right," Hazlitt said. "But in that case I can't write anything further about Bretton Woods. It is an inflationist scheme that will end badly and I can't support it." After that Hazlitt wrote no more editorials on the subject for *The Times*. However, Hazlitt was also writing a Monday column for the paper's financial page, and there he continued to criticize Bretton Woods. At that point, Sulzberger suggested he might include a line at the end of Hazlitt's Monday column: "The opinions of Mr. Hazlitt are not necessarily those of *The New York Times*."

"You can do that, Mr. Sulzberger. But," Hazlitt warned, "one consequence of such a disclaimer will be that, if you don't print a similar line on other columns, the assumption will be that they are necessarily in agreement with the views of the editor of *The Times*." Sulzberger understood Hazlitt's reasoning and dropped the idea.

Economics in One Lesson

For some time Hazlitt had been mulling over the possibility of writing a "little book" on the fallacies of short-run economic interests. He discussed the idea with Mises, by then a close friend. He also told Harper's editor for economics books about his idea. The editor offered to publish the book when it was written. *The New York Times,* for which Hazlitt was still working as an editorial writer, agreed to give him every other day off without pay to write the book. *Economics in One Lesson* was the result.

To Hazlitt, writing that book "came so easily," he said later, "that I couldn't take it very seriously.... "[W]riting these chapters was almost like writing daily editorials.... It took ... about three months of alternate days off." On the in-between days he was thinking about the book. "That meant one and a half months of actual writing."

Reader's Digest published two excerpts before the book's publication, and the book promptly became a best seller. Hazlitt had suggested that the print run be increased to satisfy the additional demand anticipated from the *Reader's Digest* publicity. Yet the publisher printed only 3,000 copies. The first week the book was out it was fifteenth on the *New York Times* best-seller list for non-fiction; the second week it was fourteenth, and then the third week it was seventh, disappearing from the list altogether in ensuing weeks—there just were no more books to be sold. After some time, when it had been reprinted and was available once more, it began to sell again, although it didn't make the *Times* list again.

Writing *Economics in One Lesson* may have come easily to Hazlitt, but its impact has been enormous. It has been translated into eight languages. By 1977 it had sold 50,000 copies in hard cover, 700,000 in all editions, and it still sells at the rate of a few thousand per year, attracting new readers to economics with its delightful style and its simple explanations and illustrations of economic fallacies.

Economics in One Lesson is clearly Hazlitt's most popular book. It established him as an economic journalist *par excellence,* the modern counterpart of the Frenchman Frederic Bastiat (1801–1850), author of *The Law*. H. L. Mencken was quoted on the book jacket of the first edition as saying that Hazlitt was "the only competent critic of the arts ... who was at the same time a competent economist, of practical as well as theoretical training, . . . one of the few economists in human history who could really write." The book has introduced countless individuals to sound economic theory.

Harper & Brothers published the first 1946 hardcover edition of *Economics in One Lesson*. Harper arranged for later paperback editions, and kept the book in print until 1974. Then, without telling Hazlitt, it let the book go out of print and canceled the contract with the paperback publisher.

When Hazlitt learned this, he approached Harper and asked about reprinting in paperback. They hesitated but said, "If you bring it up to date, we'll publish a new edition in hardback." Hazlitt revised the book. Still "they dilly-dallied," Hazlitt said, and didn't publish it in either hardback or paperback. According to Hazlitt, "They *said* they didn't think it would sell in paper. Hazlitt believed their real objection must have been ideological, since the book had been selling several thousand paperback copies a year. In time Hazlitt obtained the rights to the book, and in 1979 Arlington House put out a paperback edition.

Hazlitt left *The Times* for *Newsweek* about the time *Economics in One Lesson* came out. In Hazlitt's view his situation was improved; his "Business Tides" columns in *Newsweek* would be signed; he would no longer be writing anonymously.

Critique of Keynes

Hazlitt had been impressed with John Maynard Keynes' *The Economic Consequences of the Peace* (1919) when it first came out. At that point, Hazlitt took everything Keynes said as "gospel." But in 1923, Hazlitt read Keynes' A *Tract on Monetary Reform*. By that time Hazlitt had done a fair amount of reading in monetary theory and could recognize economic errors when he read them. He was "appalled" by how "bad" a book it was and from that time on, Hazlitt "distrusted every statement Keynes made."

B. M. Anderson commented to Hazlitt later that when Keynes discussed the quantity theory of money in A *Tract on Monetary Reform*, "he even states *that* upside down." Which he did! The actual reason prices go up is that the government prints new money and distributes it to people who spend it. As the spenders compete for goods and services by bidding against other would-be spenders they make prices go up. Yet Keynes had said that when prices go up, the government must print more money to keep pace with the prices. The great German inflation was then raging (1923) and this was precisely what the German authorities were saying, that there was (as Hazlitt later paraphrased the Germans' position) "no real inflation because the present volume of currency . . . had actually a smaller purchasing power than the former volume of currency because the depreciation per unit was greater than the multiplication of units." Keynes agreed with the Germans "that it was necessary for them to keep printing marks to keep pace with the rising prices."

Whether Keynes' success was due to personal charisma, his prestigious positions with the British government, or to the "scientific" sanction his works gave politicians to do what they wanted to do anyway—that is to spend without taxing—is immaterial. The fact remains that from the 1930s on Keynes' influence was enormous. And through it all, Hazlitt continued to be amazed by Keynes' growing reputation.

In *Economics in One Lesson,* Hazlitt demolished various Keynesian programs in a rather low-key manner. Then in 1959, in *The Failure of the "New Economics,"* he critiqued Keynes' major work, *The General Theory of Employment, Interest, and Money* (1936) in detail, citing chapter and verse. *The Failure of the "New Economics"* (1959) is much more scholarly than *Economics in One Lesson,* its market narrower, but it is by no means less important.

To refute each Keynesian error, Hazlitt expounded sound economic theory in a way academia couldn't ignore. John Chamberlain, who reviewed the book in *The Freeman,* titled his review, "They'll Never Hear the End of It." The dean of the Department of Economics at a leading university questioned Hazlitt's credentials for critiquing the noted Keynes. Mises came to Hazlitt's defense. Hazlitt, Mises responded, was "one of the outstanding economists of our age," and his anti-Keynes book was "a devastating criticism of the Keynesian doctrines."

Moral Philosophy

Henry Hazlitt was a personal friend of Mises. But he was also a student of Mises in the sense that he carefully studied his work. He attended Mises' seminar at New York University quite regularly for several years. Although Hazlitt was himself an economist and author of note by then, he said about the Mises seminars that he always found that "no matter how many times I would go, no matter how often I heard in effect the same lectures, there would always be some sentence, some incidental phrase that threw more light on the subject."

One remark by Mises which impressed Hazlitt was that questions of morality and justice always refer to social cooperation. Hazlitt agreed. But he thought the statement needed elaboration. This was a subject close to Hazlitt's heart, for he had longed to write a book on ethics since he was a youngster.

As he pondered the subject he was struck by the insight of a statement by Jeremy Bentham (1748–1832): "Legislation is a circle with the same center as moral philosophy, but its circumference is smaller." This idea became the theme of Hazlitt's book on ethics, *The Foundations of Morality* (1964).

In this book, Hazlitt sought to unify law, ethics, morality, and manners, and to show their relation to social cooperation. Following Bentham, Hazlitt presented law, ethics (morality), and manners as three aspects of the same thing. "[B]oth manners and morals rest on the same underlying principle. That principle is *sympathy, kindness consideration for others*.... Manners are minor morals." Law, he maintained, might be called "minimum ethics" with "the same center as moral philosophy." Ethics and morality cover more territory than law; they have a "far wider sphere [than law].... Morality," he wrote, "certainly calls for active benevolence beyond that called for by the law."

In *The Foundations of Morality,* Hazlitt discussed the literature on ethics and morality throughout the ages. And he described the way ethical and moral principles had been put into practice. He pointed out that the moral codes of many religions are similar and consistent with peaceful social relations. Yet their differences, as well as the cruelty and suffering inflicted on men in the name of organized religion, raise doubts as to the reliability of religious faith as a guide to ethical conduct.

Thus, Hazlitt offers a utilitarian basis for morality. The moral philosopher, he writes should seek a "foundation" for morality that does not rest on a particular religion. "[I]t is not the function of the moral philosopher, as such," Hazlitt concludes, "to proclaim the truth of this religious faith or to try to maintain it. His function is, rather, to insist on the rational basis of all morality to point out that it does not need any supernatural assumptions, and to show that the rules of morality are or ought to be those rules of conduct that tend most to increase human cooperation, happiness and well-being in this our present life."

Summing Up

In the course of his career, Hazlitt met many of the great and near great. As has been mentioned, he knew the economist, B. M. Anderson. He knew H. L. Mencken personally, and it was Mencken who recommended that Hazlitt succeed him as editor of *American Mercury* in 1933. Hazlitt was a frequent guest on the radio, debating face-to-face such socialist luminaries as former Vice President Henry A. Wallace, the late Secretary of State Dean Acheson, former U. S. Senators Paul H. Douglas and Hubert Humphrey. He is a Founding Trustee of The Foundation for Economic Education. He was, of course, a close friend of Mises and Hayek, but he also knew well all of the important personages in the libertarian/conservative movement—Leonard E. Read, Isabel Paterson, Rose Wilder Lane, John Chamberlain, William F. Buckley, Ayn Rand, Lawrence Fertig, and others.

Over the years, Hazlitt perfected a clear and lucid writing style. Writing so many editorials and short columns disciplined him to express himself succinctly and simply. Even his most important and profound books are composed of short, easy-to-understand chapters. Everything he writes may be read with pleasure and profit.

Throughout his career, Hazlitt has been an advocate of a minority point of view. He has been a constant critic of government intervention, inflation, and the welfare state, and he wrote books attacking them. His anti-Keynes, anti-Bretton Woods editorials, first published in *The New York Times,* also appeared later as a book *(From Bretton Woods to World Inflation,* 1984).

Hazlitt has spoken out repeatedly and untiringly in behalf of the freedom philosophy, limited government, free markets, and private property. At a banquet in 1964, honoring him on his 70th birthday, he spoke of the freedom movement and his part in it:

> Those of us who place a high value on human liberty . . . find ourselves in a minority (and it sometimes seems a hopeless minority) in ideology. . . . We are the true adherents of lib-

erty. . . . We are the ones who believe in limited government, in the maximization of liberty for the individual and the minimization of coercion to the lowest point compatible with law and order. It is because we are true liberals that we believe in free trade, free markets, free enterprise, private property in the means of production; in brief, that we are for capitalism and against socialism. . . .

I will confess . . . that I have sometimes repeated myself. In fact, there may be some people unkind enough to say I haven't been saying anything new for 50 years!

And in a sense they would be right. . . . I've been preaching liberty as against coercion; I've been preaching capitalism as against socialism; and I've been preaching this doctrine in every form and with any excuse. And yet the world is enormously more socialized than when I began. . . .

Is this because the majority just won't listen to reason? I am enough of an optimist, and I have enough faith in human nature, to believe that people will listen to reason if they are convinced that it is reason. Somewhere, there must be some missing argument, something that we haven't seen clearly enough, or said clearly enough, or, perhaps, just not said often enough. A minority is in a very awkward position. The individuals in it can't afford to be just as good as the individuals in the majority. If they hope to convert the majority they have to be much better; and the smaller the minority, the better they have to be. They have to think better. They have to know more. They have to write better. They have to have better controversial manners. Above all, they have to have far more courage. And they have to be infinitely patient. . . .

Yet, in spite of this, I am hopeful. . . . [We are] still free to write unpopular opinion. . . . So I bring you this message: *Be of good heart; be of good spirit. If the battle is not yet won, it is not yet lost either.*

Henry Hazlitt's Journalistic Career

1913–1916—*The Wall Street Journal*
1916–1918—*New York Evening Post*
1919–1920—Mechanics & Metals National Bank (monthly financial letter)
1921–1923—*New York Evening Mail* (financial editor)
1923–1924—*New York Herald* (editorial writer)
1924–1925—*The Sun*
1925–1929—*The Sun* (literary editor)
1930–1933—*The Nation* (literary editor)
1933–1934—*American Mercury* (editor)
1934–1946—*The New York Times* (editorial staff)
1946–1966—*Newsweek* (associate & "Business Tides" columnist)
1950–1952—*The Freeman* (co-editor)
1952–1953—*The Freeman* (editor-in-chief)
1966–1969—Columnist for the international *Los Angeles Times Syndicate*

A Bibliographical Sketch

Thinking as a Science (New York: E. P. Dutton & Co., 1916; 2nd ed., Los Angeles: Nash Publishing Corp., 1969)

Thinking clearly and logically is the secret of learning, Hazlitt says. He offers the reader many ideas for developing his powers of thinking—by concentrating, talking, and keeping a notebook handy to jot down ideas. He recommends books on how to reason and think.

In Hazlitt's 1969 epilogue, he said if he were to revise the book he would further stress, among other things, the importance of language, perseverance, learning what has already been discovered, and writing. "Good writing is the twin," he wrote, "of good thinking. He who would learn to think should learn to write." Again he recommends books.

The Way to Will Power (New York: E. P. Dutton & Co., 1922)

After asserting that there is no such *thing* as the "will," young Hazlitt proceeds to offer a sensible guide for developing "will power"—by choosing worthy goals, aiming at them with determination, and developing good study and work habits.

A Practical Program for America, ed. by Henry Hazlitt (New York: Harcourt, Brace & Co., 1932)

When this book was published, the economy was in the midst of depression and Franklin Delano Roosevelt was governor of New York and had not yet run for President. Hazlitt was then editor of *The Nation,* from which these essays were taken. Except for Hazlitt, the authors were all looking for ways to improve the economy by amending national legislation. Hazlitt advocates free trade and recommends the repeal of all barriers to trade.

The Anatomy of Criticism (New York: Simon & Schuster, 1933)

Written at a time when Hazlitt was doing many book reviews, this book presents his philosophy of criticism. The discussants in a trialogue, a three-sided conversation, present their rationales for criticizing books, novels, poetry, paintings, sculpture, and the like. After discussing the relative merits of seeking objective standards, or relying exclusively on a critic's subjective values, the discussants recognize that certain standards evolve on the basis of tradition, public opinion, ideas, ethical and moral views, and so on.

A New Constitution Now (New York: Whittlesey House/ McGraw-Hill Book Co., 1942; 2nd ed., revised, New Rochelle, N.Y.: Arlington House, 1974)

Hazlitt deplores our constitutional checks and balances that divide power and authority and make it difficult to assign responsibility. He prefers a parliamentary form of government with executive and legislative powers combined more or less as in the British cabinet system, not fully developed until well after our Constitution was written. With no fixed period of office in a parliamentary form of government, the people may throw the "ins" out if they are dissatisfied. Hazlitt suggests various changes in the franchise, the make-up of Congress and the Supreme Court, methods for amending the Constitution, and so on. He quotes John Stuart Mill, Walter Bagehot, James Bryce, and other thinkers.

In 1974, when Hazlitt revised this book, he dropped some of the minor reforms he had suggested in order to concentrate on his advocacy of a parliamentary form of government. With a parliamentary form of government, popular disaffection with an administration at any time would require it to face the electorate promptly. Then if the voters expressed a lack of confidence, that administration would fall and have to relinquish control. Hazlitt contends that this would have saved us the "nightmare" of Watergate and Richard Nixon's near-impeachment. Control would have passed from Nixon's hands without a serious crisis. Whether or not one agrees with Hazlitt, his views are worth studying.

Economics in One Lesson (New York: Harper & Brothers, 1946; Pocket Books, 1948; special edition for The Foundation for Economic Education, 1952; revised and updated paperback, New York: MacFadden-Bartell Corp., 1962; Westport, Conn.: Arlington House, 1979)

An economic "classic." The role of an economist, Hazlitt says, is to consider not only the consequences of an action that are "seen," but also its "unseen" consequences. Hazlitt proceeds to analyze the "unseen" consequences of various government programs such as legally-fixed minimum wage rates, price controls, government spending, and the like.

Will Dollars Save the World? (Irvington-on-Hudson, N.Y.: The Foundation for Economic Education, 1947)

After World War II, when the productive machinery of the warring nations was in a shambles, the world clamored for U.S. grants and loans. But, Hazlitt points out, the harm had been done not only by enemy bombing but also by inflation and economic controls. Hazlitt gives 17 reasons why Marshall Plan dollars will not save the world.

To restore production, radical policy changes must be made to repeal government interventions. "The supreme irony is that the only country in the world today that is really producing anything—and for whose goods the rest of the world is therefore clamoring—is almost the only country that does not have government production 'targets,' but merely turns out goods in the volumes and proportions determined by supply and demand, free prices and free profits." (p. 53) Hazlitt outlines a positive program to restore production in the devastated countries.

The Great Idea (New York: Appleton-Century-Crofts, 1951; rev. ed., published as *Time Will Run Back: A Novel About the Rediscovery of Capitalism,* New Rochelle, N.Y.: Arlington House, 1966; Lanham, Md.: University Press of America, Inc., 1986)

A fictional account set in the future when the entire world is under a single Communist dictator. His only son, Peter, heir to the dictatorship, had been raised by his mother who opposed Communism. When Peter's father dies and he takes over, he encounters problems due to central planning. Conservatives in the Politburo oppose changes. But with the support and advice of one sympathetic Politburo member, he succeeds in introducing private property, free market prices, competition, and freedom of opportunity. Step-by-step they dismantle the controls. Fighting erupts between the two factions and there is a mild love story. A delightful way to learn some economics. The ending of the 2nd edition is modified slightly to make it somewhat more optimistic.

The Free Man's Library (Princeton, N.J.: D. Van Nostrand Co., 1956)

An annotated bibliography of books that Hazlitt recommends to gain an understanding of the philosophy of the free market, limited government, private property system.

The Failure of the "New Economics": An Analysis of the Keynesian Fallacies (Princeton, N.J.: D. Van Nostrand Co., 1959; Lanham, Md.: University Press of America, Inc., 1983)

John Maynard Keynes' *The General Theory of Employment, Interest and Money* (1936) became the "gospel" on which practically all post-depression economic instruction has been based. Yet even Keynes' followers found it "a badly written book, poorly organized . . . not well suited for classroom use." (Paul Samuelson, quoted by Hazlitt, p. 2.) Moreover, when Hazlitt analyzed it, he was "unable to find in it a single important doctrine that is both true and original. What is original in the book is not true; and what is true is not original." (p. 6) Nevertheless the book has had a tremendous influence. Hazlitt, therefore, proceeded to do something that had never been done before, to critique the Keynes book, chapter by chapter, on the basis of subjective, marginal utility (Austrian) economic theory.

The Critics of Keynesian Economics, ed. by Henry Hazlitt. (Princeton, N.J.: D. Van Nostrand Co., 1960; Lanham, Md.: University Press of America, Inc., 1984)

In the course of writing *The Failure of the "New Economics,"* Hazlitt encountered several noteworthy articles that criticized Keynes' ideas.

This anthology of the best of those includes essays by such well-known economists as B. M. Anderson, Arthur F. Burns, F. A. Hayek, W. H. Hutt, Frank H. Knight, and Ludwig von Mises. As if to underline Keynes' lack of originality, two papers by pre-Keynes critics—Jean Baptiste Say (1767–1832) and John Stuart Mill (1806–1873) are included.

What You Should Know About Inflation (Princeton, N.J.: D. Van Nostrand Co., 1960; 2nd ed., with statistics and tables updated to 1964, D. Van Nostrand Co., 1965)

Hazlitt defines inflation as an "increase in the supply of money and credit." (p. 1) A general increase in prices, he says, is "made possible . . . only by an increased supply of money." (p. 6) To dramatize the unreliability of governments to "manage" money and maintain its value, Hazlitt quotes 12 denials by Chancellor of the Exchequer Sir Stafford Cripps that the British government would devalue the pound (pp. 22–24), denials made during the 20 months immediately prior to the British government's September 18, 1949, devaluation. Hazlitt then proceeds to attack one inflationist fallacy after another.

The Foundations of Morality (Princeton, N.J.: D. Van Nostrand Co., 1964; 2nd ed., Los Angeles: Nash Publishing, 1972)

"[M]orality is older," Hazlitt says, "than any living religion and probably older than all religion." (p. 352) The role of the moral philosopher, therefore, is not to proclaim or maintain any particular religious faith. "His function is rather, to insist on the rational basis of all morality." (p. 353)

Hazlitt sees a common denominator in law, morals (ethics), and manners. Manners are "minor morals"; they rest on the same principles as do morals or ethics—*sympathy, kindness, consideration of others.* (p. 75) Law is a "minimum ethics," a circle with the same center as moral philosophy. (p. 69)

Hazlitt covers a great deal of material in this book. He reviews the classical literature on morality and ethics, and examines the teachings of the various religions. He discusses social cooperation and the need for general rules. The moral philosophy he sets forth is "utilitarian . . . [i]n the sense that all rules of conduct must be judged by their tendency to lead to desirable rather than undesirable social results." (p. xii)

Man vs. the Welfare State (New Rochelle, N.Y.: Arlington House, 1969; Lanham, Md.: University Press of America, Inc., 1983)

The welfare state encompasses a mix of popular government interventions. In this book Hazlitt analyzes many of them—government spending, social security, progressive taxation, foreign aid, price controls, negative income taxes, planning, guaranteed employment—and he describes their devastating effects on incentives, savings, investment, and production.

As a warning of what can happen, he points to Uruguay, a "welfare state gone wild." He writes also of Herbert Spencer's prescient warning of "the coming slavery" (1884) due to Britain's incipient government intervention. In his final chapter, "What We Can Do About It," he recommends among other things that persons on relief be denied the vote so long as they remain on relief.

The Conquest of Poverty (New Rochelle, N.Y.: Arlington House, 1973; Lanham, Md.: University Press of America, Inc., 1986)

"The history of poverty is almost the history of mankind.... [U]ntil about the middle of the eighteenth century, mass poverty was nearly everywhere the normal condition of man." (pp. 13, 178) Attempts to alleviate poverty by government welfare and poor relief failed wherever and whenever tried—in Rome, in England, in France, in Germany, and in the United States. The "conquest of poverty" is a product of the capitalistic system which protected private property and enabled people to "save and invest their savings in industries producing goods for the masses." (p. 214)

The Inflation Crisis, and How to Resolve It (New Rochelle, N.Y.: Arlington House, 1978; Lanham, Md.: University Press of America, 1983)

Part I incorporates several of the more important chapters of *What You Should Know about Inflation*. In Part II Hazlitt analyzes and criticizes additional inflationist fallacies. Here are some of the chapter titles: "What Spending and Deficits Do," "What Spending and Deficits Do Not Do," "Where the Monetarists Go Wrong," "Inflation and Unemployment," "The Specter of 'Unused Capacity,'" "Indexing: The Wrong Way Out," "Why Inflation Is Worldwide," "The Search for an Ideal Money," "Free Choice of Currencies."

From Bretton Woods to World Inflation: A Study of Causes and Consequences (Chicago: Regnery Gateway, 1984)

Hazlitt's *New York Times* editorials, written at the time of the 1944 Bretton Woods Conference, form the nucleus of this book. Hazlitt pointed out then that the International Monetary Fund (IMF), established at Bretton Woods, would be inflationary, hamper world trade, and retard economic recovery. Hazlitt was distrustful of any state or bank, including the IMF, which was empowered to issue paper money. Also included in this book are several later articles by Hazlitt which amplify his 1944 conclusions.

The Wisdom of the Stoics: Selections from Seneca, Epictetus and Marcus Aurelius. Edited and with an introduction by Frances and Henry Hazlitt (Lanham, Md.: University Press of America, 1984)

In the course of Hazlitt's lifelong studies, he was impressed by the philosophy of the Stoics. Mrs. Hazlitt, Frances, researched their writings. Stoicism, founded by Zeno (c. 320–250 B.C.), a Phoenician, the editors write in their introduction, "is one of the permanent philosophies of life. . . . an indispensable element in any rational philosophy." Stoicism deals with the good and virtuous life. This book is a collection of aphorisms by three great Stoics from vastly different backgrounds. Seneca (c. 4 B.C.–65 A.D.), born in Spain, studied in Rome, gained favor, fame, fortune, then the enmity of Emperor Nero and was ordered to commit suicide. Epictetus (c. 55–130 A.D.), an ex-slave, became a favorite of Nero's, received his freedom, and later was expelled. Marcus Aurelius (121–180 A.D.) was an Emperor. The maxims assembled here offer guidance to everyday living and are suitable for daily reading.

2

A True Polymath

Edmund A. Opitz

Henry Hazlitt's *Economics in One Lesson* may be the most popular economics text ever written. It has sold more than a million copies in its numerous editions, and has been translated into all the major European languages. Hazlitt has one of the keenest economic minds around, but he's really a philosopher, one of whose specialties happens to be economics. His first two books, written before he was out of his 20's, dealt with the workings of the mind. His volume on ethics, written when he was nearly 70, is a superb exposition of utilitarian theory. He has authored a major work on constitutional theory, and produced a novel whose dialogue sparkles with sound economic teachings. Literary criticism is the subject of another volume. He has edited several books and contributed to many symposia. When H. L. Mencken retired from the *American Mercury* in 1933 he chose Hazlitt as his successor. A multi-faceted mind indeed, and a true polymath!

It was Hazlitt's good fortune—and ours—that he never took a college course in economics. Thus, he became a lifelong student of economics, and not just another academic "economist." He read voraciously, beginning in his early years, in the fields of history, literature, and philosophy. His views on the nature of man and society were derived mainly from those great Victorians, T. H. Huxley, and Herbert Spencer.

It was another and quite different Englishman, Philip H. Wicksteed, who inspired Hazlitt's lifelong interest in economics. Wicksteed was a celebrated London clergyman, Martineau's successor in 1874 at Little Portland Street Chapel, a medievalist and Dante scholar with a normal scholar's interest in economics. His huge tome entitled *The Common Sense of Political Economy* was published in 1910. It was the young Hazlitt's first lesson in marginal utility theory, a lesson which was never lost, and which grew over the years as Hazlitt pondered the

---

This tribute was written on the occasion of Mr. Hazlitt's 95th birthday.

works of Ludwig von Mises. It was Hazlitt's 1938 review of Mises' *Socialism* in *The New York Times* that first brought the Mises name before a fairly large audience. It would be gratifying to report that Mises, from then on, became the economist's economist; the truth is, however, that the Misesians even today are far outnumbered by the Keynesians and the Marxists.

And there's more. In 1959 Hazlitt took Keynes' *General Theory* apart, almost line by line, and demolished Keynesianism with devastating logic. What was true in Keynes' book was not new, he showed, and what was new was not true! Then there are his works on inflation, his critique of the welfare state, his book on poverty and wealth and, finally, an anthology of Stoic philosophy edited by Frances and Henry Hazlitt. Mrs. Hazlitt will be fondly remembered for her *Concise Bible,* well chosen passages from the King James skillfully knit together. I was honored to provide a dust jacket endorsement.

Hazlitt was a business and financial columnist for several New York newspapers during the twenties; during the next decade and beyond he was associated with *The New York Times,* specializing in matters relating to the economy. He wrote a weekly business and economics column in *Newsweek* from 1946 to 1966. *Economics in One Lesson* appeared in 1946 and continues to attract readers in increasing numbers. I was teaching two college courses in American government at this time and assigned Mr. Hazlitt's book as the best exposition of the only kind of economics compatible with the political ideals of the Declaration and the Constitution.

I was a faithful student of Hazlitt's *Newsweek* column from its early days; his 1949 review of *Human Action* persuaded me to become a student of Mises as well. It was at a Mises seminar in San Francisco in 1952 that I first encountered Hazlitt in person. Slim and aristocratic in bearing and manner, he gave off an air of precision which seemed to reflect the way he thought and wrote. But never did a man of so much scholarship wear his learning more lightly; he was affable, articulate, charming, and witty. He was companionable, appreciated a jest, and possessed a ready laugh. For many of us he is the ideal mentor.

It was inevitable that Adam Smith's invisible hand would arrange for the paths of Henry Hazlitt and Leonard Read to cross, and cross they did before the mid-Forties. An idea was developing in Leonard's mind for a novel kind of educational institution teaching sound ideas about government and the economy. Henry had suggestions and became a Founding Trustee of The Foundation for Economic Education—the only Founding member still alive, at age 95.

The body is older, but Henry's mind is still at work, following world events and thinking about his next book. He has taught millions over the course of his long life; and he's a teacher still.

3

Indefatigable Leader

Ludwig von Mises

Mr. Chairman, Ladies and Gentlemen and first of all you, our distinguished friend Hazlitt.

We are here assembled tonight to celebrate your 70th birthday. We are only a small group out of the great number of your admirers. But our meeting is not simply a private affair because you do not belong only to us, you belong to the nation and to the world. In this age of the great struggle in favor of freedom and the social system in which men can live as free men, you are our leader. You have indefatigably fought against the step by step advance of the powers anxious to destroy everything that human civilization has created over a long period of centuries.

Last week I lectured on economic policies and economics in a foreign city. After my lecture, as usual, there was a question period and a discussion of the problems which I had touched in my lectures. There was one question that startled me. It said, "You are building your reasoning upon the prejudice that freedom *is* something to be aimed at. Why? What *is* this prejudice?" I mention this fact in order to show how difficult the task is that faces today a champion of freedom. But you have successfully fought against all these prejudices and errors established for more than a hundred years in all countries of the West. In a long series of books and essays, books on philosophy, economics, and on literary criticism, and also in your brilliant novel, *The Great Idea,* you have demonstrated to the world the value of freedom and of the free market economy.

You have demonstrated again that the economic policy recommended by the liberal economists of the nineteenth century is the only policy fit to improve the material conditions of all of the people. There is no other method available for this purpose than to accelerate the accumulation of capital as against the increase in population figures.

Remarks by Ludwig von Mises on the occasion of Henry Hazlitt's 70th birthday, on November 28, 1964.

Only when the per head quota of capital invested is increasing are the material and ideal conditions of the masses improving. One has to repeat this truth again and again because, as an eminent author once said, the liars are repeating again and again their lies.

You have not only written eminent books and essays, you are also a journalist and you are writing every week in *Newsweek* a column which deals with all the important issues of our age. You are the economic conscience of our country and of our nation. And what you are saying in this country is repeated again and again in other countries and will remain victorious, repelling all the criticism levelled against it from the "left."

Edwin Cannan, the last in the long line of eminent British economists, considered as his most important contribution the article which he had written in the press, again and again criticizing the economic policies and fallacies of his own country. He collected these writings in which he had "protested," as he said, against everything that had been done ln his country, in a volume under the title *An Economist's Protest*. We hope that you will collect in the same way your weekly contributions and that this volume will one day, together with the volume of Edwin Cannan and with the immortal contributions of Frederic Bastiat, form the most precious unit in *The Free Man's Library* which you have so lucidly described and analyzed.

Every friend of freedom may today, in this post-election month, be rather pessimistic about the future. But let us not forget that there is rising a new generation of defenders of freedom. There is a real resurrection of the idea of liberty on the campuses. There is a steadily growing organization, Young Americans For Freedom, on the advisory board of which we both, you and I, and some of our friends present in this room are serving. Let us hope that these young men will succeed where we in our generation failed. But if they succeed, this wlll be to a great extent your merit, the fruit of the work that you have done in the first 70 years of your life.

HAZLITT RESPONSES

4

Reflections at 70

When I look back on my life, what strikes me is that I have been on the whole a very lucky man—and, above all, lucky in my friends.

My luck began, perhaps, in the year in which I was born, 1894. I have the advantage over most of you in knowing what it was like to live in the 19th century. Of course, I only had about six years of it, and I confess I may not even have been aware that it *was* the 19th century. But, speaking more seriously, my first 20 years were spent before the outbreak of World War I in 1914. Looking back at it, it seems now an idyllic world. There had been no major international wars for a century. There were no revolutions every week and riots every day. People could even trust their currency. There was no nuclear bomb hanging over us. There was no Communist government and not even an important organized Communist movement. Even socialism was merely a matter of academic discussion.

It was an age of innocence. How innocent it was, I well remember. At that time none of us knew, or needed to care, what was happening in such far-off places as China, or Vietnam, or the Congo. In fact, to tell the truth, we didn't pay much attention to anything that was going on outside of our own borders.

I remember those astounding days when World War I broke out. I was working at *The Wall Street Journal*. We used to get down to the job at about 8:00 in the morning and stay until about 4:00 in the afternoon. I remember the shocking day when the New York Stock Exchange failed to open its doors. It was to remain closed for many months afterward. I remember a day or two later, when England declared war on Germany. The excitement of that day, and the amount of work and confusion it imposed on myself, as a young fellow who was part stenographer and part reporter, proved exhausting. I didn't get away until about 7:30 P.M.—a day of 12 exhausting hours. As I was walking back to the trolley in the darkening streets—*The Wall*

On November 29, 1964, Henry Hazlitt was honored at a 70th birthday celebration at the New York University Club in New York City. His remarks on that occasion are reproduced here.

Street Journal was then at 44 Broad Street—the newsboys were all out on the streets shouting their extras. I can still hear the voices in my ears. They were shouting, "*Extra! Extra! Giants win!*" I do not exaggerate or invent. That was it. That was how the news of World War I came to the great metropolis of New York.

Beginnings

Perhaps you wonder how I got on *The Wall Street Journal*. Like everything else in my life, it seems to have been the result of a series of accidents.

In the last year of high school, I developed what I suppose might be called intellectual awareness. I got interested in philosophy and psychology. My great gods were Herbert Spencer and William James. I was going to go to Harvard, and major in psychology, and become a professor of psychology, writing a little philosophy on the side, like William James. But none of this was to be, because of something called a shortage of funds. So I had to compromise by going to the College of the City of New York, where the tuition was free. But even after a few months there I had to face the fact that I had to quit college and go to work to support my mother as well as myself.

However, I hadn't given up the idea of being a writer. I thought the best way to be that and still earn a living was to get on a newspaper. Well, for some reason or other, none of the major New York newspapers seemed to be very eager for my services, and the only place I could find an opening was on *The Wall Street Journal*. So I grabbed it.

The Wall Street Journal at that time (if I seem now to speak in somewhat derogatory terms of it) was comparatively obscure, and not the great national newspaper that it is today, under the editorship of Vermont Royster. I was supposed to know something about business and finance. I knew nothing about business or finance—and, moreover, I hadn't the slightest ambition to learn. My head was in the clouds, dreaming of philosophy. Every evening—in all the time I could spare, anyway, from dancing and entering dance contests—I was secretly writing a book with the ambitious title of *Thinking as a Science*.

Yes, the thing was published—and it sold, too. In fact, it outsold anything I have since written except *Economics in One Lesson* and *Will Dollars Save the World* ? And that reminds me of a wonderful piece of advice that was given by the celebrated editor Arthur Brisbane to a friend of mine who was in his first year in the newspaper game, when he asked the great man for some words of wisdom. "Young man," said Arthur Brisbane, "remember one thing. Never lose your superficiality." It was very wise advice, and every time I have forgotten it I have got into trouble.

In order to hold my job, I finally did get around to reading books on business and finance, and I began to read the standard economic textbooks of the period. Then I made the amazing discovery that economics required just as much hard thought, subtle thought, precise thought as the most abstruse problems of philosophy or psychology or physical science. A while later I stumbled upon a wonderful book in the public library. (As I say, when I look back everything important that has happened to me seems to have been accidental.) I thought it was my private discovery, and it practically was at that time. The book was titled *The Common Sense of Political Economy* by Philip H. Wicksteed. For the first time, the world of economics really opened up to me, and I caught my first glimpse of the fact—which Ludwig von Mises was later to make much more explicit—that the world of economics is almost coextensive with the whole world of human action and of human decision.

The Influence of Friends

I started to say how lucky I've been in my friends: but I have time to talk of only three or four of them.

The first one I want to talk about is Benjamin M. Anderson, who died in 1949. He was first the economist of the Bank of Commerce and later of the Chase National Bank. I was, at that time, in the early 1920s, financial editor of the *New York Evening Mail.* I used to go to see him about once a week to talk about economic developments. I read his magnificent book, *The Value of Money,* which is one of the classics of American economic writing and world monetary literature. Through his incisive mind, in my discussions with him, my thought was enormously stimulated.

But here comes another set of accidents. I got sort of pushed into the job as the book editor of the *New York Sun.* Five years later I became literary editor of *The Nation,* and so I spent the ten years from 1925 to 1934 writing on general literature.

In those ten years, among others whom I met was the British

philosopher Bertrand Russell. I first admired him through his books, and later got to know him personally. In fact, there was a time when he and his then publisher, W. W. Norton, suggested that I do a biography of him. I spent a good deal of time with him, in New York and London, in the period of 1928–1929, until one day, while reminiscing for my benefit, he suddenly said, "You know, I have had a very interesting life; I think I'd like to do my own autobiography." And he did—25 years later!

I come now to H. L. Mencken. I had admired and almost idolized Mencken as a writer long before I got to meet him, about 1930 or so. Three years later he astonished me by making the big mistake of his life: He asked me to succeed him as editor of *The American Mercury,* which for a while I did. In 1934 I got back into the economic field again. I went from my short editorship of *The American Mercury* to *The New York Times,* for which I wrote most of the financial and economic editorials for the next twelve years.

I got to know, then, first through his books and then by the great honor of meeting him personally, Ludwig von Mises. His thought has had more influence on me than the thought of any other single person in the last 25 years.

When I recall some of these great friends, when I look over this wonderful gathering and see friends who have come from abroad especially for this occasion, when I see, here and there and yonder, friends of national and international fame, when, to name only those on this dais here, I see Ludwig von Mises, William Buckley, Leonard Read, Milton Friedman, Karl Brandt, Lawrence Fertig, and Kenneth Wells, I realize how incredibly fortunate I have been in my friends.

Progress or Retrogression?

I have been, indeed, a very lucky man. But whether our generation, as such, is lucky, is another question. We live in an extraordinary age, an astonishing age by any standard. So far as any of us knows, it may even be the final age of mankind! In any case, it's very hard to say whether this is an age of unparalleled progress, or unparalleled retrogression, disintegration, and decadence. It seems to depend on where you look.

Let us look at the arts, for example. Take painting. There are probably more people painting today than ever before in the history of mankind. There is a more widespread spectator interest in painting; there is more sophisticated knowledge about it. And yet we find a complete anarchy of standards in painting. We find revolt for revolt's sake, a restless struggle for "originality" that has led to mere freakishness, to ugliness and to a pretentious unintelligibility that in most cases covers incompetence and an essential emptiness.

Much the same thing might be said about music and other arts. But each of these fields is complicated. If we take the field of architecture and engineering, for example, we are appalled by the ugly and freakish buildings that are being put up. But, on the other hand, just last week we witnessed the completion and opening of the magnificent Verrazano-Narrows Bridge.

When we come to the realm of morality we find an appalling disintegration of moral values and moral standards. But I've already written a 400-page book on that—*The Foundations of Morality*—and won't go into it further here.

Perhaps the darkest pages in the history of our era will be in politics. We find either degenerate democracy and demagogy or dictatorship. We find a constant spread of lawlessness, a constant resort to mob action, a cancerous growth in the power of the state, a turning toward more and more socialism and regimentation, and constant threats to and restrictions of liberty.

Over everything hangs the shadow of the nuclear bomb. Nobody knows what the outcome of that will be, or whether the problem is even soluble.

But when we look at the world of science, the world of technological progress and production, the creation of the necessaries and amenities of life, the achievements of today exceed anything that mankind has ever known or dreamed of in the past. We cannot dismiss this as a merely material progress. Even "mere" material progress means an immense gain in human, cultural and spiritual values. Look what it has meant in human longevity alone! A baby boy born in ancient Rome had a life expectancy of 22 years. Born in 1900, he had a life expectancy of 47 years. Born today he has a life expectancy of 70 years. I don't think any of us can afford to be ungrateful to the present age. If it hadn't been for the enormous progress that began in the Industrial Revolution 200 years ago, I doubt whether most of us in this room would ever have been born. And, if I had been one of those lucky enough to be born, I doubt that I would today be celebrating my 70th birthday, in good health and, as I like to think, not yet senile.

Great Science, Great Scientists

Our present material progress is the result, moreover, of great triumphs of the human mind, of great triumphs in theoretical sciences, of unprecedented precision, profundity, and boldness of thinking.

This is an age not only of great science; it is an age of great scientists. I have heard it said that nine-tenths of all the scientists who ever lived are living today. I don't know whether that's true or not, but it may very well be. I know that in the field I know best and which many of you know best, the field of economics, it could be pretty safely said that of all the economists who ever lived, good or bad, nine-tenths of them are alive today.

But this brings us to our problem. Those of us who place a high value on human liberty, and who are professionally engaged in the social sciences—in economics, in politics, in jurisprudence—find ourselves in a minority (and it sometimes seems a hopeless minority) in ideology. There is a great vogue in the United States today for "liberalism." Every American leftist calls himself a liberal! The irony of the situation is that we, we in this room, are the true liberals, in the etymological and only worthy sense of that noble word. We are the true adherents of liberty. Both words—liberal and liberty—come from the same root. We are the ones who believe in limited government, in the maximization of liberty for the individual and the minimization of coercion to the lowest point compatible with law and order. It is because we are true liberals that we believe in free trade, free markets, free enterprise, private property in the means of production; in brief, that we are for capitalism and against socialism. Yet this is the philosophy, the true philosophy of progress, that is now called not only conservatism, but reaction, the Radical Right, extremism, Birchism, and only Bill Buckley here knows how many other terrible things it's called.

Now this is no petty or narrow issue that ties us in this room together. For on the outcome of the struggle in which we are engaged depends the whole future of civilization. Our friend, Friedrich Hayek, in his great book, *The Road to Serfdom,* which was published 20 years ago, pointed out that it was not merely the views of Cobden and

Bright that were being abandoned, or even of Hume and Adam Smith, or even of Locke and Milton. It was not merely the liberalism of the 18th and 19th centuries that was being abandoned; it was the basic individualism that we had inherited from Christianity and the Greek and Roman world, and that was reflected in the writings of such figures as Pericles and Thucydides. This is what the world is in danger of abandoning today. Why? Why, if, as we like to think, reason is on our side? Why are we drifting deeper and deeper into socialism and the dark night of totalitarianism? Why have those of us who believe in human liberty been so ineffective?

"We Haven't Been Good Enough"

I am going to give what is no doubt a terribly oversimplified answer to that question. In the first place, we are almost hopelessly outnumbered. Our voices are simply drowned out in the general tumult and clamor. But there is another reason. And this is hard to say, above all to an audience of this sort, which contains some of the most brilliant writers and minds in the fields of economics, of jurisprudence, of politics, not only of this age but of any age. But the hard thing must be said that, collectively, we just haven't been good enough. We haven't convinced the majority. Is this because the majority just won't listen to reason? I am enough of an optimist, and I have enough faith in human nature, to believe that people will listen to reason if they are convinced that it *is* reason. Somewhere, there must be some missing argument, something that we haven't seen clearly enough, or said clearly enough, or, perhaps, just not said often enough.

A minority is in a very awkward position. The individuals in it can't afford to be just as good as the individuals in the majority. If they hope to convert the majority they have to be much better; and the smaller the minority, the better they have to be. They have to think better. They have to know more. They have to write better. They have to have better controversial manners. Above all, they have to have far more courage. And they have to be infinitely patient.

When I look back on my own career, I can find plenty of reasons for discouragement, personal discouragement. I have not lacked industry. I have written a dozen books. For most of 50 years, from the age of 20, I have been writing practically every weekday: news items, editorials, columns, articles. I figure I must have written in total some

10,000 editorials, articles, and columns; some 10,000,000 words! And in print! The verbal equivalent of about 150 average-length books!

And yet, what have I accomplished? I will confess in the confidence of these four walls that I have sometimes repeated myself. In fact, there may be some people unkind enough to say I haven't been saying anything new for fifty years! And in a sense they would be right. I have been preaching essentially the same thing. I've been preaching liberty as against coercion; I've been preaching capitalism as against socialism; and I've been preaching this doctrine in every form and with any excuse. And yet the world is enormously more socialized than when I began.

There is a character in Sterne or Smollett—was it Uncle Toby? Anyway, he used to get angry at politics, and every year found himself getting angrier and angrier and politics getting no better. Well, every year I find myself getting angrier and angrier and politics getting worse and worse.

But I don't know that I ought to brag about my own ineffectiveness, because I'm in very good company. Eugene Lyons has been devoting his life to writing brilliantly and persistently against Communism. He now even has the tremendous circulation of the *Reader's Digest* behind him. And yet, at the end of all these years that he has been writing, Communism is stronger and covers enormously more territory than when he started. And Max Eastman has been at this longer than any of the rest of us, and he's been writing a poetic and powerful prose and throwing his tremendous eloquence into the cause, and yet he's been just as ineffective as the rest of us, so far as political consequences are concerned.

Yet, in spite of this, I am hopeful. After all, I'm still in good health, I'm still free to write, I'm still free to write unpopular opinions, and I'm keeping at it. And so are many of you. So I bring you this message: *Be of good heart: be of good spirit. If the battle is not yet won, it is not yet lost either.*

Our Continuing Duty

I suppose most of you in this room have read that powerful book, George Orwell's *1984*. On the surface it is a profoundly depressing novel, but I was surprised to find myself strangely encouraged by it. I finally decided that this encouragement arose from one of the final scenes in it. The hero, Winston Smith, is presented as a rather ordinary man, an intelligent but not a brilliant man, and certainly not a courageous one. Winston Smith has been keeping a secret diary, in which he wrote: "Freedom is the freedom to say that two and two makes four." Now this diary has been discovered by the Party. O'Brien, his inquisitor, is asking him questions. Winston Smith is strapped to a board or a wheel, in such a way that O'Brien, by merely moving a lever, can inflict any amount of excruciating pain upon him (and explains to him just how much pain he can inflict upon him and just how easy it would be to break Smith's backbone). O'Brien first inflicts a certain amount of not quite intolerable pain on Winston Smith. Then he holds up the four fingers of his left hand, and says, "How many fingers am I holding up?" Winston knows that the required answer is five. That's the Party answer. But Winston can't say anything else but four. So O'Brien moves the lever again, and inflicts still more agonizing pain upon him, and says, "Think again. How many fingers am I holding up?" Winston Smith says, "Four. Four. Four fingers." Well, he finally capitulates, as you know, but not until he has put up a magnificent battle.

None of us is yet on the torture rack; we are not yet in jail; we're getting various harassments and annoyances, but what we mainly risk is merely our popularity, the danger that we will be called nasty names. So, before we are in the position of Winston Smith, we can surely have enough courage to keep saying that two plus two equals four.

This is the duty that is laid upon us. We have a duty to speak even more clearly and courageously, to work harder, and to keep fighting this battle while the strength is still in us. But I can't do better than to read the words of the great economist, the great thinker, the great writer, who honors me more than I can say by his presence here tonight, Ludwig von Mises. This is what he wrote in the final paragraph of his great book on socialism 40 years ago:

"Everyone carries a part of society on his shoulders; no one is relieved of his share of responsibility by others. And no one can find a safe way out for himself if society is sweeping towards destruction. Therefore, everyone, in his own interests, must thrust himself vigorously into the intellectual battle. None can stand aside with unconcern; the interests of everyone hang on the result. Whether he chooses or not, every man is drawn into the great historical struggle, the decisive battle into which our epoch has plunged us."

Those words—uncannily prophetic words—were written in the early 1920's. Well, I haven't any new message, any better message than that.

Even those of us who have reached and passed our 70th birthdays cannot afford to rest on our oars and spend the rest of our lives dozing in the Florida sun. The times call for courage. The times call for hard work. But if the demands are high, it is because the stakes are even higher. They are nothing less than the future of human liberty, which means the future of civilization.

5

The Art of Thinking

I have left the text of the first edition of this book practically unaltered. But I promised in the Preface that I would outline in an epilogue the changes I would make today if I were writing an entirely new book on the same subject. Here is that outline.

As thinking is primarily an activity, an art, the new book would probably not be called *Thinking as a Science,* but, perhaps, *The Art of Thinking Scientifically,* or, simply, *The Art of Thinking.*

There would be one or two major changes from the present book, at least in emphasis. I am more and more impressed, as I grow older, with how little the individual could accomplish in any direction whatever if he had to depend entirely on his own unaided efforts. He could not survive his first few years of life without the help of his parents or guardians. He could not think at all (or only at the level of a chimpanzee) if he did not inherit from the society and civilization in which he was born the priceless gift of an already created language. Without this he would not only be unable to reason logically, he would have nothing worthy to be called a "concept." He could not frame a sentence; he could not even name things. We think in words, even in conversations. Our language, concepts, and logic are part of the social inheritance of all of us.

This has several important corollaries. One of them is that before the individual can even dream of "thinking for himself," or solving a simple problem, he must first acquire at least an elementary knowledge of what mankind has already learned, discovered, or invented before him. Even if he receives what is called a good modern education, it will take him till the age of eighteen or more to acquire even the rudiments of what he needs to know.

When he was 21, Henry Hazlitt's first book had been published under the title *Thinking as a Science*. It was written, he explains, because "I primarily wanted to teach *myself* how to think more efficiently, independently, and, if possible, originally. I had already sensed that 'he who teaches, learns.'" When the book was republished 53 years later, in 1969, by Nash Publishing Corporation, Los Angeles, California, instead of extensively revising the original text, the author prepared an Epilogue, which was published in the August 1970 issue of *The Freeman,* and is reproduced here.

So my new book would emphasize far more than my previous one the need of extensive reading and study before the reader can profitably launch on "thinking for himself" or arriving at "independent" conclusions. That, of course, should always be his goal; but the road to that goal is long, hard, and often roundabout.

How to Study

My new book would therefore have a chapter on "How to Study." One of the topics considered in it would be the possibility of increasing one's reading speed, and the methods of achieving this. But my new book would emphasize what some of the teachers of the new "speed reading" methods unfortunately do not—the necessity that the student learn to "change gears," i.e., to learn to read different matter at different speeds depending on its nature, importance, and difficulty, as well as on the reader's purpose in reading it.

One of the chief problems of study, in fact, is how often the student should reread a textbook or a particular passage of it, or how often he should go over substantially the same material in other books. In studying a foreign language, for example, the reader may have to come across the same word or phrase again and again before he is able to translate it on sight, and he may have to see or hear it many more times before he can use it unprompted in a sentence framed by himself.

Knowledge of a foreign language, in short, is not really knowledge until it has been thoroughly assimilated, or *worked in*. This is no doubt widely recognized. But what is much less widely recognized is that this is not merely true of a language but of practically any other subject. A doctor is seldom a good doctor when he has just graduated from medical school, even though he may already have been over much verbal material with dreary repetition. Not until he has served as an intern, or been in private practice a couple of years, and so gone still more over the same ground and again and again encountered the same or similar problems, is he likely to achieve a quick and confident recognition and interpretation of symptoms.

A student of algebra may be taught how to extract the square root of a polynominal, and may be intelligent enough to follow the demonstration the first time, but it will probably not be until he has extracted many square roots of many polynominals that he will really feel confident he knows how. The student of languages, as well as the student of math, or a doctor, or a pianist, soon finds himself slipping backward if he ceases to study or practice. Our memories are not what they should be. A little of our knowledge is constantly oozing away. Knowledge and skill cannot be retained, let alone increased, except by constant addition, renewal, and refreshment.

I might also in this "How to Study" chapter give some hints to the reader on how to set up a study program to teach himself a particular subject, but in this epilogue I am postponing that to a later point. I may say here, however, that there are already some excellent books or pamphlets on how to study. The reader should find a wide range of choice in a college bookshop.

Language and Thought

My new book would have a chapter on "Language and Thought." I pointed out earlier that without language we would hardly be able to think at all. As the great nineteenth-century philologist Max Mueller put it: "To think is to speak low. To speak is to think aloud."

The corollary of this is tremendously important. A man with a scant vocabulary will almost certainly be a weak thinker. The richer and more copious one's vocabulary and the greater one's awareness of fine distinctions and subtle nuances of meaning, the more fertile and precise is likely to be one's thinking. Knowledge of things and knowledge of the words for them grow together. If you do not know the words, you can hardly know the thing. We are told that the Tasmanian method of counting is: "One, two, plenty." This points to a very significant truth. Man could not even *count,* certainly not beyond the number of fingers on his hands, until he had invented *names and symbols for numbers.* For in speaking of the need for language for thought, we must, of course, include symbols as an integral part of language. It is amazing how recent in human history are even the Arabic numerals, the denary system, and the elementary signs for addition, subtraction, multiplication, and division—not to speak of the myriad symbols now constantly used in algebra, geometry, trigonometry, differential and integral calculus, vector analysis, and other branches of higher mathematics. A single tiny symbol or formula—like that for zero, or *pi,* or a function, or the square root of minus one, or *dy/dx,* or Einstein's famous $E = mc^2$ (energy equals the quantity of matter multiplied by the square of the speed of light)—can condense, sum up, fix, and hold forever a discovery that it may have taken mankind centuries to arrive at.

Words Sharpen Observation

A vocabulary increases and sharpens our observation, as sharp okservation in turn leads us to increase our vocabulary. The student of nature who is learning to recognize bushes and trees finds his observation increasingly sharpened as he is told how to identify respectively an oak, maple, elm, beech, pine, spruce, or hemlock. The name both fastens down the results of observation and tells him what distinguishing traits to look for. As a result of his knowledge, a countryman very seldom calls a specific tree simply a tree. The professional forester or nurseryman habitually makes even finer distinctions, such as that between red oaks, black oaks, and white oaks, or between Norway maples, Schwedler maples, and sugar maples.

Once again, when a student of nature has a leaf described to him, or wants to describe one, he finds himself immeasurably aided by a specialized vocabulary of description for certain characteristics of edge or form—dentate, crenate, serrate, ovate, obovate, lanceolate, oblanceolate, sagittate, orbicular, and so on. The more names that are mastered, the more is observation sharpened.

This intimate interdependence of language and thought exists in all fields of knowledge, from the simple and concrete to the most abstruse and abstract.

The highest thrill of the amateur bird watcher comes when he identifies a new species for the first time. He usually does this by comparing the new bird he has just seen with the pictures or -descriptions in a bird book. But to be able to do this he has to observe very sharply everything he can—its size, shape, color, and markings, down to the minutest details, like the color and shape of its bill, its peculiarities of flight and song, and so forth.

When the bird student knows the *name* of the new species or its verbal description in a book he knows what to look for. His observation becomes keener not only for that time, but for the next time. By this process he finds his observation becoming ever more acute as his knowledge becomes fuller. The professional ornithologist, by a refinement of the same method, knows when he has discovered a species hitherto unrecognized by anyone. Whereupon he preserves his discovery, and makes it accessible to all, by giving the new species a name, accompanied by a full and precise pictorial and verbal description.

Identifying the Parts

Let us turn to still another field. The first thing the student of medicine is asked to do is to study anatomy. This means, at the beginning, to learn to recognize and name the hundreds of parts of the human body, from the *anulus inguinalis profundus* to the *vesicula seminalis*. It requires the dreary memorization of hundreds of names even to master what is called *gross* anatomv. When the student comes to some special part, like the nervous system (not to mention microscopic anatomy), he must learn hundreds of more names. And he must learn this special vocabulary if for no other reason than to know what his professors are talking about. Later on, as, say, a medical researcher, he must know this vocabulary not only to explain his findings in a medical journal, but to make them in the first place.

One of the things that used to puzzle me as a youth was why even the greatest painters and sculptors, like Leonardo da Vinci and Michelangelo, thought it necessary to study artistic anatomy. Their eyes were sharp enough: couldn't they have painted just what they saw? The answer, as I have now come to realize, is that by learning the names, position, and description of the muscles, tendons, and veins in the normal human body *they knew what to look for* and *where to look for it,* and their naturally acute vision was sharpened still more.

What is true for the supreme genius is true for those of us who are less gifted. In a charming introduction to his book on birds, John Kiernan tells the reader that he had never seen a white-breasted nuthatch until he saw, on a bird card, a picture of one going down a fence post headfirst. The next day he saw five different nuthatches at different places. They had always been around, but he had never before looked for them. He had been blind!

The reader has perhaps had the experience of looking at some object through binoculars or a magnifying glass and seeing details that he could not previously see with his naked eye; but on removing the glass he could still see them, because now he knew they were there. *The Arabian Nights* story, telling how Ali Baba could not open the door to the robbers' den until he had learned to say "open sesame," contains a profound moral. To be admitted to the realms of knowledge we must learn the right passwords.

Symbols of Communication

I remarked earlier that when I speak of "language" I do not have in mind merely words and sentences, but symbols, signs, and signals of all kinds used in human intercommunication. There are special symbols in every science; but I have particularly in mind numbers, notation, and other symbols of mathematics by which the results of mathematicians are made known to each other and without which, in fact, the mathematicians themselves could not even think mathematically. One authority, Tobias Dantzig, has written a book called *Number: The Language of Science*.

There are still further corollaries to be drawn from the inextricable interdependence of thought and language. He who seeks to be a clear and precise thinker must also seek to be a clear and precise writer. Good writing is the twin of good thinking. He who would learn to think should learn to write.

One of the most important steps, to repeat, is to enlarge one's vocabulary. The way most often consciously adopted for doing this is to study long lists of assorted words, usually polysyllabic. This may be better than nothing, but it is not the method to be preferred. It is generally more advisable to go from things and concepts to the names for them than to go from miscellaneous names to things and concepts. Vocabularies tend to grow with knowledge in general, and particularly with increasing knowledge of special subjects. Each science, discipline, art, sport, or branch of knowledge has its own special vocabulary, which is acquired with study or experience of that branch of knowledge or activity.

An abundant vocabulary is usually a by-product of wide knowledge. One good rule, both in thinking and writing, is never to use a word if you have only a vague and uncertain knowledge of its meaning. Look it up first in the dictionary to find its exact denotations and connotations—not to speak of its correct pronunciation!

Writing Improves Thinking

The reader who seeks to write well and think well should aim first at the essential qualities—coherence, clarity, precision, simplicity, and brevity. Euphony and rhythm are of course also desirable, but they are like the final rubbing on a fine piece of furniture—finishing touches justified only if the piece has been soundly made.

As a method of procedure, the apprentice writer may often find it advisable first of all to root out his faults. He should try to acquire the Five Virtues of Coherence, Clarity, Precision, Simplicity, and Brevity by vigilant abstention from the Five Vices of Incoherence, Obscurity, Vagueness, Pedantry, and Circumlocution.

For those who ask why writing is important to the thinker, one reply would be that it may be of crucial importance when the thinker wishes to present the results of his thinking to his professional colleagues or directly to the public. Newton and Leibnitz each invented the calculus independently, and Newton's discovery was earlier. But it was the calculus as presented by Leibnitz that other mathematicians began to use, mainly because Leibnitz devised a better notation.

The Abbé J. G. Mendel's biological experiments and theories on heredity, propounded in 1866, were of epoch-making importance, comparable to Darwin's theory of evolution published in *The Origin of Species* in 1859. Darwin's book brought him instant world fame, but neither Mendel nor his contribution received any recognition until 1900, thirty-four years after he had published his results and sixteen years after his death. Recognition came only when other botanists independently obtained results similar to Mendel's and in searching the literature found that both the experimental data and the general theory had been published by him a third of a century before. Mendel's original paper had reached the principal libraries in Europe and America. But it was so sparely and obscurely written that even eminent botanists at the time failed to grasp its implications.

A book on the art of thinking is not the place to dwell in detail on the art of writing. The most illuminating discussion of its length written on the subject is still Herbert Spencer's essay on "The Philosophy of Style" published in 1871. (Unfortunately, its own style is somewhat stilted and pompous.) A helpful little manual is *The Elements of*

Style by William Strunk, Jr., first published in 1918 and then republished with a delightful introduction and added chapter by Strunk's former student, E. B. White, in 1959.

Every professional writer ought to have, in addition to at least one good dictionary, four style books in his study: *The King's English,* by H. W. Fowler and F. G. Fowler, *A Dictionary of Modern English Usage,* by H. W. Fowler, *Usage and Abusage,* by Eric Partridge, and *Modern American Usage,* by Wilson Follett.

A Notebook or Journal

And every serious thinker, especially if he hopes to be a professional writer, should keep a notebook or a journal. I pointed out, in the first edition of this book, that good ideas are often elusive and must be captured in flight—in other words, that it is excellent practice always to have a pencil and pad handy, so as to jot down a good thought the moment after it lights up your mind. The complacent assumption that once a bright idea or happy phrase occurs to you it is a permanent acquisition, to be called upon only when needed, too often proves false. Even Nietzsche, one of the great seminal minds of the nineteenth century, found that: "A thought comes when it wishes, not when I wish."

When we write out our ideas, we are at the same time testing, developing, arranging, crystallizing, and completing them. We imagine ourselves not only making these ideas clear to others, but making them seem as important to others as they do to ourselves. So we try to make what was vague in our minds precise and definite; what was implicit, explicit; what was disconnected, unified; what was fragmentary, whole. We frame a generalization, then try to make it as plausible as we can; we try to think of concrete illustrations of it. And as we do this, we also expose it to ourselves—and sometimes, alas, find that it is empty, untenable, or sheer nonsense.

A lot of ideas that cannot be tested by formal experiments can be at least partly tested by writing them out. A great teacher of my acquaintance, when a student bothered him once too often by persisting in some silly proposal of his own on a subject, would suggest that the student write a paper on his idea and bring it in at the next seminar. The student seldom did so; perhaps because he was mentally lazy, but more likely because, when he attempted to write it out and to prove its validity, he found it to be hopelessly vague or a self-contradiction.

Writing Aids Concentration

One incidental advantage of the habit of writing out one's ideas is that it promotes concentration as almost no other practice does. As one who has written daily newspaper editorials or weekly magazine columns for many years, I can testify that nothing forces one to pull one's thoughts together more than deciding on a topic, sitting before the typewriter, feeding in a clean sheet of paper, and then trying to frame one's exact theme, title, and opening paragraph.

Francis Bacon summed it up with unsurpassable conciseness: "Reading maketh a full man, conference a ready man, and writing an exact man."

If the reader wants to know what the best and most stimulating notebooks and journals are like, I suggest, for a starting assortment: The *Meditations of Marcus Aurelius,* Pascal's *Pensées, The Heart of Emerson's Journals, Samuel Butler's Note-books, and* Charles Horton Cooley's *Life and the Student.* All of these, of course, can be sampled rather than read through; they are admirable bedside books.

How to Solve a Problem

In the first edition, I remarked that all thinking is problem-solving. My new book would contain a special chapter on "How to Solve a Problem."

It would begin, perhaps, by raising the problem: how to recognize a problem when you see it. The better informed, more intelligent, and more intellectually curious you are, the more problems you will become aware of. In his *Voyage of the Beagle,* Darwin describes how the savages, at one harbor in which the *Beagle* anchored, immensely admired the small boats in which his party landed, but paid no attention whatever to the big ship. They took it for granted, like a fact of nature. It was too far out of their experience.

Feebleminded barbarians. no doubt. But most of us civilized laymen daily switch on the lights, or turn on our television set, without the slightest curiosity regarding the cause of the miraculous result.

A question akin to this, which my chapter would raise, is "What *is* the problem?" Our modern social reformers are constantly preoccupied, for example, with the problem of poverty. But poverty is the original condition of man, from which he has sought to escape by the sweat of his brow, by work, production, and saving. It was when Adam Smith asked himself not what causes the poverty but what causes the *wealth of nations* that real progress on the problem began to be made. For centuries, in the same way, doctors took health for granted and assumed that the only problem is what causes disease. It was not until surgeons tried to transplant kidneys, hearts, and other organs that they became acutely troubled by the problem of what causes immunity. There is always the possibility of learning more by asking ourselves the opposite question. There are hundreds of books on *How to Play Chess.* Znosko Borowsky created a mild sensation by writing one called *How Not to Play Chess.*

Rules for Discovery

I suspect that my chapter on problem-solving would be heavily obligated to a little book by George Polya, first published in 1945, called *How to Solve It*.

Polya's book is devoted primarily to the problem of solving problems in mathematics; but it is applicable over the whole field of invention, discovery, and independent thinking.

"A great discovery," the author tells us in the preface, "solves a great problem but there is a grain of discovery in the solution of any problem. Your problem may be modest, but if it challenges your curiosity and brings into play your inventive faculties, and if you solve it by your own means, you may experience the tension and enjoy the triumph of discovery. Such experiences at a susceptible age may create a taste for mental work and leave their imprint on mind and character for a lifetime."

Polya has all sorts of instructive things to say about what questions to ask—"What is the unknown?"—about the uses of analogy, about "decomposing" and "recomposing" problems, about Descartes' rules for invention, about the indispensability of good symbols and good notation for mathematical thinking. He tells how, overnight or after a longer interval, our subconscious mind will often solve problems for us, but warns that "conscious effort and tension seem to be necessary to set the subconscious work going"—otherwise everything would be too easy.

Polya calls his whole book an effort to teach *Heuristic:* "The aim of heuristic is to study the methods and rules of discovery and invention. . . . The most famous attempts to build up a system of heuristic are due to Descartes and to Leibnitz, both great mathematicians and philosophers."

Polya's own illustrations and application are confined entirely to mathematics, for which his own enthusiasm is contagious. The reader, he says, should at least try to find out whether he has a taste for mathematics, and he may find out that "a mathematics problem may be as much fun as a crossword puzzle, or that vigorous mental work may be an exercise as desirable as a fast game of tennis. Having tasted the pleasure in mathematics he will not forget it easily and then there is a good chance that mathematics will become something for him: a hobby, or a tool of his profession, or his profession, or a great ambition."

Specialization, Perseverance, Analogy

My new book would contain a chapter on "The Dilemma of Specialization." The dilemma is this. In the modern world knowledge has been growing so fast and so enormously, in almost every field, that the probabilities are immensely against anybody, no matter how innately clever, being able to make a contribution in any one field unless he devotes all his time to it for years. If he tries to be the Rounded Universal Man, like Leonardo da Vinci, or to take all knowledge for his province, like Francis Bacon, he is most likely to become a mere dilettante and dabbler. But if he becomes too specialized, he is apt to become narrow and lopsided, ignorant on every subject but his own, and perhaps dull and sterile even on that because he lacks perspective and vision and has missed the cross-fertilization of ideas that can come from knowing something of other subjects.

I do not know the way out of this dilemma, or the exact compromise, but I hope to find it by the time I write my new book.

My new book, like the present one, will have a chapter on concentration, but it is more likely to be called "Concentration and Perseverance," for it will put far more emphasis on patience, plodding, perspiration, pertinacity, determination, effort, *work* — on again and again returning to an obstinate problem until it is solved. Scientists talk much nowadays of "serendipity"—the faculty of making desirable discoveries by accident. An example often cited is how Sir Alexander Fleming discovered penicillin because one of his laboratory technicians had carelessly left the top off a dish in which a virulent infectious organism, staphylococcus, was growing; a number of fungi had floated into the open dish, overgrown the bacteria—and killed it. The accident led Fleming to his discovery. But these "accidents" only seem to bear fruit when they happen to alert indefatigable scientists who have already been working for years on a project. As Pasteur put it: "Chance favors the prepared mind."

In my new book I would treat *Analogy* less cavalierly than I did earlier in this one, and perhaps have a separate chapter with that title. I did mention analogy in my first edition as a constructive method of making discoveries, but then went on to talk almost exclusively about its dangers and pitfalls. A. Wolf, in his *Textbook of Logic* (1938), emphasizes its achievements:

"One need only think of the most important discoveries in the history of science, in order to realize the enormous value of analogy. Our conception of the solar system (the helio-centric theory) owes a great deal to the analogy of the miniature system of Jupiter and the Medicean satellites. Some of the most important discoveries in modern mathematics are due to the analogy, discovered by Descartes, between algebra and geometry. The wave-theory of sound was suggested by the observation of water-waves; and the undulatory theory of light was suggested by the analogous air-waves which transmit sound. The theory of natural selection by the struggle for existence was suggested to Darwin by his knowledge of the artificial selection by which breeders have produced the many varieties of domestic animals. And so forth."

Like the first edition of the present volume, my new book would contain chapters on "Subjects Worth Thinking About" and on "Books on Thinking."

Subjects Worth Thinking About

But the former chapter, instead of containing a list of important but very miscellaneous problems, would call the reader's attention to some of the innumerable sciences or disciplines in which he could enjoyably and profitably interest himself—agriculture, astronomy, atomic physics, biology, building, chemistry, crystallography, electricty, engineering, fossils, gardening, geography, geology, mathematics, medicine, metallurgy, meteorology, minerology, pathology, physics, physiology, and zoology. These are all physical sciences. I name so many here because my first edition rather neglected them in its emphasis on social questions. But, of course, in my new book the reader would still be invited to consider the attractions of the social disciplines—political science, jurisprudence, economics, ethics, psychology, anthropology, or archeology.

In choosing subjects to think about or problems to solve, I must confess a personal preference for those that are useful. I admire disinterested curiosity and the achievements of "pure" science and "pure" research as much as anyone; but I cannot share the snobbery of those who seem able to express their esteem of pure science only by disparaging its practical applications. Both are admirable; and they are mutually dependent. The partisans of pure science chronically talk as if there were only a one-way dependency, and as if inventors were men of a lower order than pure scientists. They never tire of reminding us how the inventions of Marconi in wireless telegraphy and de Forest in radio were dependent on the previous theoretical discoveries of Clerk Maxwell and Hertz. All very true. But how far would pure research have been able to go in a hundred fields if it had not been for the invention, say, of the microscope? Or, for that matter, of the printing press?

As Karl R. Popper has pointed out, in his *Poverty of Historicism* (1957), one need not espouse a narrow pragmatism in order to appreciate Kant's saying: "To yield to every whim of curiosity, and to allow our passion for inquiry to be restrained by nothing but the limits of our ability, this shows an eagerness of mind not unbecoming to *scholarship*. But it is wisdom that has the merit of selecting, from among the innumerable problems which present themselves, those whose solution is important to mankind."

The Study of Economics

The reader of my new book would receive some guidance in how to take up a subject new to him, and there would be some specific illustrations. Suppose, for example, that he wanted to take up economics in a systematic way. He would be advised to begin with some short elementary text. An excellent one for the beginner today would be, say, *Essentials of Economics,* a book of only one hundred pages by Faustino Ballvé (Irvington-on-Hudson, N. Y.: Foundation for Economic Education). A collection of essays, *Planning for Freedom,* by Ludwig von Mises, is less systematic but enormously stimulating. (I would be less than mercenary if I failed to mention here also my own *Economics in One Lesson.)* The next step would be to read a book of intermediate length. One of the best is *A Humane Economy* by the late Wilhelm Roepke (Regnery).

The student would now be ready to tackle one of the most comprehensive and advanced books on the subject, of which I will mention only three. *Human Action: A Treatise on Economics* by Ludwig von Mises (Regnery, 907 pages) extends the logical unity and precision of economics beyond any other work. Some readers seem to find this excessively difficult. For these I can strongly recommend *Man, Economy, and State,* by Murray N. Rothbard (D. Van Nostrand, two volumes, 987 pages) which is equally comprehensive, and along Misesian lines, but in which the reader may find the arrangement and exposition easier to follow. Finally, I would include in this triad an older book, Philip Wicksteed's *The Common Sense of Political Economy* (1910, new edition 1933, two volumes, 871 pages), as remarkable for the ease and lucidity of its style as for the penetration and power of its reasoning.

When the reader has finished even one of the books in this advanced triad, perhaps after a couple of introductory volumes, he will be prepared to choose his own further reading in economics, and may browse among the great writers and thinkers who created the science—Hume, Adam Smith, Ricardo, Mill, Jevons, Menger, Böhm-Bawerk, Wicksell, Marshall, John Bates Clark—an enviable feast. Adam Smith's *Wealth of Nations,* though published in 1776, can still be ardently recommended no less for its literary seductiveness than for the brilliant light it still can throw even on the economic life of today.

General Rules for Exploring Any New or Strange Subject

Of course, my book could only include such specific recommendations on one or two subjects. For others there would have to be general rules. One would be to ask an expert in the subject. Another would be to consult the article on the subject in an encyclopedia and to see whether that included, as it ought to, a good list of references. A third rule would be to consult such a book as *Good Reading,* a paperback pulished by The New American Library. This is a volume sponsored by the College English Association and prepared by the Committee on College Reading. I happen to have the 19th printing which came out in 1964, but revisions have been appearing every year or two. The volume lists selected books on every conceivable subject—history, fiction, poetry, drama, biography, essays, philosophy, religion, and all the leading arts and sciences. There is also an instructive list of "100 Significant Books."

One last general piece of advice. No practice excels that of browsing along a library shelf containing books on the subject that has awakened your interest, and sampling them.

If I may be permitted a personal note, it seems to me, looking back, that the hours of purest happiness in my own youth were spent in just this way. I would avidly sample one book after another, and when the bell rang, and the library closed for the night, and I was forced to leave, I would leave in a state of mental intoxication, with my new-found knowledge and ideas whirling in my head. I would speculate eagerly on what solutions the authors I had read had come to in the passages I hadn't had time to finish. I think now that these unpremeditated efforts to anticipate an author's conclusions stimulated my thinking far more than any continuous uninterrupted reading would have done. In fact, when I came back to one of these same books the next evening, I most often felt let down. The night before, the author had seemed on the verge of some marvelous breakthrough, opening new vistas to the soul, and now he seemed to fizzle out in a truism.

Books on Thinking

The final chapter in my new book, like the final chapter in the first edition of this one, would be about "Books on Thinking."

My new references would supplement, rather than displace, those in my first edition. For example, I cited there only two "classics" on the art of thinking—John Locke's *Conduct of the Understanding,* and Arthur Schopenhauer's *Thinking for Oneself.* I should also have included the three classics mentioned in my present preface: Bacon's *Novum Organum,* Descartes' *Rules for the Direction of the Mind,* and Spinoza's *Improvement of the Understanding.* My new bibliography would of course also include a handful of good books written specifically on the art of thinking since the original edition of *Thinking as a Science* appeared. One of these would surely be *The Art of Thought,* by Graham Wallace (1926). Another would be *Thinking to Some Purpose,* by the late British logician L. Susan Stebbing. Her chief emphasis is on how to detect illogicalities in other people's thinking and how to avoid them in our own.

In addition, my new bibliography would refer the reader to passages, paragraphs, and even single sentences, widely scattered through the works of many authors, that throw light on the art of thinking. Some of these can be found in the biographies or autobiographies of great thinkers. My first edition cited material of this nature from the autobiographies of John Stuart Mill and Herbert Spencer. But there are illuminating passages in many writers less well known.

I quote here a few lines, for example, from Charles Horton Cooley's admirable notebook, *Life and the Student* (1927):

> Let our struggle be with facts, with life, rather than with other writers. We cannot have the spirit of truth and the spirit of controversy at the same time. A writer whose aim is to be unlike others is liable to a subservience of contradiction. That is, he after all gets his cue from them, takes the other end of the same rope. Originality raises new questions.

Though it starts apparently in contradiction, the advice of Morris R. Cohen in the preface to his *Reason and Nature* (1931) reinforces that of Cooley:

> The philosopher whose primary interest is to attain as much truth as possible must put aside as a snare the effort at originality. Indeed, it seems to me that the modern penchant for novelty in philosophy is symptomatic of restlessness or low intellectual vitality. . . . The principle of polarity calls attention to the fact that the traditional dilemmas, on which people have for a long time taken opposite stands, generally rest on difficulties rather than real contradictions, and that positive gains in philosophy can be made not by simply trying to prove that one side or the other is the truth, but by trying to get at the difficulty and determining in what respect and to what extent each side is justified. This may deprive our results of sweep and

popular glamour, but will achieve the more permanent satisfaction of truth.

Lessons in Logic

The art of thinking, like engineering or medicine, is based on several distinct sciences. One of these is psychology. I referred in the first edition of this book to John Dewey's *How We Think* which is still useful. But great experimental as well as theoretical progress has been made since Dewey's book was published. The reader could bring himself abreast of this by consulting the article on *Thinking and Problem Solving, Psychology of* in the 1965 edition of the *Encyclopedia Britannica.* The article itself includes an extensive list of books for further reading.

Logic, the study of the general conditions of valid inference, is of course the chief established science on which the art of thinking must be based. My recommendation for initial reading in my first edition was Stanley Jevons' *Elementary Lessons in Logic.* Because Jevons was an excellent writer as well as a first-rate thinker, this can still be read with pleasure and profit. But today I would prefer to recommend as an introductory volume A. Wolf's *Textbook of Logic* (first edition 1930, but often republished). More advanced, but still not too difficult, is L. Susan Stebbing's *Modern Introduction to Logic* (1940). Still more advanced, longer, and more difficult is *An Introduction to Logic and Scientific Method,* by Morris R. Cohen and Ernest Nagel (1934).

Scientific method is closely connected with logic. In fact, it is usual for modern books on logic (and this is true of the three just mentioned—the last explicitly in its title) to treat traditional logic in the first half of the book as "formal" or "deductive" logic, and then to devote the second half to "inductive" logic and to "scientific method" in general. This second subject includes discussions of such subjects as circumstantial evidence, the evolutionary and comparative methods, the simpler inductive methods (Mill's "five canons"), the statistical method, the deductive-inductive method, probability, laws of nature, scientific explanation, and so on. Long established as a standard work in this field is F. W. Westaway's *Scientific Method* (1919), but the literature is now very extensive.

A brilliant and penetrating book, for those who have the intellectual background, capacity, and ambition to read it, is *The Logic of Scientific Discovery* by Karl R. Popper (1961 edition).

Digression on Mathematics

It was one of the shortcomings of my first edition that it did not contain any explicit discussion of the enormously important field of mathematics. Yet at least an elementary knowledge of mathematics is essential for solving most of our daily practical problems as well as for most scientific thinking. We need arithmetic to buy and sell, to count our change, to read the time or the temperature, or to perform a hundred other daily operations. Mathematics has been called the "queen" and even the "mother" of sciences, because every science has its mathematical aspect. The accelerative development of mathematics in the last century has been both cause and consequence of the tremendous progress in the same period in the whole realm of the sciences, physical and social.

And—what was strangely not recognized until the last century—there is an inextricable connection between logic and mathematics. Mathematics may be called the quantification of logic. Mathematical logicians consider it a branch of logic. A formidable literature has grown up in the last few decades on "mathematical logic," "the algebra of logic," and "symbolic logic."

I do not mean to discourage or frighten the nonmathematical reader at this point by any implication that unless he masters higher mathematics and symbolic logic he cannot hope to contribute anything to science, philosophy, or the higher realms of thought. Great contributions to science and other knowledge will be made in the future, as they have been made in the past, by persons innocent of mathematics beyond simple arithmetic. But I do want to suggest that, other things being equal, the more you know of mathematics the more you will be likely to accomplish in science or original thought.

And mathematics can be fun. Few things can give greater enjoyment than mathematical problems, in fact, to those who relish mental exercise for its own sake.

The reader may be, like myself, one who grew up with a deep aversion to mathematics. This was chiefly, I am now convinced, because of the way it was then taught. Algebra was thrown at most of us who are now over 40 simply as something that had to be learned if we didn't want to flunk. I never remember any teacher telling me anything about the engrossing history of algebra, or even explaining why algebra was necessary in solving any problem except the artificial ones that were specially invented for the textbooks. The course in algebra seemed to me mainly a malicious contrivance to cut down the time I could give to handball.

But now, I can assure any reader who doesn't know, all is changed. There are now so many fascinating introductions to mathematics (at least for adults) that it seems almost invidious to name only a handful. For a short introduction covering the whole field, I would especially recommend David Bergamini's *Mathematics* (1963) in the admirable Life Science Library series. *Mathematician's Delight* by W. W. Sawyer (1943) is a charming introduction available in paperback. Two single volumes that teach the actual operations of the conventional part of the field are *Mathematics for the Practical Man* by George Howe (1957), and Lancelot Hogben's best-selling *Mathematics for the Million* (1937) —if you don't mind its belligerent Marxism. There is an excellent five-volume set on *Mathematics for Self-Study* (1931, 1962) by J. E. Thompson, covering in separate volumes arithmetic, algebra, geometry, trigonometry, and calculus. Finally there are the magnificent four volumes of *The World of Mathematics* edited by James R. Newman (1956).

Science, Philosophy, and Logic

I am still talking, the reader will remember, about studies that are directly likely to help him in the art of thinking—though the discussion inevitably splashes over into the domain of the chapter on "Subjects Worth Thinking About."

To continue with aids to the art of thinking: The reader will get both knowledge and stimulation from reading histories of science, lives of great scientists and inventors and discussions of their methods; histories of engineering, and histories of inventions and discoveries. Again I can mention only a few books. Two more from the handsomely illustrated Life Science Library series: *The Engineer,* by C. C. Furnas, Joe McCarthy and others (1966), and *The Scientist,* by Henry Margenau, David Bergamini, and the editors of *Life* (1964). The latter book will introduce the reader to a wide variety of sciences. In the realm of technology the reader may consult anything from the five-volume *History of Technology* (1954–58), edited by C. Singer to the *Popular History of American Invention* (1924), edited by W. Kaempffert.

Of course I should include philosophy also among the subjects whose study would contribute directly to the stimulation and improvement of one's thinking. But my list of recommendations has already grown so long that I shall here mention only two. The first is Bertrand Russell's brilliant *History of Western Philosophy* (1945). The second is *An Introduction to Philosophical Analysis* (second edition, 1967), by John Hospers. This text will bring the reader abreast of the kind of problems that professional philosophers now discuss.

At this point some reader may ask, earnestly or skeptically: But if I do some or all of this reading, will it really make me a better thinker than if I devote my leisure wholly to detective stories or golf? To this I can confidently reply: Yes. But to the further question: *How much* will it help me?, I can not reply with any confidence at all. The answer depends on the native intelligence of the individual reader, the nature of his gifts and interests, and a score of other factors.

Improving the Prospects

Is it really necessary to study formal logic, for example? Tristram Shandy, Lawrence Sterne's hero, commenting on the gap between his father's argumentative powers and his ignorance of formal logic, says: "It was a matter of just wonder with my worthy tutor, and two or three fellows of that learned society, that a man who knew not so much as the names of his tools, should be able to work after that fashion with them." In 1685, in the great hall of Dublin University, the young Jonathan Swift, having failed once before to take his bachelor's degree on account of his ignorance of logic, came up again without having condescended to read logic. He was asked how he could reason well without rules, and replied that he did reason pretty well without them. Reluctantly, though as the outcome proves, justifiably, his examiners gave him the degree. On the reverse side of the coin we may cite examples of even great professional logicians, like John Stuart Mill, sometimes falling into logical howlers.

The only reply I can think of to these examples is that though ignorance of logic may not prevent correct reasoning, or knowledge of it guarantee correct thinking, that knowledge nonetheless helps. The probability is that in the long run a man who has studied formal logic will reason better, and make fewer errors, than if he had not.

Remembering the technical names and descriptions of the more common fallacies, for example, will help him to detect such fallacies in the reasoning of others and avoid them in his own.

I have much less doubt about the usefulness of mathematics. True, even a prolonged study of higher mathematics will not make a man into an original or even effective thinker if he lacks the innate qualities. But a study of mathematics is of great importance in training a man to *think mathematically* about a problem or a subject.

On the negative side the importance of mathematical study is overwhelming. Without a knowledge of at least elementary arithmetic none of us would be competent to manage his daily affairs. Without a knowledge of double entry bookkeeping and cost accounting, a business firm would never know just how much money it was making or losing. And without a knowledge of higher mathematics, few modern physical scientists could hope to make contributions to their subjects, or even understand what had already been discovered. Morris R. Cohen tells us that in dealing with experimental physics, the lack of advanced mathematical knowledge discomforted the acute and powerful mind of Hobbes.

Even if the case for the usefulness of mathematics were not so overwhelming, its study could still be infinitely rewarding. In a famous 15-page essay, "The Study of Mathematics," included in his *Mysticism and Logic* (1918), Bertrand Russell writes:

> Mathematics, rightly viewed, possesses not only truth, but supreme beauty ... sublimely pure, and capable of a stern perfection such as only the greatest art can show....
>
> For the health of the moral life, for ennobling the tone of an age or a nation, the austerer virtues have a strange power, exceeding the power of those not informed and purified by thought. Of these austerer virtues the love of truth is the chief, and in mathematics, more than elsewhere, the love of truth may find encouragement for waning faith. Every great study is not only an end in itself, but also a means of creating and sustaining a lofty habit of mind; and this purpose should be kept always in view throughout the teaching and learning of mathematics.

The Joy of Thinking

But I ought not to try to proselytize for any one subject, among the hundreds, indeed (as encyclopedias and great libraries remind us) the thousands, that compete for the interest of the inquiring mind. Some of the world's most brilliant intellects have had no gift for mathematics. Most of us, moreover, have neither the surplus time nor energy to divert from the interests that already preoccupy our attention. And most of us, also, will feel less frustrated if we devote ourselves to less abstract and abstruse subjects which are nonetheless rewarding and absorbing. Not everyone can be a Newton or a Darwin, but everyone, by a little effort and persistence, can improve his intellectual attainments and satisfactions—and his enjoyment of life.

I would like to end this epilogue where I began, and to repeat that if I were writing a new book on the art of thinking I would emphasize, as I failed to do in my first edition, that no man can hope to do original work or even profitable thinking in any science or branch of knowledge until he has gone to the trouble to learn *what has already been discovered* in that branch of knowledge. He must know *the previous state of the question*. Then he will see whether he can make any contribution of his own. When the great Isaac Newton was asked how he had been able to make such tremendous contributions to human knowledge and thought, and to see so much farther than other men, he answered modestly: "I stood on the shoulders of giants." In other words, he was able to build on what his predecessors had discovered.

We who live today are in one respect in a more enviable position than any other generation in history. We stand on the shoulders of giants, like Newton and his successors, who stood on the shoulders of other giants before them. A thousand professional mathematicians today, though they have nothing approaching his genius, know more mathematics than Newton, who invented the calculus. And they know it because Newton, Leibnitz, the Bernoullis, Euler, Lagrange, Gauss, Riemann, Hamilton, and a hundred lesser figures have taught them. So an intelligent college student today is in a position to learn more about calculus than Newton, more about economics than Adam Smith, more about evolution than Darwin.

The present generation has been privileged beyond all others in acquiring this great intellectual heritage. It is a cardinal sin for any individual to neglect to acquire at least some small part of it for himself.

It is more than a sin; it is a folly. It is a failure to take advantage of one of the greatest sources of human enjoyment.

For we may say of thought in general what Tarrasch said of chess: Thinking, like Love, like Music, has the power to make men happy.

The way to this happiness is what I have tried to show in this book.

OF THE MARKET ORDER

6

The ABC of a Market Economy

There are basically only two ways in which economic life can be organized. The first is by the voluntary choice of families and individuals and by voluntary cooperation. This arrangement has come to be known as the free market. The other is by the orders of a dictator. This is a command economy. In its more extreme form, when an organized state expropriates the means of production, it is called socialism or communism. Economic life must be primarily organized by one system or the other.

It can, of course, be a mixture, as it unfortunately is in most nations today. But the mixture tends to be unstable. If it is a mixture of a free and a coerced economy the coerced section tends constantly to increase.

One qualification needs to be emphasized. A "free" market does not mean and has never meant that everybody is free to do as he likes. Since time immemorial mankind has operated under a rule of law, written or unwritten. Under a market system as any other, people are forbidden to kill, molest, rob, libel or otherwise intentionally injure each other. Otherwise free choice and all other individual freedoms would be impossible. But an economic system must be dominantly either a free or a command system.

Ever since the introduction and spread of Marxism the great majority of people who publicly discuss economic issues have been confused. Recently a very eminent person was quoted as denouncing economic systems that respond "only to the forces of the market place," and are governed "by the profit motive of the few rather than the needs of the many." He warned that such a system could put "the world's food supply into even greater jeopardy."

The sincerity of these remarks is beyond question. But they show how phrases can betray us. We have come to think of "the profit-motive" as a narrowly selfish drive confined to a small group of the already-rich whose profit comes at the expense of everybody else. But in its widest sense the profit-motive is one that all of us share and must

From the February 1985 issue of *The Freeman*.

share. It is our universal motive to make conditions more satisfactory for ourselves and our families. It is the motive of self-preservation. It is the motive of the father who is not only trying to feed and house himself but his wife and his children, and to make the economic conditions of his whole family, if possible, constantly better. It is the dominant motive of all productive activity.

Voluntary Cooperation

This motive is often called "selfish." No doubt in part it is. But it is hard to see how mankind (or any animal species) could have survived without a minimum of selfishness. The individual must make sure he himself survives before the species can survive. And the so-called profit motive itself is seldom solely selfish.

In a primitive society the "unit" is seldom the individual but the family, or even the clan. Division of labor begins within the family. The father hunts or plants and harvests crops; the mother cooks and bears and nurses children; the children collect firewood, and so forth. In the clan or the wider group there is even more minute subdivision and specialization of labor. There are farmers, carpenters, plumbers, architects, tailors, barbers, doctors, lawyers, clergymen, and so *ad infinitum*. They supply each other by exchanging their services. Because of his specialization, production increases more than proportionately to numbers; it becomes incredibly efficient and expert. There develops an immense system of voluntary productive cooperation and voluntary exchange.

Each of us is free (within certain limits) to choose the occupation in which he himself specializes. And in selecting this he is guided by the relative rewards in this occupation, by its relative ease or difficulty, pleasantness or unpleasantness, and the special gifts, skills, and training it requires. His rewards are decided by how highly other people value his services.

Free-Market Economy

This immense cooperative system is known as a free-market economy. It was not consciously planned by anybody. It evolved. It is not perfect, in the sense that it leads to the maximum possible balanced production and/or distributes its rewards and penalties in exact proportion to the economic deserts of each of us. But this could not be expected of any economic "system." The fate of each of us is always affected by the accidents and catastrophes as well as the blessings of nature—by rainfall, earthquakes, tornadoes, hurricanes, or what not. A flood or a drought may wipe out half a crop, bringing disaster to those growers directly hit by it, and perhaps record-high prices and profits to the growers who were spared. And no system can overcome the shortcomings of the human beings that operate it—the relative ignorance, ineptitude, or sheer bad luck of some of us, the lack of perfect foresight or omniscience on the part of all of us.

But the ups and downs of the market economy tend to be self-correcting. Over-production of automobiles or apartments will lead to fewer of them being produced the following year. A short crop of corn or wheat will cause more of that crop to be planted the following season. Even before there were government statistics, producers were guided by relative prices and profits. Production will tend to be constantly more efficient because the less efficient producers will tend to be weeded out and the more efficient will be encouraged to expand output.

The people who recognize the merits of this system call it the market economy or free enterprise. The people who want to abolish it have called it—since the publication of *The Communist Manifesto* in 1848—capitalism. The name was intended to discredit it—to imply that it was a system developed for and by the "capitalists"—by definition the disgustingly rich who used their capital to enslave and "exploit" the "workers."

The whole process was grossly distorted. The enterpriser was putting his accumulated savings at risk at what he hoped was an opportunity. He had no prior assurance of success. He had to offer the going wage or better to attract workers from their existing employments. Where the more successful enterprisers were, the higher wages also tended to be. Marx talked as if the success of every new business undertaking was a certainty, and not a sheer gamble. This resulted in his condemning the enterpriser for his very risk-taking and venturesomeness. Marx took profits for granted. He seemed to assume that wealth could never be honestly earned by successful risk-taking but had to be inherited. He ignored the record of constant business failures.

But the label "capitalism" did pay unintended tribute to one of the system's supreme merits. By providing rewards to some of the people who risked investing their capital, it kept putting into the hands of the workers more and constantly better tools to increase per capita production more and more. The system of private property and capitalism is the most productive system that has ever existed.

The Communist Manifesto was an appeal to "the masses" to envy and hate the rich. It told them that their only salvation was to "expropriate the expropriators," to destroy capitalism root and branch by violent revolution.

Marx attempted a rationalization of this course, built upon what he saw as inevitable deductions from a doctrine of Ricardo. That doctrine was in error; in Marx's hands the error became fateful. Ricardo concluded that all value was created by "labor" (which might almost be true if one counted labor from the begin ning of time—all the labor of everybody that went into the production of houses, land clearing, grading, plowing, and the creation of factories, tools and machines. But Marx chose to use the term as applying only to *current* labor, and the labor only of hired employees. This completely ignored the contribution of capital tools, the foresight or luck of investors, the skill of management, and many other factors.

The Errors of Marx

The theoretical errors of Marx have since been exposed by a score of brilliant writers. In fact, his preposterous conclusions could also have been proved wrong even at the time *Das Kapital* appeared by a patient examination of the available contemporary knowledge of incomes, payrolls and profits.

But the day of organized, abundant, and even "official" statistics had not yet come. To cite only one of the figures we now know: In the ten years from 1969 to 1978, inclusive, American "nonfinancial" corporations were paying their employees an average of 90.2 percent of the combined total available for division between the two groups, and only 9.8 percent to their stockholders. The latter figure refers to profits after taxes. But only about half of this amount—4.1 percent—was on the average of those ten years paid out in dividends. (These figures compared with public-opinion polls taken at the time which showed a consensus of most Americans that corporate employees got only 25 percent of the total available for division and the stockholders 75 percent.)

Yet the fierce diatribes of Marx and Engels led to the Russian Revolution of 1917, the slaughter of tens of thousands, the conquest and communization by Russia of some half dozen neighboring countries, and the development and production of nuclear weapons that threaten the very survival of mankind.

Economically, communism has proved a complete disaster. Not only has it failed to improve the welfare of the masses; it has appallingly depressed it. Before its revolution, the great annual problem of Russia was to find sufficient foreign markets for its crop surpluses. Today its problem is to import and pay for less than adequate foodstuffs.

Yet *The Communist Manifesto* and the quantity of socialist propaganda which it inspired continue to exert immense influence. Even many of those who profess themselves, quite sincerely, to be violently "anticommunist," feel that the most effective way to combat communism is to make concessions to it. Some of them accept socialism itself—but "peaceful" socialism—as the only cure for the "evils" of capitalism. Others agree that socialism in a pure form is undesirable, but that the alleged "evils" of capitalism are real—that it lacks "compassion," that it does not provide a "safety net" for the poor and unfortunate; that it does not redistribute the wealth "justly"—in a word, that it fails to provide "social justice."

And all these criticisms take for granted that there is a class of people, our officeholders, or at least other politicians whom we could elect in their place, who could set this all right if they had the will to do so.

And most of our politicians have been promising to do exactly that for the last half century.

The trouble is that their attempted legislative remedies turn out to be systematically wrong.

It is complained that prices are too high. A law is passed forbidding them to go higher. The result is that fewer and fewer items are produced, or that black markets develop. The law is ignored, or finally repealed.

It is said that rents are too high. Rent ceilings are imposed. New apartments cease to be built, or at least fewer of them. Old apartment buildings stand vacant, and fall into decay. Higher rents are eventually legally allowed, but they are practically always set below what market rates would be. The result is that tenants, in whose supposed interest the rent controls were imposed, eventually suffer as a body even more than landlords, because there is a chronic shortage of housing.

Wages are supposed to be too low. Minimum wages are fixed. The result is that teen-agers, and especially black teen-agers, are thrown out of work and on the relief rolls. The law encourages strong unions and compels employers to "bargain collectively" with them. The result is often excessive wage-rates, and a chronic amount of unemployed.

Unemployment relief and Social Security schemes are put into effect to provide "safety nets." This reduces the urgency for the unemployed to find new or better-paid work and reduces their incentive to look. Unemployment payments, Social Security and other such safety nets continue to grow. To pay for these, taxes are increased. But they do not raise the expected revenue because the taxation itself, reducing profit incentives and increasing losses, reduces enterprise and production. The spending and safety nets are increased. Deficit spending appears and increases. Inflation appears, demoralizing production further.

Sad to relate, these consequences have appeared in country after country. It is hard to find a single country today that has not become a bankrupt Welfare State, its currency constantly depreciating. Nobody has the courage to suggest dismantling it or to propose reducing its handouts or safety nets to affordable levels. Instead the remedy proposed everywhere is to "tax-the-rich" (which turns out everywhere to include the middle-classes) still more, and to redistribute the wealth.

Guided by Profit

Let us return to our point of beginning. The eminent person that I quoted then is mistaken when he tells us that we are governed by the profit-motive of the few rather than the needs of the many. The profit motive is simply the name for the practically universal motive of all men and all families—the motive to survive and to improve one's condition. Some of us are more successful at this effort than others. But it is precisely the profit-motive of the many that must be our main reliance for supplying the needs of the many.

It is strange that so little recognition is given to the fact that a man cannot grow richer without making others richer, whether that is his intent or not. If he invests and starts a new and successful business, he must hire an increasing number of workers, and raise wages by his own increased demand. He is supplying his customers either with a better product than they had before, or as good a product at a cheaper price, in which case they have more money left to buy other things. Even if he uses his own receipts only to increase his own consumer demand, he helps provide more employment or higher pay; but if he reinvests his profits to increase the output of his business, he directly provides more employment, more production, more goods.

So let us be thankful for the successful profit-motive in others. Of course, none of us should respond "only to the forces of the market place." Fortunately few of us do. Americans are not only among the richest people in the world today but among the most generous. It is only when each of us has provided for more than his own needs that he can acquire a surplus to help meet the needs of others. Voluntary cooperation is the key.

7

Private Ownership: A Must

If capitalism did not exist, it would be necessary to invent it—and its discovery would be rightly regarded as one of the great triumphs of the human mind. But as "capitalism" is merely a name for freedom in the economic sphere, the theme might be stated more broadly: The will to freedom can never be permanently stamped out.

Under complete world totalitarianism (in which there was no free area left from which the totalitarian area could appropriate the fruits of previous or current discovery and invention, or in which its own plans could no longer be parasitic on knowledge of prices and costs as determined by capitalistic free markets) the world would in the long run not only stop progressing but actually go backward technically as well as economically and morally—as the world went backward and remained backward for centuries after the collapse of Roman civilization .

A centrally directed economy cannot solve the problem of economic calculation, and without private property, free markets, and freedom of consumer choice, no organizational solution of this problem is possible. If all economic life is directed from a single center, solution of the problem of the exact amounts that should be produced of thousands of different commodities, and of the exact amount of capital goods, raw materials, transport, etc., needed to produce the optimum volume of goods in the proper proportion, and the solution of the problem of the *coordination and synchronization* of all this diverse production, becomes impossible. No single person or board can possibly know what is going on everywhere at the same time. It cannot know what real costs are. It has no way of measuring the extent of waste. It has no real way of knowing how inefficient any particular plant is, or how inefficient the whole system is. It has no way of knowing just what goods consumers would want if they were produced and made available at their real costs.

Henry Hazlitt's novel, originally appearing in 1951 as *The Great Idea,* was revised and republished in 1966 as *Time Will Run Back* with a new Preface from which this article was drawn and published in the June 1967 issue of *The Freeman.*

The System Breaks Down

So the system leads to wastes, stoppages, and breakdowns at innumerable points. And some of these become obvious even to the most casual observer. In the summer of 1961, for example, a party of American newspapermen made an 8,000-mile conducted tour of the Soviet Union. They told of visiting collective farms where 17 men did the work of two; of seeing scores of buildings unfinished "for want of the proverbial nail"; of traveling in a land virtually without roads.

In the same year even Premier Khrushchev complained that as of January 1 there were many millions of square feet of completed factory space that could not be used because the machinery required for them just wasn't available, while at the same time in other parts of the country there were the equivalent of hundreds of millions of dollars worth of machinery of various kinds standing idle because the factories and mines for which this machine was designed were not yet ready.

At about the same time G. I. Voronov, a Communist party Presidium member, said: "Who does not know that the national economy suffers great difficulties with the supply of metals, that the supply of pipes is inadequate, that insufficient supplies of new machinery and mineral fertilizers for the countryside are produced, that hundreds of thousands of motor vehicles stand idle without tires, and that the production of paper lags ?"[1]

In 1964 *Izvestia* itself was complaining that the small town of Lide, close to the Polish border, had first been inundated with boots, and then with caramels—both products of state factories. Complaints by local shopkeepers that they were unable to sell all these goods were brushed aside on the ground that the factories' production schedules had to be kept.

Such examples could be cited endlessly, year by year, down to the month that I write this. They are all the result of centralized planning.

The most tragic results have been in agriculture. The outstanding example is the famine of 1921–22 when, directly as a result of collectivization, controls, and the ruthless requisitioning of grain and cattle, millions of peasants and city inhabitants died of disease and starvation. Revolts forced Lenin to adopt the "New Economic Policy." But once more in 1928 more "planning" and enforced collections of all the peasants' "surpluses" led to the famine of 1932–33, when more millions died from hunger and related diseases. These conditions, in varying degree, come down to the present moment. In 1963 Russia again suffered a disastrous crop failure. And in 1965, this agrarian nation, one of whose chief economic problems in Tsarist days was how to dispose of its grain surplus, was once more forced to buy millions of tons of grains from the Western capitalist world.

Problems in Industry

The industrial disorganization has been less spectacular, or better concealed—at least if we pass over that in the initial phase between 1918 and 1921. But in spite of extravagant claims of unparalleled "economic growth," Russia's problems of industrial production have been chronic. Since factory output goals are either laid down in weight or quota by the planners, a knit-wear plant recently ordered to produce 80,000 caps and sweaters produced only caps, because they were smaller and cheaper to make. A factory commanded to make lamp shades made them all orange, because sticking to one color was quicker and less trouble. Because of the use of tonnage norms, machine builders used eight-inch plates when four-inch plates would easily have done the job. In a chandelier factory, in which the workers were paid bonuses based on the tonnage of chandeliers produced, the chandeliers grew heavier and heavier until they started pulling ceilings down.

The system is marked by conflicting orders and mountains of paperwork. In 1964 a Supreme Soviet Deputy cited the example of the Izhora factory, which received no fewer than 70 different official instructions from nine state committees, four economic councils, and two state planning committees—all of them authorized to issue production orders to that plant. The plans for the Novo-Lipetsk steel mill took up 91 volumes comprising 70,000 pages, specifying precisely the location of each nail, lamp, and washstand.

Yet in 1964, in Russia's largest republic alone, deliveries of 257 factories had to be suspended because their goods were not bought. As a result of the consumer's stiffening standards and increased inclination to complain, $3 billion worth of unsellable junk accumulated in Soviet inventories.[2]

Remedial Measures

Such conditions have led to desperate remedial measures. In the last couple of years, not only from Russia but from the communist satellite countries, we get reports of massive decentralization programs, of flirtations with market mechanisms, or more flexible pricing based on "actual costs of production" or even on "supply and demand." Most startling, we hear that "profits" is no longer a dirty word. The eminent Russian economist Liberman has even argued that profit be made the foremost economic test. "The higher the profits," he has said, "the greater the incentive" to quality and efficiency. And equally if not more miraculous, the Marxian idea that interest represents mere exploitation is being quietly set aside, and in an effort to produce and consume in accordance with real costs, interest (usually at some conventional rate like 5 percent) is being charged not only on the use of government money by shops and factories, but against the construction costs of plants.

On the surface all this looks indeed revolutionary (or "counter-revolutionary"); and naturally I am tempted to hope that the communist world is on the verge of rediscovering and adopting a complete capitalism. But several weighty considerations should warn us against setting our hopes too high, at least for the immediate future.

The "New Economic Policy"

First, there is the historical record. This is not the first time that the Russian communists have veered toward capitalism. In 1921, when mass starvation threatened Russia and revolt broke out, Lenin was forced to retreat into his "New Economic Policy," or NEP, which allowed the peasants to sell their surplus in the open market, made other concessions to private enterprise, and brought a general reversion to an economy based on money and partly on exchange. The NEP was actually far more "capitalistic," for the most part, than recent reforms. It lasted till 1927. Then a rigidly planned economy was reimposed for almost 40 years. But even within this period, before the recent dramatic change, there were violent zigs and zags of policy. Khrushchev announced major reorganizations no fewer than six times in ten years, veering from decentralization back to recentralization in the vain hope of finding the magic balance.

He failed, as the present Russian imitation of market mechanisms is likely to fail, because the heart of capitalism is private property, particularly private property in the means of production. Without private property, "free" markets, "free" wages, "free" prices are meaningless concepts, and "profits" are artificial. If I am a commissar in charge of an automobile factory, and do not own the money I pay out, and you are a commissar in charge of a steel plant, and do not own the steel you sell or get the money you sell it for, then neither of us really cares about the price of steel except as a bookkeeping fiction. As an automobile commissar I will want the price of the cars I sell to be set high and the price of the steel I buy to be set low so that my own "profit" record will look good or my bonus will be fixed high. As a steel commissar you will want the price of your steel to be fixed high and your cost prices to be fixed low, for the same reason. But with all means of production owned by the state, how can there be anything but artificial eompetition determining these artificial prices in such "markets"?

In fact, the "price" system in the USSR has always been chaotic. The bases on which prices are determined by the planners seem to be both arbitrary and haphazard. Some Western experts have told us (e.g., in 1962) that there were no fewer than five different price levels or price-fixing systems in the Soviet Union, while others were putting the number at nine. But if the Soviet planners are forced to fix prices on some purely arbitrary basis, they cannot know what the real "profits" or losses are of any individual enterprise. Where there is no private ownership of the means of production there can be no true economic calculation.

Elusive Costs of Production

It is no solution to say that prices can be "based on actual costs of production." This overlooks that costs of production are themselves prices—the prices of raw materials, the wages of labor, etc. It also overlooks that it is precisely the *differences* between prices and costs of production that are constantly, in a free market regime, redirecting and changing the balance of production as among thousands of different commodities and services. In industries where prices are well above marginal costs of production, there will be a great incentive to increase output, as well as increased means to do it. In industries where prices fall below marginal costs of production, output must shrink. Everywhere supply will keep adjusting itself to demand.

But in a system only half free—that is, in a system in which every factory was free to decide how much to produce of what, but in which the basic prices, wages, rents, and interest rates were fixed or guessed at by the sole ultimate owner and producer of the means of production, the state—a decentralized system could quickly become even more chaotic than a centralized one. If finished products M, N, O, P, etc. are made from raw materials A, B, C, D, etc. in various combinations and proportions, how can the individual producers of the raw materials know how much of each to produce, and at what rate, unless they know how much the producers of finished products plan to produce of the latter, how much raw materials they are going to need, and just *when* they are going to need them? And how can the individual producer of raw material A or of finished product M know how much of it to produce unless he knows how much of that raw material or finished product others in his line are planning to produce, as well as relatively how much ultimate consumers are going to want or demand? In a communistic system, centralized or decentralized, there will always be unbalanced and unmatched production, shortages of this and unusable surpluses of that, duplications, time lags, inefficiency, and appalling waste.

Private Property the Key

It is only with private property in the means of production that the problem of production becomes solvable. It is only with private property in the means of production that free markets, with consumer freedom of choice and producer freedom of choice, become meaningful and workable. With a private price system and a private profit-seeking system, private actions and decisions determine prices, and prices determine new actions and decisions; and the problem of efficient, balanced, coordinated, and synchronized production of the goods and services that consumers really want is solved.

Yet it is precisely private property in the means of production that communist governments cannot allow. They are aware of this, and that is why all hopes that the Russian communists and their satellites are about to revert to capitalism are premature. Only a few months ago the Soviet leader, Kosygin, told Lord Thomson, the British newspaper publisher: "We have never rejected the great role of profits as a mechanism in economic life ... [But] our underlying principle is inviolate. There are no means of production in private hands."[3]

The communist rulers cannot permit private ownership of the means of production not merely because this would mean the surrender of the central principle of their system, but because it would mean the restoration of individual liberty and the end of their despotic power. So I confess that the hope that some day an idealistic Peter Uldanov, miraculously finding himself at the pinnacle of power, will voluntarily restore the right of property, is a dream likely to be fulfilled only in fiction. But it is certainly not altogether idle to hope that, with a growth of economic understanding among their own people, the hands of the communist dictators may some day be forced, more violently than Lenin's were when the mutiny at Kronstadt, though suppressed, forced him to adopt the New Economic Policy.

Yet any attempt to decentralize planning while retaining centralized ownership or control is doomed to failure. As a recent writer explains it:

> If the state owns or controls the major resources of the economy, to allow for local autonomy in their utilization invites utter chaos. The Soviet planners, then, are caught on the horns of a serious dilemma. They find that their economy is becoming too complex and diverse to control minutely from above; yet they cannot really achieve the tremendous productiveness of a decentralized economy without relinquishing complete ownership or control of the nation's resources.[4]

---

1. See *New York Times,* October 29, 1961.
2. For the foregoing and other examples, see *Time,* February 12, 1965.
3. *New York Herald-Tribune,* September 27, 1965.
4. G. William Trivoli in *National Review,* March 22, 1966.

8

Rights

The concept of Rights is in origin a legal concept. In fact, in most European languages the term for Law is identical with the term for Right. The Latin *jus,* the French *droit,* the Italian *diritto,* the Spanish *derecho,* the German *Recht* signify both the legal rule that binds a person and the legal right that every person claims as his own. These coincidences are no mere accident. Law and Right are correlative terms. They are two sides of the same coin. All private rights are derived from the legal order, while the legal order involves the aggregate of all the rights coordinated by it. As one legal writer puts it: "We can hardly define a right better than by saying that it is the *range of action assigned to a particular will within the social order established by law.*"[1]

In other words, just because every person under the rule of law is divested of an unlimited liberty of action, a certain liberty of action *within* the legal limits is conceded and guaranteed to him by right.

When a man claims something as a right, he claims it as *his own* or *as due to him.* The very conception of a legal right for one man implies an *obligation* on the part of somebody else or of everybody else. If a creditor has a right to a sum of money owed to him on a certain day, the debtor has an obligation to pay it. If you have a right to freedom of speech, to privacy, or to the ownership of a house, everyone else has an *obligation* to respect it. A legal right for me implies a legal duty of others not to interfere with my free exercise of it.

Among legal rights almost universally recognized and protected today are the right to freedom from assault, or from arbitrary arrest or imprisonment; the right to be protected from arbitrary intrusion into one's home; the right to freedom of speech and publication (within certain established limits); the right to hold property; the right to compensation for damages inflicted by trespassers; the right to demand fulfillment of a contract; and many others.

The notion of legal right has its counterpart in legal duty. In their legal relations men either *claim* or *owe.* If A exerts an acknowledged

This article was published in the September 1964 issue of *The Freeman.*

right, he has the legal power to require that B (or that B, C, D, etc.) shall act or forbear to act in a certain way—shall do something or abstain from doing something.

Neither legally nor morally can "property rights" be properly contrasted with "human rights":

The right of ownership is, strictly speaking, quite as much a personal right—the right of one person against other persons—as a right to service, or a lease. It may be convenient for certain purposes to speak of rights over things, but in reality there can only be rights *in respect of* things *against* persons. . . . Relations and intercourse arise exclusively between live beings; but goods as well as ideas are the object and the material of such relations; and when a right of ownership in a watch or a piece of land is granted to me by law, this means not only that the seller has entered into a personal obligation to deliver those things to me, but also that every person will be bound to recognize them as mine.[2]

"Every single legal rule may be thought of as one of the bulwarks or boundaries erected by society in order that its members shall not collide with each other in their actions."[3] As every legal rule appears as a necessary adjunct to some relation of social intercourse, it is often difficult to say whether the rule precedes the rights and duties involved in the relation, or vice versa. Both of these sides of law stand in constant cross-relations with each other.

Constitutional Guarantees

In the last three centuries there has been an expansion of legal rights and an increasingly explicit recognition of their existence and importance. To protect the individual against abuses in statute law or by law-enforcement officials, "bills of rights" have been incorporated into written constitutions. The most famous of these is the Bill of Rights adopted in 1790 in the American Constitution.

The Bill of Rights is another name for the first ten Amendments. It guarantees freedom of worship, of speech, and of the press; the right of the people peaceably to assemble, and to petition the government for a redress of grievances; the right of the people to be secure in their persons, houses, papers, and effects, against unreasonable searches and seizures; the right of every person not to be compelled in any criminal case to be a witness against himself; nor to be deprived of life, liberty, or property, without due process of law; nor to have his property taken for public use, without just compensation; the right of the accused, in all criminal prosecutions, to a speedy and public trial by an impartial jury; the right to be protected against excessive bail and excessive fines, and cruel and unusual punishments.

This list is not complete. To the rights specified in the first ten Amendments, additional rights were later added in the Fourteenth Amendment. Some rights, in fact, are specified in the original Constitution. The privilege of the writ of *habeas corpus* cannot be suspended unless in cases of rebellion or invasion the public safety may require it. Congress is prohibited from passing any bill of attainder or *ex post facto* law. Any state also is prohibited from passing any bill of attainder, *ex post facto* law, or law impairing the obligation of contracts.

We shall return later to fuller consideration of some of these rights, and of their scope and limitations.

Natural Rights

Especially in the last two centuries, there has been a broadening of the concept of legal rights to the notion of "natural" rights. This was already implicit and sometimes explicit, however, in the thought of Plato and Aristotle, of Cicero and the Roman jurists, and becomes more explicit and detailed in the writings of Locke, Rousseau, Burke, and Jefferson.[4]

The term *Natural Rights,* like the term *Natural Law, is* in some respects unfortunate. It has helped to perpetuate a *mystique* which regards such rights as having existed since the beginning of time; as having been handed down from heaven; as being simple, self-evident, and easily stated; as even being independent of the human will, independent of consequences, inherent in the nature of things. This concept is reflected in the Declaration of Independence: "We hold these truths to be self-evident, that all men are created equal, that they are endowed by their Creator with certain unalienable Rights, that among these are Life, Liberty, and the pursuit of Happiness."

A Goal or Ideal

Yet though the term *Natural Rights* easily lends itself to misinterpretation, the *concept is* indispensable; and it will do no harm to keep the term as long as we clearly understand it to mean *ideal* rights, the legal rights that every man *ought* to enjoy. The historic function of the doctrine of Natural Rights has been, in fact, to insist that the individual be guaranteed legal rights that he did not have, or held only uncertainly and precariously.

By a further extension, we are justified in talking not only of "natural" *legal* rights but of *moral* rights. Yet clarity of thought demands that we hold fast to at least one part of the *legal* meaning of "rights." We have seen that every right of one man implies acorresponding *obligation* of others to do something or refrain from doing something so that he may be protected in and even *guaranteed* that right. If we abandon this two-sided concept the term *right* becomes a mere rhetorical flourish without definite meaning.

Pseudo-Rights

Before we examine the real nature and function of "natural" or moral rights it will clarify our ideas to look at some illegitimate extensions of the concept.

These have been rife for the last generation. An outstanding example is the Four Freedoms announced by President Franklin D. Roosevelt in 1941. The first two of these—"freedom of speech and expression," and "freedom of every person to worship God in his own way"—are legitimate freedoms and legitimate rights. They were, in fact, already guaranteed in the Constitution. But the last two—"freedom from want . . . everywhere in the world" and "freedom from fear . . . anywhere in the world" are illegitimate extensions of the concept of freedom or the concept of rights.

It will be noticed that the first two are freedoms of (or *to*), and the second two are freedoms from. Had Roosevelt used the synonym "liberty," he would still have been able to promise "liberty *to*," but English idiom would hardly have allowed him to promise "liberty *from*."[5] "Freedom to" is a guaranty that no one, including the government, will be allowed to *interfere* with one's freedom of thought and expression; but "freedom *from*" means that it is considered the duty of *someone else* to *supply* one's wants or to *remove* one's fears. Aside from the fact that this is a demand impossible of fulfillment (in a world of daily dangers and in a world in which we have not collectively produced enough to meet all our wants), just how does it become someone else's duty to supply my wants or to banish my fears? And how do I decide just *whose* duty it is?

Human Rights and the U.N.

Another outstanding example of a demand for pseudo-rights is found in the Universal Declaration of Human Rights adopted by the General Assembly of the United Nations in 1948. This declaration states, for example, that "everyone has the right to rest and leisure, including reasonable limitation of working hours and periodic holidays with pay." Assuming that this is even possible for *everyone* (in South America, Asia, Africa, and in the present state of civilization), whose obligation is it to provide all this? And how far does each provider's alleged obligation extend?

The same questions may be asked of all the rhetorical demands for alleged rights that we now hear almost daily—"the right to a minimum standard of living"; "the right to a decent wage"; "the right to a job"; "the right to an education"; and even "the right to a *comfortable* living"; "the right to a *satisfactory* job," or "the right to a *good* education." It is not only that all these alleged rights have vague quantitative boundaries—that they do not specify how high a wage is considered "decent" or *how much* education "the right to an education" implies. What makes them pseudo-rights is that they imply that it is somebody else's *obligation* to supply those things. But they do not usually tell us *whose* obligation, or precisely how it comes to be *his*. My "right to a job" iplies that it is somebody else's *duty* to give me a job, apparently regardless of my qualifications or even whether I would do more damage than good on the job.

Absolute vs. Prima Facie Rights

Unfortunately, disposing of some of the more obviously pseudo-rights does only a little to simplify our problem. Natural rights or moral rights are not always self-evident, are not necessarily simple, and are seldom if ever absolute. If legal rights are the correlates of legal rules, moral rights are the correlates of moral rules. And as moral duties may sometimes conflict with each other, so may moral rights. My legal and moral rights are limited by your legal and moral rights. My right to freedom of speech, for example, is limited by your right not to be slandered. And "your right to swing your arm ends where my nose begins."

The temptation to simplify moral rights is great. One moral philosopher, Hastings Rashdall, tried to reduce them all to one single right—the right to equality of consideration:

> Not only does the principle of equal consideration not necessarily prescribe any actual equality of Well-being or of the material conditions of Well-being: when properly understood, it does not favor the attempt to draw up *a priori* any detailed list of the "rights of man." It is impossible to discover any tangible concrete thing, or even any specific "Liberty of action or acquisition," to which it can be contended that every individual or human being has a right under all circumstances. There are circumstances under which the satisfaction of any and every such right is a physical impossibility. And if every assertion of right is to be conditioned by the clause "if it be possible," we might as well boldly say that every man, woman, and child on the earth's surface has a right to £1000 a year. There is every bit as much reason for such an assertion as for maintaining that every one has a right to the means of subsistence, or to three acres and a cow, or to life, or to liberty, or to the Parliamentary franchise, or to propagate his species, or the like. There are conditions under which none of these rights can be given to one man without prejudice to the equal rights of others. There seems, then, to be no "right of man" which is unconditional, except the right to consideration—that is to say, the right to have his true Well-being (whatever that true Well-being be) regarded as of equal importance in all social arrangements with the Well-being of everybody else.
>
> Elaborate expositions of the rights of man are, at best, attempts to formulate the most important actual or legal rights which an application of the principle of equality would require to be conceded to the generality of men at a particular state of social development. They are all ultimately resolvable into the one supreme and unconditional right—*the right to consideration;* and all particular applications of that principle must be dependent upon circumstances of time and place.[6]

A Vague Criterion

In its negative contention—in emphasizing how many devoutly to-be-wished-for conditions may be falsely called rights—this passage is highly instructive. But in its affirmative contention—in its effort to prove that all rights may be subsumed under equality of consideration—the passage cannot be called successful. No doubt "equality of consideration" is *one* moral right. But it is a very vague one. Suppose we think of it for a moment as a claimed *legal* right. Suppose a chair of philosophy falls vacant at Harvard and M, N, and O are among those who secretly aspire to be appointed to the post. And suppose, instead, that A gets the appointment and M, N, and O discover that A was, in fact, the only man even *considered* for the post? How could any one of the unsuccessful hopefuls go about legally *proving* that he did not get equality of consideration? (And in just what would "equality of consideration" have consisted?) He could say that the appointing group was influenced by *irrelevant* considerations—by considerations apart from what were strictly A's qualifications for the post—or that his, M's, qualifications for the post were not even considered. But could the appointing group reasonably be expected to consider equally *everybody's* qualifications for the post? Or is Rashdall's criterion merely another form of Bentham's "everybody to count for one, nobody to count for more than one"? And just how would either criterion help a man to decide a specific moral problem—such as, in a ship-wreck at sea, whether to save his wife or a stranger? Or even (if conditions made this the only alternative) whether to save his wife or two strangers?

We must try to think of moral rights with at least as much care and precision as legislators, judges, and jurists are compelled to think of legal rights. We cannot be satisfied with any vague and easy rhetorical solutions. Legal rights actually constitute an intricate and interrelated structure of rights worked out by centuries of judicial reasoning applied to centuries of human experience. Contrary to Justice Holmes's facile epigram: "The life of the law has not been logic; it has been experience,"[7] the life of the law has been *both* logic and experience. The law is the product of logic and reason *brought to bear* on experience.

Few Rights Are Absolute

As everyone's rights are conditioned by the equal rights of others, as the rights of each must be harmonized and coordinated with the equal rights of all, and as one right may not always and everywhere be compatible with another, there are few if any *absolute* rights. Even the right to life and the right to freedom of speech are not absolute. John Locke often wrote as if the rights to life, liberty, and property *were* absolute, but he made exceptions and qualifications in the course of his discussion: "Every one as he is bound to preserve himself . . . so by the like reason, *when his own preservation comes not in competition,* ought he as much as he can to preserve the rest of mankind, and not *unless it be to do justice on an offender,* take away or impair the life, or what tends to the preservation of the life, the liberty, health, limb, or goods of an other."[8] (My italics.)

Even the right to freedom of speech does not extend to libel, slander, or obscenity (though there may be difficult problems of definition concerning the latter). And nearly everyone will concede the limits to free speech as defined by Justice Holmes in a celebrated opinion:

> The most stringent protection of free speech would not protect a man in falsely shouting fire in a theatre, and causing a panic. It does not even protect a man from injunction against uttering words that may have all the effect of force. The question in every case is whether the words are used in such circumstances and are of such a nature as to create a clear and present danger that they will bring about the substantive evils that Congress has a right to prevent. It is a question of proximity and degree.[9]

Adherence to Principle the Ultimate Foundation

The suggestion has been made, following the analogy of the concept of "prima facie duties" (which we owe to Sir David Ross), that though we have no absolute rights, we do have *prima facie* rights. That is, we have a *prima facie* right to life, liberty, property, etc., which must be respected in the absence of some conflicting right or other consideration. But just as the law must be more precise than this, so must moral philosophy. Legal rights are of course subject to certain conditions and qualifications. But *within* those necessary qualifications, legal rights are or ought to be *inviolable*. And so, of course, should moral rights be inviolable.

This inviolability does not rest on some mystical yet self-evident "law of nature." It rests ultimately (though it will shock many to hear this) on utilitarian considerations. But it rests, not on *ad hoc* utilitism, on expediency in any narrow sense, but on *rule* utilitism, on the recognition that the highest and only permanent utility comes from an unyielding adherence to *principle*. Only by the most scrupulous respect for each other's imprescriptible rights can we maximize social peace, order, and cooperation.

---

1. Paul Vinogradoff, *Common-Sense in* Law (Home University Library; New York: Henry Holt, 1914), pp. 61–62. I am indebted to Vinogradoff's whole discussion of the nature of rights in positive law.

2. *Ibid.,* pp, 68–69.

3. *Ibid., p. 70.*

4. A scholarly and illuminating history can be found in Leo Strauss, *Natural Right and History* (Uiversity of Chicago Press. 1953).

5. See George Santayana, *Dominations and Powers* (New York: Scribner's, 1951), p. 58n.

6. *The Theory of Good and Evil (O*xford University Press, 1907), p. 1,227.

7. Justice Oliver Wendell Holmes, Jr. *The Common Law* (1881).

8. *Two Treatises of Civil Government* (1689), Book II, Chap. 2, sec. 6.

9. *Schenck v. United States,* 249 U.S. 52.

9

The Case for the Minimal State

Since at least as far back as Plato, many of the world's great minds have devoted themselves to the problems of politics. But they have not come up with any answers that have satisfied more than a narrow and transient majority in some country here or there. Today there are about 150 national governments in the world; but no two operate on exactly the same principles. If a free expression of opinion could be obtained in any one country, it would probably be found that at least a substantial minority was unhappy with some important part of the existing political arrangement or its operation.

We may distinguish at least three major political problems, which have existed since the beginning of time:

1. Should there be a government at all, and if so, exactly what should be the extent and nature of its permitted powers? Should these powers be precisely specified and limited, or is there an indeterminate area between certain minimum and maximum powers that may safely be left to popular choice?

2. Once the proper limits to the province and powers of the state have been decided upon, how can we stop the politicians in office from using their existing powers to extend and increase their powers?

3. By what method should the holders of office and power be chosen? For what terms, and so forth? How should their individual powers be allotted and delimited; and what provision should be made to assure that they responsibly execute those powers and no others?

It will be noticed that the political problem is twofold. It is not only to find what the best arrangements would be for choosing or changing political leaders or their powers, but for assuring that these arrangements are adhered to. This is one of the chief reasons (if not the chief) why the political problem has almost nowhere been better than temporarily solved. The ambition of men for political power has immemorially led them not only to demagoguery and deceit, but to force, war and murder, to achieve and increase it. It is because of this that I have elsewhere raised the question whether the principal prob-

From the November 1979 issue of *The Freeman*.

lems of politics are in fact solvable. ("Is Politics Insoluble?" *Modern Age,* Fall 1976.)

This is not on its face an encouraging quest. But the answer is so important for the future of mankind (let alone the immediate future of our own country) that we are bound to extend every effort to try to get as near to a workable solution as we can.

One promising procedure is to examine the answers that have been offered historically by the great political thinkers of the past to try to determine where they went wrong or what important problems they neglected to answer. We could do this chronologically beginning with the earlier answers, but I think it would be more interesting if we began with one of the latest answers and tried to find whether it satisfied us, and if not, why.

So I shall begin by examining the answer offered by Professor Robert Nozick of Harvard in 1974 in his book *Anarchy, State, and Utopia.* This book has attracted more attention than any other in the last five years that attempted to solve the problem of the proper province of the state. It won the National Book Award in 1975.

Away from Anarchy

Not least interesting about it is that it begins with a patient and open-minded discussion of an anarchy—of the possibility of getting along with no government at all. It considers the suggestion of the New Anarchists, for example, that honest and peaceable citizens could solve the problem of protecting their property and persons by joining and paying dues to private protective associations. Nozick shows how there would tend to grow up competing protective associations, that some of these might be little better than gangster associations, that some would be stronger than others, that it would not give anyone adequate protection to become a member of one of the weaker associations, and that in time one association would tend to establish a monopoly. But if such an association had the power of excluding some people from membership, or failed to act with complete morality and impartiality, it would be intolerable. Hence society would be forced to adopt a "minimal" state.

Nozick announces his main conclusions on the very first page of his Preface:

> Our main conclusions about the state are that a minimal state, limited to the narrow functions of protection against force, theft, fraud, enforcement of contracts, and so on, is justified; that any more extensive state will violate persons' rights not to be forced to do certain things, and is unjustified; and that the minimal state is inspiring as well as right. Two noteworthy implications are that the state may not use its coercive apparatus for the purpose of getting some citizens to aid others, or in order to prohibit activities to people for their own good or protection.

Now, this conclusion, though it would be regarded as extreme not only by popular opinion but by the great majority of political writers in every country today, is one that has a respectable history, and will be regarded sympathetically by a large number of declared libertarians. But I am troubled, most of the time, by the kind of arguments by which Nozick reaches his conclusion. Going a little further, I am frequently troubled by Nozick's style. It seems at times almost deliberately obscure. It is interrupted by diversions, digressions, parentheses, involutions, excessive footnotes—by a sort of self-heckling. He constantly confronts us with logic-chopping, with technicalities, and with abstractions without any helpful concrete references or illustrations.

Natural Law

Coming to problems of substance, I am bothered by his explicit rejection of any form of utilitarianism, and his attempt to substitute "natural law" justifications of his position. Here he seems to have been influenced by his Harvard colleague John Rawls—though he rejects Rawls' conclusions in many other respects. But as not only Nozick but an astonishing number of young libertarians have recently been taking this natural-law position, it is worth examining in some detail.

Nozick dismisses utilitarianism because his conception of it, like that of Rawls and others, is essentially a caricature. He sees the utilitarian as a fellow who judges conduct by its immediate effect on the balance of pain and pleasure, and makes a mechanical pain pleasure calculus of the results of a particular action, without considering "justice" and other values. One or two of the older utilitarians may have been guilty of giving such an impression, but this has little to do with the doctrine in its modern form.

I have suggested in my book, *The Foundations of Morality* (1964, 1972), not only that the utilitarianism of Bentham, and even of Mill and Sidgwick, has been in important respects superseded, but that it would increase clarity of thought to abandon the old term entirely. I have recommended substituting the term "rule-utilitism" because it comes much closer to describing a satisfactory moral system.

We should not take or judge an action in accordance with what we think would be its consequences considered as an isolated act. Not only can we never be certain what such consequences would be, but with such a moral code (or lack of code) we would never be able to depend on each other's conduct, and we would fall far short of that social cooperation by which we most fully promote our own and each other's ends. Moral action, for the most part, is action in accordance with accepted *principles* or *rules*. It is only when each of us can be depended upon to act consistently in accordance with such principles or rules that we can depend on each other. It is only when we can rely on each other to keep our promises, to tell the truth, to refrain from theft, fraud and violence, and to help each other in emergencies, that we can best promote that social cooperation so essential to attaining our individual ends.

These moral rules evolved during the centuries, long before they were explicitly formulated or codified, and certainly long before any moral philosopher explicitly formulated any single rationale or test by which good rules could be distinguished from bad ones or the best from the second best. But the doctrine of utility, first put forward by David Hume and later elaborated by Bentham, Mill, Sidgwick, and others, was the first test that unified and clarified the whole area of morals.

The Pleasure-Pain Balance—An Unsolved Problem

The first attempts to generalize the proper aim of all moral rules—such as rules conducive to promoting "the greatest happiness of the greatest number," proved to have some awkward shortcomings. Was the goal of "pleasure" or "happiness" sufficiently inclusive? Or sufficiently noble? And when an action promoted one man's happiness—or even a hundred men's happiness —but at the cost of another man's pain or misery, by what kind of moral arithmetic could we determine the net balance? The utilitarians have never satisfactorily solved this problem—but neither has anybody else. Fortunately, because an acceptable moral code prescribes principles or rules of action rather than particular acts, there are very few occasions when the need for such moral arithmetic seriously arises.

More important than this, rule utilitists are not necessarily bound by any pain-pleasure principle, or even any happiness-maximizing principle. They can simply accept as the principles of moral action those rules that would lead to the most satisfactory or desirable results for society, without trying to be more explicit as to the exact way of measuring such results. Anti-utilitists, rejecting such a criterion, would then be obliged to contend that their substitute criterion should be applied instead, even though it admittedly prescribed moral rules that would lead to less satisfactory or less desirable results for society.

Justice and Utility

One favorite contention of some anti-utilitists is that the utilitist criterion must be abandoned because it does not include "justice." That this contention is being seriously pressed today is odd historically, because John Stuart Mill devoted the whole last third of his famous essay *Utilitarianism* in 1863 to discussing "The Connection Between Justice and Utility." He concluded that: "Justice is a name for certain moral requirements, which, regarded collectively, stand higher in the scale of social utility, and are therefore of more paramount obligation, than any others."

But those who make "justice" the supreme if not the sole criterion of moral judgment regard it as a requirement that must be met for its own sake, regardless of what consequences it may lead to. The motto of these people is: *Fiat justitia, ruat caelum:* "Let there be justice, though the heavens fall." But the real reason for insisting on justice is to prevent the heavens from falling.

Those who insist that justice is solely an end in itself, and never a means to social peace and cooperation or other ends beyond itself, are also nearly always those who take a simplistic view of it. Everybody is supposed to know what "justice" is: it is simply "fairness," and we all know what is "fair." But through the centuries it has been the main function of thousands of legislators and jurists to decide what is justice both in abstract types of cases and in particular cases and circumstances.

Most of the non-utilitists and anti-utilitists in the past have been champions of Natural Law. The doctrine of Natural Law, it is true, has a very respectable history. It was promulgated or accepted by Plato and Aristotle, by the Stoics, by St. Thomas Aquinas, by Hugo Grotius and Samuel Pufendorf, by John Locke, by Jean-Jacques Rousseau, and by some of the Founding Fathers when they drafted or defended the American Constitution. But it has always owed a large part of its appeal to its ambiguity. The physical laws of nature, of cause and effect, determine everything, including, in one sense, human action. But this is something quite different from "natural laws" that are supposed to *prescribe* how men should conduct themselves.

A Nebulous Concept

The central difficulty with Natural Law is that no two of its votaries seem to have been able to agree regarding precisely what it enjoins. For Aristotle it sanctioned the subordination of women to men and of slaves to Athenian citizens. For the Stoics it prescribed equalitarianism. For many it meant the plain dictates of "right reason," though nobody could quite agree regarding what right reason prescribed. For others it meant the "divine will," with even more disagreement regarding what *this* commanded. Still others derived Natural Law from the law that existed in a "state of nature." But for some this meant savagery and for others a sort of Garden of Eden. According to the Declaration of Independence "the Laws of Nature" made certain "unalienable" rights "self-evident."

Finally, Jeremy Bentham, toward the end of the eighteenth century, was moved to exclaim that Natural Law was "nonsense on stilts." In his *Principles of Morals and Legislation* (1780), he wrote (Ch. 2):

"A great multitude of people are continually talking of the Law of Nature; and then they go on giving you their sentiments about what is right and what is wrong: and these sentiments, you are to understand, are so many chapters and sections of the Law of Nature."

This is not too unfair a description of those who are trying to revive the doctrine of Natural Law even today. They try to deduce its prescriptions from certain moral "axioms" taken from Locke or of their own devising. A typical one goes: "Every man owns himself; therefore ____." It is also clear that some of the rules that the natural-law champions "deduce" are, in fact, disguised or crypto-utilitist rules. Thus John Rawls, an avowed anti-utilitarian, in trying to deduce the principles of justice (in his *A Theory of Justice),* begins by assuming a society of persons "who in their relations to one another recognize certain rules of conduct as binding;" and "these rules specify a system of cooperation designed to advance the good of those taking part in it (p. 4)." He goes on to remark that "social cooperation makes possible a better life for all than any would have if each were to live solely by his own efforts" and so on. But rules designed to "advance the good" and make possible "a better life for all" are precisely utilitist rules. The ideal of justice is an inherent part of rule utilitism, not a separate or competing concept.

No Firm Foundation

The great difficulty with Natural Law, on the other hand, is not only that there is no agreed-upon code, but no agreement on the principles upon which such a code could be constructed. The greater part of the Natural Law votaries are really intuitionists in their moral philosophy.

I apologize for having given so much space to a seemingly irrelevant discussion of the relative merits of utilitist versus Natural Law standards. But it is not only Nozick who explicitly rejects utilitist tests in favor of Natural Law, but an increasing number of young libertarians who have apparently been influenced by him.

So far practically all I have written on Nozick's book has been negative. Why, then, am I discussing his book at all?

I do this because, while I think that Nozick often fails to base his reasoning on genuine first principles, and while his logic often seems to me unduly technical or irrelevant, he more than makes up for this by many brilliant arguments on special points. I shall cite a few of these.

Nozick is especially good in analyzing the rhetorical nonsense behind many of the leftists' recent objections to capitalism. A fashionable objection today is that workers lose their self-esteem by being frequently ordered about, under the authority of others unselected by them, and by having to work at tasks that they do not regard as "meaningful." Nozick points out that even members of a symphony orchestra are constantly ordered about by their conductor, and not consulted about the overall interpretation of their work, but nevertheless retain a high self-esteem.

More seriously, he points out that fragmentation and specialization of tasks are not problems peculiar to capitalist modes of production, but would go with any industrial society. The reason is that they tend to lead to the lowest costs and the highest efficiency and production. Suppose (which is most probable) that dividing a firm's work force into "meaningful" segments, rotating the workers into different tasks, and so on, could only be accomplished at the cost of less efficiency and production (as judged by market criteria)? Would the workers be willing to accept lower pay in order to do this more "meaningful" labor? Or would consumers be willing to pay higher prices for the same goods, or get less of them, in order that this more "meaningful" work could be provided? Who would be willing to pay for such a reform, and how much? Would a socialist government *forbid* "non-meaningful" work?

Labor Theory Refuted

As a more important example, let us take Nozick's refutation (on pages 253 to 262) of Marx's labor theory of value and his general exploitation theories. Similar refutations have been made before, notably by Böhm-Bawerk, but Nozick's is an especially compact one. Marxist theory, he concedes "does *not* hold that the value of an object is proportional to the number of simple undifferentiated labor hours that went into its production; rather, the theory holds that the value of an object is proportional to the number of simple undifferentiated *socially necessary* labor hours that went into its production."

But then, it turns out (though Marx himself never got around to seeing or acknowledging this clearly) that the amount of labor that really is "socially necessary" is determined by the utility and value of the particular commodity that is made! As Nozick concludes: "*What* is socially necessary, and how much of it is, will be determined by what happens on the market! There is no longer any labor theory of value; the central notion of socially necessary labor time is itself defined in terms of the processes and exchange ratios of a competitive market! . . . One might be left with the view that Marxian exploitation is the exploitation of people's lack of understanding of economics."

"Distributive Justice"

I come to my final example. This is Nozick's theory of "entitlements." He has argued that "the minimal state is the most extensive state that can be justified," and that "any state more extensive violates people's rights." He then addresses himself to the argument that a more extensive state is justified in order to achieve "distributive justice."

One trouble with this whole conception, he points out, is that it implicitly assumes that goods have already been "distributed" by some central source or according to some single principle, and that the duty of the state is to redistribute them according to some *other* "patterned" principle. But this overlooks the whole history of how the present "distribution" of goods came about. "Things come into the world already attached to people having entitlements over them. From the point of view of the historical entitlement conception of justice in holdings, those who start afresh to complete 'to each according to his ______' treat objects as if they appeared from nowhere, out of nothing."

How did the existing "distribution" of things come about? It came about because some people *made* the things they now hold, or because they were paid their marginal contribution to output in wages, or because they inherited property, or the objects (or money) were given to them by their parents, their spouses, or their friends. So even if the state made some "patterned" redistribution of wealth—"to each according to his needs," or to each equally—that pattern would very quickly be upset by some people continuing to create more than others, or some people giving freely to others, or some people voluntarily paying well for certain services, or to see or hear a particular professional athlete or performer, and so on. As Nozick sums up: "The socialist society would have to forbid capitalist acts between consenting adults."

The system of entitlements is defensible, he argues, "when constituted by the individual aims of individual transactions. No overarching aim is needed, no distributional pattern is required."

He goes on later to contend persuasively that: "Taxation of earnings from labor is on a par with forced labor (p. 169)."

Unfinished Arguments

But in spite of many excellences, Nozick's argument for his minimal state is in the end not quite convincing. A good part of the reason for this is revealed in his own description of his procedure in his Preface:

"Part I justifies the minimal state; Part II contends that no more extensive state can be justified. I proceed by arguing that a diversity of reasons which purport to justify a more extensive state, don't. Against the claim that such a state is justified in order to achieve or produce distributive justice among its citizens, I develop a theory of justice (the entitlement theory) which does not require any more extensive state, and use the apparatus of this theory to dissect and criticize other theories of distributive justice which do envisage a more extensive state.... Other reasons that some might think justify a more extensive state are criticized, including equality, envy, workers' control, and Marxian theories of exploitation

But his book, he goes on, is not "a political tract" but a "philosophical exploration." It does not pretend to be "a finished, complete, and elegant whole," but "a less complete work, containing unfinished presentations, conjectures, open questions and problems, leads, side connections, as well as a main line of argument. There is room for words on subjects other than last words."

No doubt there is. But it is precisely because Nozick has elected to write a book with a rambling and "unfinished" argument, with so many digressions, that many readers will find it unsatisfying and even occasionally irritating, that they will lose the thread of the main argument, and though finding it often persuasive, will in the end not find it quite conclusive.

I am not saying that it could not have been made so. Nozick does convincingly make his argument against anarchy. Others before him have advocated precisely his minimal state, "limited to the narrow functions of protection against force, theft, fraud, enforcement of contracts, and so on." It is an attractive ideal. But it has never been held by more than a tiny minority. If its appeal is ever to be widened to reach an effective number of thought leaders it must be by a broadly understandable but orderly chain of reasoning, without confusing digressions and without serious missing links, that makes its conclusion seem inescapable.

10

The Sphere of Government

Nineteenth-Century Theories

1. John Stuart Mill*

I remarked in "The Case for the Minimal State" *(The Freeman,* November 1979) that we might get some help in dealing with the central problems of government power by examining the answers offered over the years by the great political thinkers. But I suggested it might be more interesting to do this rather in the reverse of their chronological order, and begin with the latest answers first. We accordingly began with the recent book by Robert Nozick, *Anarchy, State, and Utopia.* I should like now to turn to some of the answers offered in the nineteenth century.

To try to present the whole of nineteenth-century thought on this subject would in itself require at least a full-length book and probably a repetitious one. So I shall confine myself to the answers offered by three or four outstanding writers who seem to me to offer representative approaches, beginning with John Stuart Mill and Herbert Spencer.**

Mill's main discussion of the problem occurs in Volume II (Book V, Chapters I and IX) of his *Principles of Political Economy,* first published in 1848. When one recalls that Mill was brought up in the laissez-faire tradition, some of his conclusions may seem surprising.

He begins by distinguishing between the "necessary" and the "optional" functions of government. The first are those which "are either inseparable from the idea of government, or are exercised habitually and without objection by all governments." The second are those functions of which the "expediency of its exercising them does not amount to necessity" and "on which diversity of opinion does or may exist."

---

*From the January 1980 issue of *The Freeman*.

**Mr. Hazlitt's treatment of Herbert Spencer begins on page 114.

Mill's Extended List of Necessary Functions of Government

The necessary functions of government, he insists, are "considerably more multifarious than most people are at first aware of." The contention, for example, that "governments ought to confine themselves to affording protection against force and fraud," and "that, these two things apart, people should be free agents," is much too narrow. What about, for example, the laws of inheritance? Not only is the government obliged to decide what happens to an estate when there is no will; it must pass on the validity of a will; it must decide among litigants.

Again, the government must enforce contracts. It must decide what contracts are fit to be enforced. (A contract to do something contrary to law? A contract to sell oneself into slavery?) The state must also establish civil tribunals to settle disputes. It must keep a registry of facts, such as births, deaths, marriages, wills and contracts, and judicial proceedings.

It must decide on the legal competency of children, or alleged lunatics, and provide for guardians. It may undertake the function of coining money, and of prescribing a set of standard weights and measures. It may make or improve harbors, build lighthouses, make surveys for accurate maps and charts, raise dykes to keep the sea out, or embankments to keep rivers in. National governments may build roads, and municipal governments may pave, light, and clean the streets. "Examples might be indefinitely multiplied without intruding on any disputed ground."

In a later chapter, Mill considers some of the reasons for limiting government power. "There is a part of the life of every person who has come to years of discretion, within which the individuality of that person ought to reign uncontrolled either by any other individual or by the public collectively. . . . A second general objection to government agency is that every increase of the functions devolving on the government is an increase in its power—which may soon become 'arbitrary.' . . . A third general objection to governmental agency rests on the principle of the division of labor. Every additional function undertaken by the government is a fresh occupation imposed upon a body already overcharged with duties. A natural consequence is that most things are ill done; much not done at all."

There follows a long description of the reasons why, in general, private enterprise and initiative are more efficient than government in carrying on any enterprise. In every instance these reasons are more than sufficient, Mill concludes, to throw "the burden of making out a strong case, not on those who resist, but on those who recommend, government interference. Laisser-faire, in short, should be the general practice: every departure from it, unless required by some great good, is a certain evil." He supplements this with a recital of the incredible restraints on business imposed historically in seventeenth-century France and elsewhere.

But then Mill turns to what he regards as the "exceptions" to the generally beneficent rule of laissez-faire:

> The proposition that the consumer is a competent judge of the commodity, can be admitted only with numerous abatements and exceptions. . . . The uncultivated cannot be competent judges of cultivation. Those who need most to be made wiser and better, usually desire it least, and if they desired it, would be incapable of finding the way to it by their own lights. . . . Education, therefore, is one of those things which it is admissible in principle that a government should provide for the people. . . .
>
> With regard to elementary education, the exception to ordinary rules may, I conceive, justifiably be carried still further . . . . It is therefore an allowable exercise of the powers of government, to impose on parents the legal obligation of giving elementary instruction to children. This, however, cannot fairly be done, without taking measures to insure that such instruction shall be always accessible to them, either gratuitously or at a trifling expense.

The one safeguard Mill insists on is that "the government must claim no monopoly for its education."

More Exceptions

Mill continues with his "exceptions" to the principle of laissez-faire. "Insane persons are everywhere regarded as proper objects of the care of the state." "It is right that children and young persons . . . should be protected, as far as the eye and hand of the state can reach, from being overworked." "Cruelty to animals" should be forbidden. "The law should be extremely jealous" of all "engagements for life"—including marriage. If it grants a monopoly for a private road, canal, or railway, the state "should retain, and freely exercise, the right of fixing a maximum of fares and charges."

The state should have the right to diminish the hours of adult labor.

Mill approves the Poor Laws, and endorses the principles of the Poor Law of 1834. "The claim to help, created by destitution, is one of the strongest that can exist." But the problem is "how to give the greatest amount of needful help, with the smallest encouragement to undue reliance on it." For "if the condition of a person receiving relief is made as eligible as that of the laborer who supports himself by his own exertions, the system strikes at the root of all individual industry and self-government." Yet we cannot depend on "voluntary charity"; "In the first place, charity almost always does too much or too little: it lavishes its bounty in one place, and leaves people to starve in another. Secondly, since the state must necessarily provide subsistence for the criminal poor while undergoing punishment, not to do the same for the poor who have not offended is to give a premium on crime."

Mill goes on to recommend government subsidies for colonization, for "scientific researches," and for other modes "of insuring to the public the services of scientific discoverers."

And as a final argument for extending goverment power still further, he adds: "The intervention of government cannot always practically stop short at the limit which defines the cases intrinsically suitable for it. In the particular circumstances of a given age or nation, there is scarcely anything really important to the general interest, which it may not be desirable, or even necessary, that the government should take upon itself, not because private individuals cannot effectually perform it, but because they will not."

An Open-Ended Formula

This last argument is capable of serving as an excuse for almost any arbitrary government intervention whatever. Mill ends by granting most of the contentions of the present-day statists. As he keeps adding to his list of "exceptions" to the general rule of laissez-faire, he gradually seems to forget all his earlier warnings against piling an unmanageable number of functions on the state and building excessive powers that can more easily be abused. In many of his exceptions he unconsciously takes it for granted that the state will necessarily do better than private initiative. He overlooks the possibility that scientists may be subsidized on the basis of favoritism or that the subsidized projects will be selected on the basis of political rather than scientific appeal.

After having warned us that the state may carry out its delegated powers very badly, he assumes in particular instances that they will carry out these powers very well. He rightly approved the restrictive principles of the Poor Law of 1834, which required from the applicant for relief, as Nassau Senior put it, "monotonous and uninteresting" toil in a workhouse, so that he would retain an incentive to become again as soon as possible an independent laborer. What Mill did not foresee was the immense political difficulty of retaining such a disciplinary system once relief was embarked upon. He did not foresee that this disciplinary system would soon come to be regarded by a large part of the public as needlessly harsh and even heartless. The sentimental but powerful pen of Charles Dickens, for example, was shortly to make the retention of the workhouse system impossible. The almost inevitable tendency in any relief system is for demagogic politicians to remove one by one all the original restraints and safeguards and to load the relief rolls to the point where work incentives are destroyed, the national budget becomes chronically unbalanced, and a progressive inflation sets in.

Even more broadly, what Mill overlooked was that once these broad powers of control were put in the hands of the state, under a popularly-elected government, that government would be very unlikely to adhere to the sound economic (and anti-interventionist) principles that Mill, and other economists of his school, were recommending in their textbooks, but would enact popular prejudices leading to inflation, to price controls, to "soak-the rich" taxes, to the redistribution of wealth and income, to anti-capitalistic and anti-productive policies of every other kind, and incidentally to the eventual destruction of liberty.

In his essays on *Liberty,* on *Representative Government,* and on *The Subjection of Women,* Mill made important contributions to political theory. But on the central question of what ought to be the limits of government power, he clearly granted too much. He left unanswered the great problem: How can we retain interventionist democratic government and yet prevent majority rule from degenerating into mob rule?

2. Herbert Spencer*

Herbert Spencer (1820–1903) was the 19th century's philosopher of evolution. He aspired to universal knowledge. What he called his Synthetic Philosophy ran to ten volumes. They included *First Principles* (1862), followed by volumes on *The Principles of Biology, The Principles of Psychology, The Principles of Sociology,* and *The Principles of Ethics.* Spencer also wrote at least eight other books.

But his earliest published work was a pamphlet, *The Proper Sphere of Government,* which he wrote at the age of 22, and his first important book was *Social Statics,* published in 1851. These publications advocated what would today be called, and was in fact called at the time, "an extreme form of laissez faire."

The limitation of state power remained one of Spencer's dominant interests till the end of his life. In a later edition of *Social Statics* he omitted a chapter entitled: "The Right to Ignore the State," but essentially his ideas on the subject of state power changed very little as he grew older. In 1884 he published a small volume entitled *The Man Versus the State.* In 1891 appeared Part IV of *The Principles of Ethics:* "The Ethics of Social Life: Justice," and he declared this to represent his definitive views on the subject. Let us summarize and analyze them.

After some prior discussion, Spencer arrives at what he calls "a formula of justice: . . . Every man is free to do that which he wills, provided he infringes not the equal freedom of any other man." This is almost exactly the maxim that he had laid down in his *Social Statics* 40 years earlier, but I regret that it seems to me vague and unsatisfactory

In *The Principles of Ethics* Spencer was aware of criticisms that must in the meantime have been made of it by others, for he immediately proceeds to deal with one of them:

> A possible misapprehension must be guarded against. There are acts of aggression which the formula is presumably intended to exclude, which apparently it does not exclude. It

*From the August 1980 issue of *The Freeman*.

> may be said that if A strikes B, then, so long as B is not debarred from striking A in return, no greater freedom is claimed by the one than by the other; or it may be said that if A has trespassed on B's property, the requirement of the formula has not been broken so long as B can trespass on A's property. Such interpretations, however, mistake the essential meaning of the formula. . . . It does not countenance a superfluous interference with another's life, committed on the ground that an equal interference may balance it. . . .[1]

Now this will hardly do. If a formula does not in fact countenance actions that it does countenance on its face, then it has not been satisfactorily formulated. It is not a satisfactory rule or guide to policy, and it must be revised or rejected. It must clearly exclude aggression against or harm to others.

But it must also carefully delimit the nature of the "aggression" or "harm." If A and B are applying for the same job or courting the same girl, and A is the successful competitor, the prospects of B may be correspondingly damaged. But as long as A "played fair," and did not resort to violence or fraud, no one would consider that B had any just cause for complaint. There are many similar cases, but there are also border line cases. If A and B have neighboring properties and A puts up an ugly house that B considers an eyesore threatening his property value, has B just cause for suit? If A puts up a fire hazard or a chemical factory that pollutes B's air or water, nearly everyone would consider B's case much stronger. It is problems like these that legislators and courts have to try to solve by passing scores of laws and making thousands of decisions in individual cases.

More a Formula for Liberty than for Justice

Spencer's formula strikes me more as an attempted definition of liberty than as a maxim of justice. And if it is so, then I much prefer the formula of John Locke in 1690: "Freedom of men under government is to have a standing rule to live by, common to every one of that society, and made by the legislative power erected in it; a liberty to follow my own will in all things, where the rule prescribes not: and not to be subject to the inconstant, uncertain, unknown, arbitrary will of another man."[2]

Montesquieu stated essentially the same formula more briefly in 1748: "Liberty is the right to do what the laws allow. If a citizen had a right to do what they forbid it would no longer be liberty, for everyone else would have the same right."[3]

So all practicable liberty is liberty under law. But the shortcoming of both Locke's and Montesquieu's formulas is that they fail to state explicitly that the restraints that the laws impose must be just, definite, and minimal. But even a formula that embodied these specifications would again fall short unless it spelled out what these just and minimal restraints would be. This is the dilemma that confronts all efforts to frame a concise definition of either justice or liberty.

The nearest to a good, short specification that I can at present remember is Thomas Jefferson's call for "a wise and frugal government, which shall restrain men from injuring one another, which shall leave them otherwise free to regulate their own pursuits of industry and improvement, and shall not take from the mouth of labor the bread it has earned."[4]

But I have perhaps allowed myself to be carried too far astray on this point. Spencer's case for the minimal state does not rest solely or even mainly on his own "formula for justice." Though he does not embrace the doctrine of Natural Law, he does believe that man has certain inherent rights which we recognize by "a priori intuition" or "a priori cognition." He proceeds to write a series of ten chapters on The Right to Physical Integrity, The Rights to Free Motion and Locomotion, to the Uses of Natural Media, The Right of Property, of Incorporeal Property, of Gift and Bequest, of Free Exchange and Free Contract, to Free Industry, of Free Belief and Worship, and of Free Speech and Publication. No government, he argues, has any legitimate power to violate or abridge these rights.

A Modern Ring

At the end of Part IV Spencer comes to seven chapters (23 to 29) on the nature, constitution, and duties of the state, and on the limits of state duties. When he discusses the constitution of the state, he might have been writing about one of the chief problems that disturb us today:

> If it is true that a generation ago landowners and capitalists so adjusted public arrangements as to ease themselves and to press unduly upon others, it is no less true that now artisans and laborers, through representatives who are obliged to do their bidding, are fast remolding our social system in ways which achieve their own gain through others' loss. Year after year more public agencies are established to give what seem gratis benefits, at the expense of those who pay taxes, local and general, and the mass of the people, receiving the benefits and relieved from the cost of maintaining the public agencies, advocate the multiplication of them.
>
> It is not true, then, that the possession of political power by all ensures justice to all. Contrariwise, experience makes obvious that which should have been obvious without experience, that with a universal distribution of votes the larger class will inevitably profit at the expense of the smaller class. Those higher earnings which more efficient actions bring to the superior, will not be all allowed to remain with them, but part will be drafted off in some indirect way to eke out the lower earnings of the less diligent or the less capable; and insofar as this is done, the law of equal freedom must be broken."[5]

He sums up:

> One conclusion, however, is clear. State burdens, however proportioned among citizens, should be borne by all. Every one who receives the benefits which government gives should pay some share of the costs of government and should directly and not indirectly pay it. . . .
>
> Had each citizen to pay in a visible and tangible form his proportion of taxes, the sum would be so large that all would insist on economy in the performance of necessary functions and would resist the assumption of unnecessary functions, whereas at present, offered as each citizen is certain benefits for which he is unconscious of paying, he is tempted to approve of extravagance; and is prompted to take the course, unknowingly if not knowingly dishonest, of obtaining benefits at other men's expense.

> During the days when extensions of the franchise were in agitation, a maxim perpetually repeated was—"Taxation without representation is robbery." Experience has since made it clear that, on the other hand, representation without taxation entails robbery. (pp. 219–20)

A Duty to Protect

In his chapter on "The Duties of the State," Spencer concludes that there is in effect just one: to protect the citizenry against external and internal aggression—against foreign enemies and against its law breakers. And in the following chapter on "The Limits of State Duties," he asserts:

> The question of limits becomes the question whether, beyond maintaining justice, the state can do anything else without transgressing justice. On consideration we shall find that it cannot. . . .
>
> If justice asserts the liberty of each limited only by the like liberties of all, then the imposing of any further limit is unjust; no matter whether the power imposing it be one man or a million of men. . . . We do not commonly see in a tax a diminution of freedom; and yet it clearly is one. The money taken represents so much labor gone through, and the product of that labor being taken away. . . . "Thus much of your work shall be devoted, not to your own purposes, but to our purposes," say the authorities to the citizens; and to whatever extent this is carried, to that extent the citizens become slaves of the government. (pp. 241–43)

Examples Galore

Though Spencer insisted constantly on the priority and necessity of deductive reasoning, few political writers have been so industrious and specific in citing and piling up concrete examples of the bungling, contradictions, and abuses of power in carrying out the multitudinous functions that governments have taken on. Long before he got to *The Principles of Ethics*, he had detailed scores of these not only in *Social*

Statics, but in such essays as "Over-Legislation," "State Tamperings with Money and Banks," "The Collective Wisdom," and many others.

So in the *Principles* he continued to cite case after specific case. Of drafting laws, for example:

"The judges themselves exclaim against the bungling legislation they have to interpret: one judge saying of a clause that he 'did not believe its meaning was comprehended either by the draftsman who drew it' or 'the parliament that adopted it,' and another declaring that 'it was impossible for human skill to find words more calculated to puzzle everybody.' As a natural consequence we have everyday appeals and again appeals—decisions being reversed and re-reversed." (pp. 252–253) One would think Spencer was writing of conditions in America today, rather than those of England in 1890.

Of the coinage: "In this we have frequent changes where changes are undesirable. We have mixed systems: decimal, duodecimal, and nondescript. Until recently we had two scarcely distinguishable pieces for threepence and fourpence" etc. (p. 253)

Socialistic Legislation

In a discussion on "socialistic legislation," Spencer excoriates the then Prime Minister, Lord Salisbury, for sneering at basic principles and saying: "We ought first to discuss every subject on its own merits." This is the method, comments Spencer,

> which has been followed by those legislators who, throughout past thousands of years, have increased human miseries in multitudinous ways and immeasurable degrees by mischievous laws. Regard for "the merits of the case" guided Diocletian when he fixed the prices of articles and wages of workers, and similarly guided rulers of all European nations who, century after century, in innumerable cases, have decided how much commodity shall be given for so much money, and in our own country guided those who, after the Black Death, framed the Statute of Labourers [to hold down wages], and presently caused the peasant revolt. The countless acts which, here and abroad, prescribed qualities and modes of manufacture, and appointed searchers to see that things were made as directed,

> were similarly prompted by considerations of "the merits of the case": evils existed which it was obviously needful to prevent. . . .
>
> Each one of those multitudinous regulations enforced by swarms of officials, which in France nearly strangled industry, and was a part cause of the French Revolution, seemed to those who established it, a regulation which "he merits of the case" called for; and no less did there seem to be called for the numberless sumptuary laws which, generation after generation, kings and their ministers tried to enforce. (pp. 260–61)

The Remarkable Contrast

After citing many more such examples, Spencer sums up the contrast between the amazing accomplishments of free and spontaneous social cooperation and the immense harm wrought by multitudinous government interventions:

> The average legislator, equally with the average citizen, has no faith whatever in the beneficent working of social forces, notwithstanding the almost infinite illustrations of this beneficent working. He persists in thinking of a society as a manufacture and not as a growth: blind to the fact that the vast and complex organization by which its life is carried on, has resulted from the spontaneous cooperations of men pursuing their private ends. Though, when he asks how the surface of the earth has been cleared and made fertile, how towns have grown up, how manufactures of all kinds have arisen, how the arts have been developed, how knowledge has been accumulated, how literature has been produced, he is forced to recognize the fact that none of these are of governmental origin, but have many of them suffered from governmental obstruction; yet, ignoring all this, he assumes that if a good is to be achieved or an evil prevented, Parliament must be invoked. He has unlimited faith in the agency which has achieved multitudinous failures, and has no faith in the agency which has achieved multitudinous successes. (pp. 266–67)

In expounding these views, Spencer, so far as the bulk of public opinion was concerned, was an isolated figure. Similar ideas were being voiced by a handful of others, notably Auberon Herbert (1838–1906), but the vigorous opposition of Thomas H. Huxley (1825–1895) probably came much nearer to expressing the political philosophy of the great mass of the British public in the 1880s and 1890s, to the extent that they bothered to formulate any philosophy.

---

1. *Principles of Ethics,* Vol. II (Indianapolis: Liberty Classics), Ch. 6, p. 62.
2. *Two Treatises of Civil Government* (Everyman's: E. P. Dutton), Second Treatise, sec. 21, p. 127.
3. *The Spirit* of *the Laws, XI.*
4. First Inaugural Address (March 4, 1801).
5. *Principles of Ethics,* II, pp. 212–13.

11

How Should Prices Be Determined?

"How should prices be determined?" To this question we could make a short and simple answer: Prices should be determined by the market.

The answer is correct enough, but some elaboration is necessary to answer the practical problem concerning the wisdom of government price control.

Let us begin on the elementary level and say that prices are determined by supply and demand. If the relative demand for a product increases, consumers will be willing to pay more for it. Their competitive bids will both oblige them individually to pay more for it and enable producers to get more for it. This will raise the profit margins of the producers of that product. This, in turn, will tend to attract more firms into the manufacture of that product, and induce existing firms to invest more capital into making it. The increased production will tend to reduce the price of the product again, and to reduce the profit margin in making it. The increased investment in new manufacturing equipment may lower the cost of production. Or—particularly if we are concerned with some extractive industry such as petroleum, gold, silver, or copper—the increased demand and output may raise the cost of production. In any case, the price will have a definite effect on demand, output, and cost of production just as these in turn will affect price. All four—demand, supply, cost, and price—are interrelated. A change in one will bring changes in the others.

Direct and Indirect Price Interrelationships

Just as the demand, supply, cost, and price of any single commodity are all interrelated, so are the prices of all commodities related to each other. These relationships are both direct and indirect. Copper mines may yield silver as a by-product. This is connexity of production. If the price of copper goes too high, consumers may substitute alumi-

From the February 1967 issue of *The Freeman*.

num for many uses. This is a connexity of substitution. Dacron and cotton are both used in drip-dry shirts; this is a connexity of consumption.

In addition to these relatively direct connections among prices, there is an inescapable interconnexity of all prices. One general factor of production, labor, can be diverted, in the short run or in the long run, directly or indirectly, from one line into any other line. If one commodity goes up in price, and consumers are unwilling or unable to substitute another, they will be forced to consume a little less of something else. All products are in competition for the consumer's dollar: and a change in any one price will affect an indefinite number of other prices.

No single price, therefore, can be considered an isolated object in itself. It is interrelated with all other prices. It is precisely through these interrelationships that society is able to solve the immensely difficult and always changing problem of how to allocate production among thousands of different commodities and services so that each may be supplied as nearly as possible in relation to the comparative urgency of the need or desire for it.

Because the desire and need for, and the supply and cost of, every individual commodity or service are constantly changing, prices and price relationships are constantly changing. They are changing yearly, monthly, weekly, daily, hourly. People who think that prices normally rest at some fixed point, or can be easily held to some "right" level, could profitably spend an hour watching the ticker tape of the stock market, or reading the daily report in the newspapers of what happened yesterday in the foreign exchange market, and in the markets for coffee, cocoa, sugar, wheat, corn, rice, and eggs; cotton, hides, wool, and rubber; copper, silver, lead, and zinc. They will find that none of these prices ever stands still. This is why the constant attempts of governments to lower, raise, or freeze a particular price, or to freeze the interrelationship of wages and prices just where it was on a given date ("holding the line") are bound to be disruptive wherever they are not futile.

Price Supports for Export Items

Let us begin by considering governmental efforts to keep prices up, or to raise them. Governments most frequently try to do this for commodities that constitute a principal item of export from their countries. Thus Japan once did it for silk and the British Empire for natural rubber; Brazil has done it and still periodically does it for coffee; and the United States has done it and still does it for cotton and wheat. The theory is that raising the price of these export commodities can only do good and no harm domestically because it will raise the incomes of domestic producers and do it almost wholly at the expense of the foreign consumers.

All of these schemes follow a typical course. It is soon discovered that the price of the commodity cannot be raised unless the supply is first reduced. This may lead in the beginning to the imposition of acreage restrictions. But the higher price gives an incentive to producers to increase their average yield per acre by planting the supported product only on their most productive acres, and by more intensive employment of fertilizers, irrigation, and labor. When the government discovers that this is happening, it turns to imposing absolute quantitative controls on each producer. This is usually based on each producer's previous production over a series of years. The result of this quota system is to keep out all new competition; to lock all existing producers into their previous relative position, and therefore to keep production costs high by removing the chief mechanisms and incentives for reducing such costs. The necessary readjustments are therefore prevented from taking place.

Meanwhile, however, market forces are still functioning in foreign countries. Foreigners object to paying the higher price. They cut down their purchases of the valorized commodity from the valorizing country, and search for other sources of supply. The higher price gives an incentive to other countries to start producing the valorized commodity. Thus, the British rubber scheme led Dutch producers to increase rubber production in Dutch dependencies. This not only lowered rubber prices, but caused the British to lose permanently their previous monopolistic position. In addition, the British scheme aroused resentment in the United States, the chief consumer, and stimulated the eventually successful development of synthetic rubber. In the same way, without going into detail, Brazil's coffee schemes and America's cotton schemes gave both a political and a price incentive to other countries to initiate or increase production of coffee and cotton, and both Brazil and the United States lost their previous monopolistic positions.

Meanwhile, at home, all these schemes require the setting up of an elaborate system of controls and an elaborate bureaucracy to formulate and enforce them. This has to be elaborate, because each individual producer must be controlled. An illustration of what happens may be found in the United States Department of Agriculture. In 1929, before most of the crop control schemes came into being, there were 24,000 persons employed in the Department of Agriculture. Today there are 109,000. These enormous bureaucracies, of course, always have a vested interest in finding reasons why the controls they were hired to enforce should be continued and expanded. And of course these controls restrict the individual's liberty and set precedents for still further restrictions.

None of these consequences seem to discourage government efforts to boost prices of certain products above what would otherwise be their competitive market levels. We still have international coffee agreements and international wheat agreements. A particular irony is that the United States was among the sponsors in organizing the international coffee agreement, though its people are the chief consumers of coffee and therefore the most immediate victims of the agreement. Another irony is that the United States imposes import quotas on sugar, which necessarily discriminate in favor of some sugar exporting nations and therefore against others. These quotas force all American consumers to pay higher prices for sugar in order that a tiny minority of American sugar cane producers can get higher prices.

I need not point out that these attempts to "stabilize" or raise prices of primary agricultural products *politicalize* every price and production decision and create friction among nations.

Holding Prices Down

Now let us turn to governmental efforts to *lower* prices or at least to keep them from rising. These efforts occur repeatedly in most nations, not only in wartime, but in any time of inflation. The typical process is something like this. The government, for whatever reason, follows policies that increase the quantity of money and credit. This inevitably starts pushing up prices. But this is not popular with consumers. Therefore, the government promises that it will "hold the line" against further price increases.

Let us say it begins with bread and milk and other necessities. The first thing that happens, assuming that it can enforce its decrees, is that the profit margin in producing necesssities falls,—or is eliminated,—for marginal producers, while the profit margin in producing luxuries is unchanged or goes higher. This reduces and discourages the production of the controlled necessities and relatively encourages the increased production of luxuries. But this is exactly the opposite result from what the price controllers had in mind. If the government then tries to prevent this discouragement to the production of the controlled commodities by keeping down the cost of the raw materials, labor and other factors *of* production that go into them, it must start controlling prices and wages in ever-widening circles until it is finally trying to control the price of everything.

But if it tries to do this thoroughly and consistently, it will find itself trying to control literally millions of prices and trillions of price cross-relationships. It will be fixing rigid allocations and quotas for each producer and for each consumer. Of course these controls will have to extend in detail to both importers and exporters.

Necessary Price Flexibility

If a government continues to create more currency on the one hand while rigidly holding down prices with the other, it will do immense harm. And let us note also that even if the government is not inflating the currency, but tries to hold either absolute or relative prices just where they were, or has instituted an "incomes policy" or "wage policy" drafted in accordance with some mechanical formula, it will do increasingly serious harm. For in a free market, even when the so-called price "level" is not changing, all prices are constantly changing in relation to each other. They are responding to changes in *costs* of production, in supply, and of demand for each commodity or service.

And these price changes, both absolute and relative, are in the overwhelming main both necessary and desirable. For they are drawing capital, labor and other resources out of the production of goods and services that are less wanted and into the production of goods and services that are more wanted. They are adjusting the balance of production to the unceasing changes in demand. They are producing thousands of goods and services in the relative amounts in which they are socially wanted. These relative amounts are changing every day.

Therefore the market adjustments and price and wage incentives that lead to these adjustments must be changing every day.

Price Control Distorts Production

Price control always reduces, unbalances, distorts, and discoordinates production. Price control becomes progressively harmful with the passage of time. Even a fixed price or price relationship that may be "right" or "reasonable" on the day it is set can become increasingly unreasonable or unworkable. What governments never realize is that, so far as any individual commodity is concerned, the cure for high prices is high prices. High prices lead to economy in consumption and stimulate and increase production. Both of these results increase supply and tend to bring prices down again.

Very well, someone may say; so government price control in many cases is harmful. But so far you have been talking as if the market were governed by perfect competition. But what of monopolistic markets? What of markets in which prices are controlled or fixed by huge corporations? Must not the government intervene here, if only to enforce competition or to bring about the price that real competition would bring if it existed?

Unwarranted Fears of Monopoly

The fears of most economists concerning the evils of "monopoly" have been unwarranted and certainly excessive. In the first place, it is very difficult to frame a satisfactory definition of economic monopoly. If there is only a single drug store, barber shop, or grocery in a small isolated town (and this is a typical situation), this store may be said to be enjoying a monopoly in that town. Again, everybody may be said to enjoy a monopoly of his own particular qualities or talents. Yehudi Menuhin has a monopoly of Menuhin's violin playing; Picasso of producing Picasso paintings; Elizabeth Taylor of her particular beauty and sex appeal; and so for lesser qualities and talents in every line.

On the other hand, nearly all economic monopolies are limited by the possibility of substitution. If copper piping is priced too high, consumers can substitute steel or plastic: if beef is too high, consumers can substitute lamb; if the original girl of your dreams rejects you, you can always marry somebody else. Thus, nearly every person, producer, or seller may enjoy a quasi monopoly within certain inner limits, but very few sellers are able to exploit that monopoly beyond certain outer limits. There has been a tremendous literature within recent years deploring the absence of perfect competition; there could have been equal emphasis on the absence of perfect monopoly. In real life competition is never perfect, but neither is monopoly.

Unable to find many examples of perfect monopoly, some economists have frightened themselves in recent years by conjuring up the specter of "oligopoly," the competition of the few. But they have come to their alarming conclusions only by inserting in their own *hypotheses* all sorts of imaginary secret agreements or tacit understandings between large producing units, and deducing what the results could be.

Now the mere *number* of competitors in a particular industry may have very little to do with the existence of effective competition. If General Electric and Westinghouse effectively compete, if General Motors and Ford and Chrysler effectively compete, if the Chase Manhattan and the First National City Bank effectively compete, and so on (and no person who has had direct experience with these great companies can doubt that they dominantly do), then the result for consumers, not only in price, but in quality of product or service, is not only as good as that which would be brought about by atomistic competition but much better, because consumers have the advantage of large-scale economies, and of large-scale research and development that small companies could not afford.

A Strange Numbers Game

The oligopoly theorists have had a baneful influence on the American antitrust division and on court decisions. The prosecutors and the courts have recently been playing a strange numbers game. In 1965, for example, a Federal district court held that a merger that had taken place between two New York City banks four years previously had been illegal, and must now be dissolved. The combined bank was not the largest in the city, but only the third largest; the merger had in fact enabled the bank to compete more effectively with its two larger competitors; its combined assets were still only one-eighth of those represented by all the banks of the city; and the merger itself had reduced the number of separate banks in New York from 71 to 70. (I should add that in the four years since the merger the number of *branch* bank offices in New York City had *increased* from 645 to 698). The court agreed with the bank's lawyers that "the general public and small business have benefited" from bank mergers in the city. Nevertheless, the court continued, "practices harmless in themselves, or even those conferring benefits upon the community, cannot be tolerated when they tend to create a monopoly; those which restrict competition are unlawful no matter how beneficent they may be."

It is a strange thing, incidentally, that though politicians and the courts think it necessary to forbid an existing merger in order to increase the number of banks in a city from 70 to 71, they have no such insistence on big numbers in competition when it comes to political parties. The dominant American theory is that just two political parties are enough to give the American voter a real choice; that when there are more than this it merely causes confusion, and the people are not really served. There is this much truth in this political theory as applied in the economic realm. If they are really competing, only two firms in an industry are enough to create effective competition.

Monopolistic Pricing

The real problem is not whether or not there is "monopoly" in a market, but whether there is monopolistic pricing. A monopoly price can arise when the responsiveness of demand is such that the monopolist can obtain a higher net income by selling a smaller quantity of his product at a higher price than by selling a larger quantity at a lower price. It is assumed that in this way the monopolist can realize a higher price than would have prevailed under "pure competition."

The theory that there can be such a thing as a monopoly price, higher than a competitive price would have been, is certainly valid. The real question is, *how useful is* this theory either to the supposed monopolist in deciding his price policies or to the legislator, prosecutor, or court in framing antimonopoly policies? The monopolist, to be able to exploit his position, must know what the "demand curve" *is* for *his* product. He does not know; he can only guess; he must try to find out by trial and error. And it is not merely the unemotional price response of the consumers that the monopolist must keep in mind; it is what the effect of his pricing policies will probably be in gaining the goodwill or *arousing* the resentment of the *consumer*. More importantly, the monopolist must consider the effect of his pricing policies in either encouraging or discouraging the entrance of competitors into the field. He may actually decide that his wisest policy in the long run would be to fix a price no higher than he thinks pure competition would set, and perhaps even a little lower.

In any case, in the absence of competition, no one *knows* what the "competitive" price would be if it existed. Therefore, no one knows exactly how much higher an existing "monopoly" price is than a "competitive" price would be, and no one can be sure whether it is higher at all!

Yet antitrust policy, in the United States, at least, assumes that the courts can know how much an alleged monopoly or "conspiracy" price is above the competitive price that might-have-been. For when there is an alleged conspiracy to fix prices, purchasers are encouraged to sue to recover three times the amount they were allegedly forced to "overpay."

Avoid Price-Fixing

Our analysis leads us to the conclusion that governments should refrain, wherever possible, from trying to fix either maximum or minimum prices for anything. Where they have nationalized any service—the post office or the railroads, the telephone or electric power—they will of course have to establish pricing policies. And where they have granted monopolistic franchises—for subways, railroads, telephone or power companies—they will of course have to consider what price restrictions they will impose.

As to antimonopoly policy, whatever the present condition may be in other countries, I can testify that in the United States this policy shows hardly a trace of consistency. It is uncertain, discrimnatory, retroactive, capricious, and shot through with contraditions. No company today, even a moderate-sized company can know when it will be held to have violated the antitrust laws, or why. It all depends on the economic bias of a particular court or judge.

There is immense hypocrisy about the subject. Politicians make eloquent speeches against "monopoly." Then they will impose tariffs and import quotas intended to protect monopoly and keep out competition; they will grant monopolistic franchises to bus companies or telephone companies; they will approve monopolistic patents and copyrights, they will try to control agricultural production to permit monopolistic farm prices. Above all, they will not only permit but impose labor monopolies on employers, and legally compel employers to "bargain" with these monopolies; and they will even allow these monopolies to impose their conditions by physical intimidation and coercion.

I suspect that the intellectual situation and the political climate in this respect is not much different in other countries. To work our way out of this existing legal chaos is, of course, a task for jurists as well as for economists. I have one modest suggestion: We can get a great deal of help from the old common law, which forbids fraud, misrepresentation, and all *physical* intimidation and coercion. "The end of the law," as John Locke reminded us in the seventeenth century, "is not to abolish or restrain, but to preserve and enlarge freedom." And so we can say today that in the economic realm, the aim of the law should not be to constrict, but to maximize price freedom and market freedom.

12

Market Prices vs. Communist Commands

A correspondent recently asked me why it was that Soviet Russia seemed to be suffering in recent years from chronic "crop failures," and found itself forced to import increased quantities of foodstuffs from the United States and other capitalistic countries. She understood, she wrote, that the most frequent explanation offered for this was that Russia operated under "communism" and that the countries exporting food to her were "capitalistic." But she wanted to know more in detail just why these different results came about.

I started to answer on the assumption that my explanation would be simple and brief, but soon found myself getting into complications.

In its simplest form, of course, the explanation *can* be brief. Under "capitalism" (Karl Marx's vocabulary)—that is to say, under a free market system—the individual farmer is rewarded by earning a profit if he grows the right things in the right amounts, and is penalized by a loss if he grows the wrong things. He is daily guided in his plans and operations by the prices of farm commodities in the "market." (Sometimes this may mean the national speculative markets on the commodity exchanges, where prices change from minute to minute, and sometimes it may mean merely the local market in his own district.)

The average farmer, of course, has little conception of how many prices of how many commodities, and grades of commodities, this involves. We could begin by citing such leading U.S. crops as corn, oats, barley, sorghum, wheat, rye, flaxseed, cotton, cottonseed, tobacco, hay, beans, peas, peanuts, soybeans, potatoes, seed crops, sugar cane, sugar beets, pecans, almonds, walnuts, filberts, oranges, tangerines, grapefruits—but the list goes on and on.

We can get an inkling of the number of commodities from the daily newspapers. *The Wall Street Journal,* for example, daily lists "Cash Prices" of more than 90 commodities, of which the majority are farm commodities. In that paper's long list of "Futures Prices" on the commodity exchanges, there are some 350 prices listed of a single

---

From the February 1983 issue of *The Freeman.*

grade of about 45 different commodities with six to ten different delivery dates.

If we add to these "national" prices the prices in local markets, we get a total that can run into the millions.

How Many Prices?

How many prices of all different commodities and services are there, in fact, at any given moment in an economy like the United States? Nobody knows. But in 1943 Chester Bowles, then head of the Office of Price Administration (OPA), was asked this question by a Congressional committee. He came up with an estimate of 8 million. A few days later this answer was withdrawn as much too low. It depended on how you defined a "commodity" and how you defined a "price." No definite answer was ever substituted.

But if, for the sake of argument, the figure were only 8 million prices, how could any bureaucracy, without previous actual market prices to guide it, go about safely fixing even one of them? For such prices, and their interrelationships—which would reach 8 million times 8 million, or 64 trillion—would reflect the past production and demand, absolute and proportional, for the 8 million commodities and services; they would embody everybody's expectations at the moment based on individual scraps of knowledge; and would largely determine the future absolute and relative supply and demand. No computer could solve this problem. Without a set of previous real and recent market prices, without informed expectations, the bureaucracy would have to make 64 trillion blind guesses.

Each farmer in planning his next year's acreage of each of the crops he plans to raise, is guided by the current or expected market price of each commodity. So thousands of different commodities and grades of commodities are planted in the proportions decided upon by each farmer on his assumptions regarding which will bring him the maximum profit (or, it may be, the minimum loss). In each case, to repeat, he is rewarded by the success of his estimates or penalized for his mistakes. He can change his plans any day, up to the actual day of plowing or planting.

We have been talking about the workings of an ideal free market system. This unfortunately does not exist in the United States. For many years, for example, the federal government has been subsidizing the production of milk by guaranteeing minimum prices, and thereby bringing about huge wasteful surpluses paid for by the taxpayers . . . . But that is another story.

Working in the Dark

Let us turn now to the problem confronting a communist nation. Such a nation, in the present world, is not totally without price guides. It is parasitic on capitalism, because it knows the prices being quoted for various commodities in capitalist countries. It can make plausible guesses (by figuring presumptive transportation costs in the same way) concerning how to convert these into equivalent prices in its own country. (Much depends on whether it allows a free exchange rate for its currency in the foreign exchange market.)

Apart from this, a communist bureaucracy is working in the dark. It must make blind guesses concerning the size and proportions it wants of the thousands of commodities to which it assigns production quotas for individual farmers. If by oversight or intention it omits some commodities from its production schedules, those commodities will not be produced at all.

The situation is slightly alleviated when the bureaucracy allows individual farmers to devote a certain proportion of their acreage to raising crops for their own consumption. But from the bureaucracy's standpoint, this has a disadvantage. It allows cheating on the part of individual farmers who try to get as much "free" acreage as they can in the hope of having some surplus foodstuffs to sell off on a black market. These farmers, of course, are forced to guess how much they can successfully cheat, and just what surplus production of each commodity would pay the maximum return.

But as the farmers under communism, by and large, do not individually profit from raising the "right" amount of a given crop, and are not proportionately penalized for raising the "wrong" amount, both bureaucrats and farmers are working in the dark. The individual farmers are deprived of the incentives and deterrents that would guide them in a market economy. The bureaucrats' overall plan must chronically go wrong. They do not know the absolute amount of each commodity that it would be most productive to raise nor the *relative* size of each crop. Any relative surplus in the size of one crop must—with a given working force, acreage and capital—force a corresponding shortage in the production of another.

The communists, in short, cannot engage in what the late Ludwig von Mises labeled "economic calculation." Their production plans, therefore, must be unbalanced, haphazard, and wasteful. If they put their emphasis on producing "enough" of commodities A, B, and C, for example, they will almost certainly do so only at the expense of a corresponding shortage of commodities D, E, F, and G.

The Inevitable Errors

The inevitable errors in the communists' overall plans of production must occur as well in their methods of production. In a country operating with a free-market system, of course, individually mistaken and costly methods of production can also be pursued, but through the play of individual profit or loss the more efficient producers will be constantly increasing their share in production and the inefficient will be forced out of the field. Every year something new will be learned. In a non-inflationary free economy there will be a tendency for production methods to be constantly improved and costs to be cut.

So when we examine closely how the two systems, communism and free market economy, work in detail—the one controlled by bureaucrats imposing by fiat a single overall production plan from the top, the other operating through the free and flexible production and consumption choices of millions of individuals, with their individual decisions constantly modified and coordinated by a system of free market prices—we can see why the capitalistic system is so enormously productive, and why the overall production plans of the communist bureaucrats must go wrong *chronically* and *necessarily,* and not merely because of bad luck or bad weather.

It remains to ask why the communist bureaucracies have not recognized this, or even, apparently, acknowledged it to themselves. The most obvious answer is that they have a vested interest in not acknowledging it: they would be overthrown. But a full answer goes much deeper. They did not originally adopt their doctrines through mere analysis and reason, but through an appeal to hatred, envy, vindictiveness, and cupidity: To quote the conclusion of the *Communist Manifesto* (1848): "The workers have nothing to lose but their chains. They have a world to win. Workers of the world, unite!"

Wrong Theories by Marx

Das Kapital, which purports to give the economic reasoning which led to the *Manifesto's* conclusion, did not begin to appear until a quarter century later—1873 for the first volume, 1885 for the second, and 1894 (eleven years after Marx's death) for the third and final volume.

Kapital is obscurely written and nearly unreadable. It is built on a distortion of the errors of Ricardo. It ascribes the creation of all economic goods solely to "labor," overlooking or explaining away the contribution of nature, land, capital, human intelligence, or any other factor. It tries to ignore, also, the thousands of different degrees of specialized labor skills by reducing them all to a single homogenized goo called "the [average?] socially necessary working time" required to produce different commodities and services.

It is only, Marx tells us, the number of hours of this "socially necessary working time" that has gone into a commodity that determines its comparative value in the market. Any profit that goes to an employer above his payroll is in effect stolen from his "exploited" workers.

I shall not go on to explain or expose all the fallacies and contradictions embodied in Marx's theories. That was magnificently done by Eugen von Böhm-Bawerk in his book *Karl Marx and the Close of His System,* originally published in 1896. Only the emergence of "Austrian economics" (beginning about 1870) made such a conclusive refutation of Marx possible. If my reader has not yet read Böhm-Bawerk's book, I recommend that he make up his loss without socially or personally unnecessary delay.

13

The Distribution of Income

For more than a century socialist writers have leveled two main charges against capitalism: 1. It is not productive (or only wastefully productive, or far less productive than some imaginable socialist system would be). 2. It leads to a flagrantly unjust "distribution" of the wealth that it does produce; the workers are systematically exploited; "the rich get richer and the poor get poorer."

Let us consider these charges. That the capitalist system could ever have been accused of being unproductive, or of being very inefficiently productive, will seem incredible to most economic students of the present day, familiar with the record of the last generation. It will seem even more incredible to those familiar with the record since the middle of the eighteenth century. Yet the improvement in that early period remained hidden even from some astute contemporary observers. Thomas Malthus in 1798 (the date of the first edition of his *Essay on Population)* seemed hardly aware of the productive transformation already achieved in the first half of the Industrial Revolution.[1]

Yet much earlier, in 1776, Adam Smith had shown keen awareness of improvement: "The uniform, constant, and uninterrupted effort of every man to better his condition ... is frequently powerful enough to maintain the natural progress of things toward improvement, in spite of the extravagance of government, and of the greatest errors of administration."[2]

Smith rightly attributed this progress to the steady increase of capital brought about by private saving—to the "addition and improvement to those machines and instruments which facilitate and abridge labor."

"To form a right judgment" of this progress, he continued, "one must compare the state of the country at periods somewhat distant from one another. [So as not be deceived by short periods of recession.] ... The annual produce of the land and labor of England, for example, is certainly much greater than it was a little more than a century ago at the restoration of Charles II." And this again was cer-

From the October 1971 issue of *The Freeman*.

tainly much greater "than we can suppose it to have been about a hundred years before, at the accession of Elizabeth." Quite early in *The Wealth of Nations* we find Smith referring to the conditions of his own period as being comparatively, as a result of the increasing division of labor, a period of "universal opulence which extends itself to the lowest ranks of the people."[3]

If we leap ahead another century, we find the economist Alfred Marshall writing in the 1890s:

"The hope that poverty and ignorance may gradually be extinguished, derives indeed much support from the steady progress of the working classes during the nineteenth century. The steam engine has relieved them of much exhausting and degrading toil; wages have risen; education has been improved and become more general. A great part of the artisans have ceased to belong to the 'lower classes' in the sense in which the term was originally used; and some of them lead a more refined and noble life than did the majority of the upper classes even a century ago."[4]

Statistical Comparisons

For more recent years we have the great advantage of getting beyond more or less impressionistic comparisons of economic progress to fairly reliable statistical comparisons. Our chief care here must be to avoid making such comparisons in terms of dollar income at current prices. Because of the continuous monetary inflation in the United States since the 1930s, this would give a very misleading impression. To get a true picture of the real improvement in production and welfare, in so far as these are measurable, allowance must be made for price increases. Statisticians do this by deflating recent prices and incomes in accordance with index numbers of average prices—in other words, by making their comparisons in terms of so-called "constant" dollars.

Let us begin with some over-all figures. In the 59 years between 1910 and 1969 it is estimated that the real gross national product of the United States (the GNP) increased at an average rate of 3.1 percent a year compounded.[5] At such a rate the production of the country has been more than doubling every 24 years.

Let us see how this has looked expressed in billions of 1958 dollars:

Year	GNP
1929	$203.6
1939	209.4
1949	324.1
1959	475.9
1969	727.1

Source: Department of Commerce.

In the ten years from 1939 to 1949, then, the real gross national product of the country increased 55 percent; in the twenty years from 1939 to 1959 it increased 127 percent; in the thirty years from 1939 to 1969 it increased 242 percent.

If we now express this in terms of disposable per capita personal income (at 1958 prices) for these same years, the comparison is less striking because we are allowing for the growth in population, but the progress is still remarkable:

Year	Per capita income
1929	$1,236
1939	1,190
1949	1,547
1959	1,881
1969	2,517

Source: Department of Commerce.

In other words, disposable per capita personal income at constant prices increased 112 percent—or more than doubled—in the generation from 1939 to 1969.

This disposes effectively of the charge that capitalism is unproductive, or unacceptably slow in increasing production. In the thirty years from 1939 to 1969 the United States was still the most capitalistic country in the world; and the world had never before witnessed anything comparable with this vast production of the necessities and amenities of life.

Which Groups Gain Most?

The foregoing figures do nothing, it is true, to answer the charge that capitalism distributes its gains unjustly—that it benefits only the already rich, and leaves the poor, at best, no better off than they were before. These charges are at least partly answered, however, as soon as we compare the *median* incomes of families in constant (1969) prices:

Year	Families (millions)	Median Income
1949	39.3	$4,779
1959	45.1	6,808
1969	51.2	9,433

Source: Department of Commerce.

As the *median* income means that there were just as many families earning more than the amount cited as those earning less, it follows that the 97 percent increase of median real incomes in this twenty-year period must have been shared in by the mass of the people.

Other sets of figures confirm this conclusion. If we compare weekly wages paid in manufacturing, we find that these rose from $23.64 in 1939 to $129.51 in 1969—an increase of 448 percent. As the cost of living was constantly rising during this period, this of course greatly exaggerates labor's gains. Yet even after we restate these wages in terms of constant (1967) prices, we find the following changes in average gross weekly earnings:

Wages	Year (in 1967 prices)
1939	$ 56.83
1949	75.46
1959	101.10
1969	117.95

Source: Department of Labor.

So, far from wages falling to keep pace with increases in living costs, real wages rose 108 percent in this thirty-year period.

Was the worker getting his "fair share," however, in the general increase in production—or was he getting a smaller share compared with, say, the owners of industry?

Dividing the Pie

Let us begin by looking at the sources of personal income. Of the nation's total personal income of $801 billion in 1970, $570.5 billion, or 71 percent, was in wages and salaries and other labor inome. Income from farming came to $16.2 billion, or 2 percent; business and professional income was $51.4 billion, or 6.4 percent. Rental income received by persons was $22.7 billion, or 2.8 percent; dividends came to $25.2 billion, or 3.1 percent; interest received by persons was $65.2 billion, or 8.1 percent. (Source: Economic Indicators, June, 1971, Council of Economic Advisers.) If we total these last three items we get $113.1 billion, or 14.1 percent, of "unearned" income. (The income from farming and from business was partly "earned" and partly "unearned," in undeterminable proportions.)

It is doubtful how much all this tells us about the distribution of income between the "rich" and the "poor." Total wage and salary disbursements include the salaries of high-paid executives and of television and motion-picture stars. On the other hand, rentals, dividends, and interest payments include many millions of moderate-sized individual sums that may represent the major part or the sole means of support of widows and orphans and persons too old or too ill to work. (There are some 30 million American stockholders, for example, and 25 million savings-bank accounts.)

A very significant figure, however, is the comparison of how much the employees get from the corporations with how much the owners get. Let us look first at a few facts about profits. In the five-year period 1965 to 1969 inclusive, all manufacturing corporations of the United States earned profits after Federal income taxes of only 5.2 cents per dollar of sales. Manufacturing corporation profits after taxes as a percentage of stockholders' equity look a little better—they averaged 12.3 percent for the same five years. (Source: *Economic Report of the President,* February, 1971, p. 284.)

Both of these figures, however, overstate the real profits of the corporations. In a period of continuous inflation like the present, the corporations are forced by the tax laws to make inadequate deductions for depreciation of plant and equipment, based on original cost, and not sufficient to cover replacement costs. Profits as a percentage of equity are overstated for still another reason: they are stated in dollars of depreciated purchasing power compared with the dollars that were originally invested.

Lion's Share to Employees

What is more significant (and constantly forgotten) is that the employees of the corporations draw far more from them than the owners. This is exactly the opposite of what is commonly believed. Surveys by the Opinion Research Corporation have found that the median opinion of those polled was that the employees of American corporations receive only 25 cents out of each dollar available for division between the employees and the owners, and that the remaining 75 cents goes to profits. The facts are quite the opposite. In 1970, for example, of the U. S. corporation income available for distribution between the workers and the owners, nine-tenths went to the workers and only one-tenth to the owners. Here is how, in billions of dollars, the division appeared over a series of years:

DIVISION OF U.S. CORPORATE INCOME BETWEEN EMPLOYEES AND STOCKHOLDERS

Year	Profits After Tax	Payrolls	% for Payroll
1970	$36.4	$366.0	91.0
1969	40.0	350.5	89.8
1968	44.2	319.2	87.8
1967	43.0	291.8	87.2
1966	46.7	275.5	85.5
1960	24.8	188.8	88.4
1955	25.4	144.6	85.1

Derived from Office of Business Economics, U.S. Department of Commerce.

If we average out the five years from 1966 to 1970, we find that compensation to employees came to 88.2 percent of the corporation income available for division, and only 11.8 percent, or less than an eighth, went to profits available for share owners.

So if American workers are being "exploited" by the capitalists it is certainly not evident from the figures. One important fact that the anticapitalist mentality so often forgets is that corporation earnings do not constitute a common pool. If manufacturing corporations earn an average of 12 percent on their equity, it does not mean that every corporation earns this average profit margin. Some will earn 20 percent on equity, some 10 percent, some 3 percent—and many will suffer losses. (Over a 40-year period an average of 45 percent of companies—by number—reported losses annually. As a general rule, small companies suffered losses more frequently than did the large corporations.)

Another point to be kept in mind: When profits are large, it does not mean that they are at the expense of the workers. The opposite is more likely to be true. In 1932 and 1933, for example, the two years when the nation's corporations as a whole showed a net loss, the workers also suffered their worst years from unemployment and wage cuts. In a competitive capitalistic economy, aggregate profits and aggregate wages tend to go up or down together. It is to the long-run interest of the workers as well as of stockholders for profits to be high.

A Look at Family Incomes

Turning from the sources of income, we come now to increases in family incomes over recent years and to the division of income as between various segments of the population. Because of rising prices, comparisons between different years of family incomes in current dollars have little meaning. Here is a comparison, however, of the percent distribution of white families by income level, in constant (1968) dollars, between 1950 and 1968:

Family Income	1950	1968
Under $3,000	23.4%	8.9%
$3,000-$4,999	26.8	11.0
$5,000-$6,999	22.9	14.3
$7,000-$9,999	16.6	24.0
$10,000-$14,999	10.2	26.1
$15,000 and over	10.2	15.7
Median income	$4,985	$8,936

Source: U. S. Department of Commerce, Bureau of the Census.

The sharp drop in the percentage of families with "constant" incomes under $3,000 is especially noteworthy. The rise in the over all "real" median income in this eighteen-year period was 79 percent.

The percent of aggregate income received by each fifth of the number of families in the country, and the percent of aggregate income received by the top 5 percent of families, has changed much less over the years, but such change as has occurred has been toward a more equal distribution:

Families	1947	1960	1968
Lowest fifth	5.0%	4.9%	5.7%
Second fifth	11.8	12.0	12.4
Middle fifth	17.0	17.6	17.7
Fourth fifth	23.1	23.6	23.7
Highest fifth	43.0	42.0	40.6
Top 5 percent	17.2	16.8	14.0

Source: U. S. Department of Commerce, Bureau of the Census.

If the reader wishes to know how the various fifths of the population ranged in actual incomes in 1968, and in which fifth or bracket his own family income fell, he can learn it from the following table:

Families	Income Range	% of Income Received
Lowest fifth	Under $4,600	5.7
Second fifth	$4,600-$7,400	12.4
Middle fifth	$7,400-$10,000	17.7
Fourth fifth	$10,000-$13,500	23.7
Highest fifth	$13,500 and over	40.6
Top 5 percent	$23,000 and over	14.0
Top 1 percent	$42,500 and over	5.0

Derived from Herman P. Miller, *Rich Man, Poor Man* (Crowell, 1971), p. 15.

How Government Intervention Affects Each Group

A study published on March 18, 1971 by two Census Bureau statisticians, Herman P. Miller, director of the Census Bureau's population studies, and Roger A. Herriot, concluded that the processes of government now shift income from rich to poor with substantially greater effect than is commonly believed. They contended that most families pay direct and indirect taxes at about the same rate—30 percent—regardless of income level; but that when payments from government (such as unemployment insurance) are taken into account, the result is a markedly progressive redistribution of income. For example, families with earned income of less than $2,000 a year in 1968, according to the study, paid an estimated 50 percent of their income for all taxes—but got back 106.5 percent in government payments. So their "net" tax was not a tax at all, but a benefit of 57 percent. Families with over $50,000 a year, meanwhile, paid 45 percent in total taxes and got back less than 1 percent. So their net tax was 44.7 percent of income.[6]

The income comparisons here presented fail to give any support whatever to the socialist contention that under a capitalist system the tendency is for the rich to get richer and for the poor to get poorer—or at any rate for the proportional "gap" between the rich and poor to increase. What the figures show, on the contrary, is that in a healthy, expanding capitalist economy the tendency is for both the rich and the poor to get richer more or less proportionately. If anything, the position of the poor tends to improve better than proportionately.

This becomes even clearer if, instead of merely comparing incomes in terms of dollars, we look at the comparative gains of the poor that have been brought about by the technological progress that has in turn to so large an extent been brought about by capitalism and capital accumulation. As Herman P. Miller has pointed out:

> Looking back, there is good reason to wonder why the 1920s were ever regarded as a golden age. . . . Take for example a simple matter like electric power. Today electricity in the home is taken for granted as a more or less inalienable right of every American.
>
> Practically every home—on the farm as well as in the city—is electrified. Even on southern farms, ninety-eight out of every hundred homes have electricity. In 1930, nine out of every ten farm homes were without this "necessity." And the country was much more rural than it is now.
>
> A more striking example is provided by the presence of a toilet in the home. . . . As recently as 1940, about 10 percent of city homes and 90 percent of farms lacked toilet facilities within the structure. This is not Russia or China that is being described, but these United States only thirty years ago.

Even the skeptical Paul Samuelson conceded in 1961 that "the American income pyramid is becoming less unequal."[8]

Technological Progress

There can be little doubt that the technological progress of the last two generations has meant more to the families at the bottom of this pyramid than to those at the top. It is the overwhelming majority of Americans that now enjoy the advantages of running water, central heating, telephones, automobiles, refrigerators, washing machines, phonographs, radios, television sets—amenities that millionaires and kings did not enjoy a few generations ago.

Here are some of the figures of the percentage of American households owning cars and appliances in 1969:

ANNUAL INCOME GROUPS

	All Households	Under $3,000	$3,000-$3,999
One or more cars	79.6%	44.7%	67.0%
TV, B&W	79.0	77.5	83.5
TV, Color	31.9	9.5	16.9
Washing Machine	70.0	49.8	60.9
Refrig. or freezer	82.6	75.0	76.8

Source: U. S. Department of Commerce Bureau of the Census.

In view of the fact that government statisticians officially placed the "poverty threshold" for 1969 at $3,721 for a family of four, and $4,386 for a family of five, the percentage of families with incomes less than this who own cars and appliances is remarkable. In 1969, in addition, 90 percent of all American households had telephone service.

To these figures on the distribution of physical appliances we must add many intangibles. The most important of these is the enormous increase in the number of those who have enjoyed the advantage of an education. Broadly speaking, the percentage increase has been greatest for those at the bottom of the pyramid. A century ago (1870), only 57 percent of all children between 5 and 17 years of age attended school. By the turn of the century this had risen to 76 percent, by 1920 to 82 percent, and by 1960 to 89 percent. It was as low as this in 1960 only because children were starting school at 6 years of age instead of at 5. Nearly 97 percent of all children between 7 and 17 years of age were in school in 1960. Even more dramatic are the figures on schooling at a higher level. In 1870, only 2 percent of the relevant age group graduated from high school. This tripled to 6 percent by 1900, tripled again to 17 percent by 1920, and again to 50 percent by 1940. It had reached 62 percent by 1956. Enrollment in institutions of higher education—junior colleges, colleges, and universities—was less than 2 percent of the relevant age group in 1870, and more than 30 percent in 1960.[9]

Serving the Masses

The long-run historical tendency of capitalism has been to benefit the masses even more than the rich. Before the Industrial Revolution the prevailing trades catered almost exclusively to the wants of the well-to-do. But mass production could only succeed by catering to the needs of the masses. And this could be done only by dramatically reducing the costs and prices of goods to bring them within the buying power of the masses. So modern capitalism benefited the masses in a double way—both by greatly increasing the wages of the masses of workers and greatly reducing the real prices they had to pay for what was produced.

Under the feudal system, and nearly everywhere before the Industrial Revolution, a man's economic position was largely determined by the economic position of his parents. To what extent is this true in the United States of the present day? This is a difficult question to answer in quantitative terms, because one of the intangibles a man tends to "inherit" from his parents is his educational level, which so largely influences his adult earning power. But some of the partial answers we do have to this question are surprising. Herman P. Miller tells us:

"In 1968 fewer than one family out of a hundred in the top income group lived entirely on unearned income—interest, dividends, rents, royalties, and the like. The other ninety-nine did paid work or were self-employed in a business or profession. Nearly all of these families were headed by a man who worked at a full-time job. In 1968 over four-fifths of these men worked full time throughout the year."[10]

They also seemed to work longer hours than the average worker. Among the rich, also, "relatively few admit to having inherited a substantial proportion of their assets. Even among the very rich—those with assets of $500,000 or more—only one-third reported that they had inherited a substantial proportion of their assets; 39 percent claimed to have made it entirely on their own, and an additional 24 percent admitted to having inherited a small proportion of their assets."[11]

International Comparisons

I have said nothing so far of the comparison of American incomes with those of other nations. In absolute figures—in gross national product per capita, in ownership of passenger cars and TV sets, in use of telephones, in working time required to buy a meal—these comparisons have been all heavily in favor of the United States. In 1968, the per capita gross national product of the country came to $4,379, compared with $3,315 in Sweden, $2,997 in Canada, $2,537 in France, $1,861 in the United Kingdom, $1,418 in Italy, $1,404 in Japan, $566 in Mexico, and $80 in India.[12]

More immediately relevant to our subject is a comparison of the distribution of income in the United States with that in other countries. In this respect also the result has been largely in favor of the United States. A comparison of conditions in the 1950's made by Simon Kuznets found that the top 5 percent of families received 20 percent of the U. S. national income. Industrialized countries like Sweden, Denmark, and Great Britain showed approximately the same percentage. It was in the "underdeveloped" countries where the greatest internal disparities existed in incomes. For example, in El Salvador the top 5 percent of families received 36 percent of the national income, in Mexico 37 percent, in Colombia 42 percent. This comparison is one more evidence that capitalism and industrialization tend to reduce inequalities of income.

I have entitled this article "The Distribution of Income," and have been using that phrase throughout; but I have done so with reluctance. The phrase is misleading. It implies to many people that income is first produced, and *then* "distributed"—according to some arbitrary and probably unjust arrangement.

A Misleading Phrase

Something like this idea appears to have been in the back of the minds of the older economists who first began to arrange their textbooks under these headings. Thus, Book I of John Stuart Mill's *Principles of Political Economy* (1848) is entitled "Production," and Book II, "Distribution." Mill wrote, at the beginning of this second book:

> The principles which have been set forth in the first part of this Treatise are, in certain respects, strongly distinguished from those on the consideration of which we are now about to enter. The laws and conditions of the production of wealth partake of the character of physical truths. There is nothing optional or arbitrary in them. . . .

> It is not so with the Distribution of Wealth. That is a matter of human institution solely. The things once there, mankind, individually or collectively, can do with them as they like.... The distribution of wealth, therefore, depends on the laws and customs of society.

This distinction, if not altogether false, is greatly overstated. Production in a great society could not take place—on the farms, in the extraction of raw materials, in the many stages of processing into finished goods, in transportation, marketing, saving, capital accumulation, guidance by price and cost and supply and demand—without the existence of security, law and order, and recognized property rights—the same rules and laws that enable each to keep the fruits of his labor or enterprise. Goods come on the market as the property of those who produced them. They are not first produced and then distributed, as they would be in some imagined socialist society. The "things" are not "once there." The period of production is never completed, to be followed by some separate period of distribution. At any given moment production is in all stages. In the automobile industry, for example, some material is being mined, some exists in the form of raw materials, some in finished or semifinished parts; some cars are going through the assembly line, some are on the factory lots awaiting shipment, some are in transport, some are in dealers' hands, some are being driven off by the ultimate buyers; most are in use, in various stages of depreciation and wear and need of replacement.

Everyone Gains

In brief, production, distribution, and consumption all go on continuously and concurrently. What is produced, and how much of it, and by what method, and by whom, depends at all times on the relative sums that those engaged in the process are receiving or expect to receive in profits or wages or other compensation. Production depends no less than distribution on "the laws and customs of society." If farmer Smith raises 100 bushels of potatoes and farmer Jones 200 bushels, and both sell them for the same price per bushel, Jones does not have twice as much income as Smith because it has been "distributed" to him. Each has got the market value of what he produced.

It would be better to speak of the *variation* between individual incomes than of their "distribution." I have used the latter term only because it is customary and therefore more readily understood. But it can be, to repeat, seriously misleading. It tends to lead to the prevalent idea that the solution to the problem of poverty consists in finding how to expropriate part of the income of those who have earned "more than they need" in order to "distribute" it to those who have not earned enough. The real solution to the problem of poverty, on the contrary, consists in finding how to increase the employment and earning power of the poor.

---

1. See "The Problem of Poverty" in *The Freeman,* June 1971, pp. 325–6.
2. *The Wealth of Nations,* Book II, Ch. III.
3. Book I, Ch. I.
4. *Principles of Economics,* Eighth edition, pp. 3–4.
5. Based on estimates by the Department of Commerce expressed in "constant" (1958) dollars.
6. The estimate that families with earned incomes of less than $2,000 a year paid a total in taxes of 50 percent of their income seems on its face extremely high, but I cite the conclusions of the study as given.
7. *Rich Man, Poor Man* (New York: Thomas Y. Crowell Co., 1971), pp. 44–45.
8. *Economics: An Introductory Analysis,* 5th edition (New York: McGraw Hill Book Co.), p. 114.
9. Author's source: Rose D. Friedman, *Poverty: Definition and Perspective* (Washington: American Enterprise Institute, 1965), p. 11.
10. *Rich Man, Poor Man,* p. 150.
11. *Ibid.,* p. 157.
12. *Statistical Abstract of the United States,* 1970, p. 810.

THE ROAD NOT TAKEN

14

The Road Not Taken

The Foundation for Economic Education, which publishes *The Freeman,* was set up in 1946. This seems to me as appropriate a time as any to review what has happened since its establishment in the realm of the government interventions and economic controls—the prohibitions and compulsions—that FEE was set up to combat.

In 1946, of course, these controls were already established over a wide-ranging area. A formidable network of what might be called "traditional" controls was already in existence in the early 1930s; but this was enormously extended and tightened by the advent of the New Deal. It was then established that the government could repudiate with impunity its most solemn pledges —the gold clause, for example; that it could abrogate contracts containing or assuming this clause; that it could allow labor unions to resort to violence and vandalism with relative immunity (as in the Norris-LaGuardia Act of 1932); that the government could act as a union organizing agency, and force employers to "bargain collectively" with such unions—that is, to make at least some concessions to their demands—as in the Wagner Act of 1935. And so on.

But let us now come to 1946, the year FEE was founded. That was the year when the International Monetary Fund, which had been set up by the Bretton Woods Agreement of 1944, began to operate. The IMF had been set up ostensibly—believe it or not—to "stabilize" currencies. And this was to be done by phasing that absurd and tyrannical thing, the gold standard, out of the monetary system. Instead, the member countries pledged themselves to keep their currencies convertible at a fixed rate only into the dollar. If the dollar were kept convertible into gold, it was assumed, that would be sufficient to stabilize the whole world currency system and make the value of each national money unit dependable.

Of course none of the Fund's general rules were expected to be obeyed too strictly. That would have interfered with the freedom of each country's monetary authorities to manipulate their currency in the

---

From the February 1979 issue of *The Freeman*.

way that seemed to them most expedient at any given moment. Therefore, it was explicitly provided in the Fund's Articles of Agreement that any country could devalue its own currency at least 10 percent in any one step, and it was explicitly stipulated that "the Fund shall raise no objection." In addition, it was understood that the Fund was to come to the rescue of any country whose currency got into trouble, even through its own inflationary policies. The stronger currencies were to support the weaker ones, thus insuring that the stronger would also be weakened.

The Results of Bretton Woods

We all know now what this finally led to. The American monetary authorities could not bring themselves to take seriously the grave responsibility they had assumed in agreeing to make the dollar the world's anchor currency. Keeping the dollar convertible into gold, even if only at the demand of foreign central banks, seemed to them a mere technical requirement, an unnecessary annoyance and burden imposed upon them by some still persisting superstitions about gold. As the U.S. increased its paper-money issue, conversion became increasingly inconvenient. It practically stopped de facto in 1968, and in August 1971, it was stopped openly and officially. Since then practically every nation's currency has become an irredeemable paper currency. Every currency fluctuates every day in terms of every other. Money values, world trade, and capital flows become more and more disorderly and unpredictable.

And all this has happened because the world's so-called statesmen and national monetary managers, when they met at Bretton Woods in 1944, were thinking only of their own immediate problems, and had no understanding of what the consequences of their patched-up scheme would be in the long run.

The same kind of shortsightedness has been the common characteristic of nearly all the government interventions of the last 30 years. We may select our examples almost at random.

Minimum Wage Laws

Take minimun wage laws. A national minimum wage was first enacted in this country in 1938. At that time the average hourly wage in American manufacturing was about 63 cents. Congress set a legal minimum of 25 cents. In 1945, the year before FEE was set up, the average factory wage had risen to $1.02 an hour, and Congress raised the legal minimum to 40 cents.

It all seemed very reasonable, very compassionate, very necessary, to those who urged and those who voted for it. Could the country tolerate ruthless exploitation of unskilled workers with no bargaining power? Could it tolerate "starvation" wages? The obvious remedy seemed to be to prohibit such wages. Employers were forbidden to offer jobs at wages below the new legal minimum.

An ironic thing happened. As increased capital investment, increased productivity, and competition among employers (all with a little help from inflation) kept raising the average hourly dollar wage, and making each existing legal minimum wage level obsolete, Congress acted as if its prescribed minimums had brought this rise about. It kept amending the law every few years. It kept raising its minimum wage faster than the market was raising the average wage. It acted on the principle that whatever average wage the market produced, it would never be high enough. Congress has acted as if by constantly boosting the legal minimum it could hurry the market along. The minimum wage, at $2.65 an hour in 1978 and $2.90 in 1979, is scheduled to keep going up to $3.35 an hour on January 1, 1981.

Is this helping the poor? Is it helping the unskilled worker? The results show that it is doing exactly the opposite. Minimum wage laws overlook the obvious. It should be obvious that the first thing that must happen when a law prescribes that no one shall be paid, say, less than $106 for a 40-hour week, is that no one who is not worth $106 a week to the employer will be employed at all.

And if statistics can show anything they show this. The minimum wage laws were passed to help especially the unskilled, the teen-agers, and the blacks. We have no comparative figures on the unskilled as such, but we do have comparative figures on the teen-agers and the blacks. There has always been a tendency for teen-age unemployment to run at a somewhat higher rate than that of men and women 20 years old and over, but it took the minimum wage levels and their successive increases to make the contrast a startling one.

It is difficult to get comparative statistics going back beyond 1948. In that year the unemployment rate for both white and non-white teen-agers stood at 10 percent. But as the minimum wage rate was jacked up year by year, not only did the overall teen-age rate of unemployment keep rising, but it kept rising much more for black teen-agers than for white. In 1954 unemployment for black teen-agers stood at 14.9 percent against 13 percent for white. By 1968 the black teen-ager unemployment rate had risen to 26.6 percent against 11.6 percent for whites. In 1977 it rose to 37 percent for black teen-agers against 15 percent for white. Between 1977 and 1978 unemployment for 16- to 17-year-old blacks rose from 38.7 percent to 50.4 percent.

So the minimum wage law and its successive hikes has simply driven into unemployment the very people it was most designed to help. The potential production of these people has been lost to the economy.

And what is the response to this consequence by the Congressmen who voted for the law and for the annual increases? They have simply ignored it. They would consider it political suicide, in fact, to oppose the minimum wage law.

Unemployment Insurance

A similar history can be traced for unemployment insurance. This was one of the great New Deal "reforms" adopted in 1935. The argument for it was appealing. Workers suffered terrific hardships when they were laid off. Even when they were working, they lived in dread of sudden unemployment. Certainly they should be assured of unemployment compensation when they were forced to look for new jobs.

The first State-Federal unemployment insurance programs, beginning about 1940, were surrounded with safeguards. Unemployment compensation was to be about one-half of the worker's previous earnings, but it was to run typically for only 16 weeks, and there was to be at least a two-week waiting period for the worker, after losing his job, before he would be eligible for that compensation. But gradually, all these safeguards were weakened or removed. The typical waiting period was reduced from two weeks to one, and in some States to none at all. The period for paying the compensation was extended from 16 weeks to 20, then to 26 weeks, then to 39 (in an emergency, of course), then in some States to 65 weeks. In 1969 President Nixon called upon the States to provide for maximum weekly benefits of two-thirds of the previous average weekly wages instead of one-half.

The result of prolonging and increasing unemployment compensation, naturally, has been to prolong and increase unemployment. It was found a year or so ago by a committee of the State Senate of New York that a number of New Yorkers repeatedly worked the minimum 20 weeks required and then collected 65 weeks of unemployment benefits. Though unemployment compensation may be only one-half of previous working salary, the unemployment compensation is tax-free, so the net loss from not working is sometimes quite tolerable. In a typical case in Pennsylvania, for example, a man whose previous weekly take-home pay was $140 can draw $96 a week in tax-free compensation. A study made by the U.S. Department of Labor itself found that "an increase in unemployment benefits leads to an increase in the duration of unemployment." This country can have as much unemployment as it wants to pay for.

Rent Control

Still another example of our shortsighted legislation is rent control. This is usually imposed in the early stages of an inflation. As the inflation goes on, the discrepancy between the rent the landlord is allowed to charge, and the rent necessary to yield him a return comparable with that in other investments, becomes greater and greater. The landlord soon has neither the incentive to make repairs and improvements, nor the funds to make them.

When the rent control is first imposed, the government promises that new buildings will be exempt from it; but this assurance is soon repudiated by a new law. It becomes unprofitable to build new rental housing. New mortgage money for it becomes increasingly difficult to obtain. Landlords of old housing often can no longer supply even heat and other essential services. Some cannot even pay their taxes; their property has in effect been expropriated; they abandon it and disappear. Old rental housing is destroyed quicker than new housing is built.

Some favored tenants, already in possession, are momentary beneficiaries, but tenants or would-be tenants as a whole, in whose interest the legislation has been professedly passed, become the final victims. The irony is that the longer rent control is continued, and the more unrealistic the fixed rents become as compared with those that would yield an adequate return, the more certain the politicians are that any attempt to repeal the rent control would be "politically suicidal."

The Energy Crisis

The limits of space compel me to pass over any analysis of a score of other government interventions in recent years in the economic field, and to come immediately to the two or three that mainly characterize the economic situation today, not only in our own country, but throughout the world.

In 1974 the Organization of Petroleum Exporting Countries—the OPEC quadrupled crude oil prices. It is instructive to notice that this was done by a combination of governments. They did what private industry is always accused of doing—forming a monopolistic conspiracy—but what the hundreds of private oil-well owners and companies would never have been able to impose and enforce no matter how much most of them might have wanted to do so.

This OPEC action produced a profound economic shock throughout the world. And what was the response of our own government? Did it retain or insist on a free market to give the greatest possible incentive to petroleum production and exploration on the one hand and economy in consumption on the other? No. It did the exact opposite. It imposed an elaborate and incredibly complicated set of price controls on domestic crude oil and on natural gas, to encourage continued wasteful consumption and to reduce the incentives to output and exploration. It preferred to protect the short-term interest of American consumers at the cost of their real long-term interest, and at the cost of both the short-term and long-term interest of American producers.

Rampant Inflation

Now let us turn to the government policies that most obviously affect us in all our daily activities—government finances and monetary inflation. Throughout our history as a nation, when we were on the gold standard, federal government surpluses were the rule. Deficits—except in the two world wars —were rare and comparatively small. But in 1931, we began to run chronic deficits—in the first few years by accident, and then by deliberate policy. In the last ten years or so, these deficits have been acceleratively larger. These deficits—again since the early 1930s—have been accompanied by mounting monetary inflation. The dollar's purchasing power has been reduced, for example, to about 22 cents compared with that of 1940.

To bring this inflation to an end, what policy must we follow in the immediate future? Obviously what needs to be done is to bring the budget back to balance at the earliest possible moment. Obviously what needs to be done is to halt the accelerative increase in money and credit, to stop printing more paper dollars. But the situation is now so bad that practically no politician dares to suggest this course.

About half of our Federal expenditure programs consist in the transfer of income from the wealthy or the middle-classes to the so-called needy. In other words, they force the productive to support the unproductive. In the official budget these programs are not gathered under a single head. But there is a table, on page 191 of the official budget for fiscal 1979, called "National Need: Providing Income Security," which estimates the total of such expenditures for fiscal 1979 at $160 billion. Who is there—among our officeholders—who is going to suggest cutting these expenditures? And by how much? And who is there who is going to suggest halting the reckless expansion of our money supply and risking a recession? The situation is so bad that no politician dares to suggest where to begin in correcting it. Once more, that is considered the path of political suicide.

The Dilemma

This is the ominous dilemma that confronts us. Some of my readers must have recognized that the title of this article is taken from the title of a poem—"The Road Not Taken"—by Robert Frost. The last stanza of that poem reads:

> I shall be telling this with a sigh
> Somewhere ages and ages hence:
> Two roads diverged in a wood, and I—
> I took the one less travelled by,
> And that has made all the difference.

Perhaps most of us have had a similar experience, either figuratively or literally. You may have driven on a throughway, for example, toward a destination to which you had never driven before, and may have been told, or may have figured out from a map, that you should get off, say, at Exit 23. And then, suddenly and too late, you realize that you have driven past Exit 23. You can't turn back. You must look for the next exit, which may be miles ahead, and hope you will know what to do when you get there. You realize that you are going to be late, so you start almost unconsciously to speed up, but are aware that you are only going faster in the wrong direction.

We have reached such a dilemma in our political and economic life. We have taken the wrong road, and we have been on it so long that getting back on the right one seems almost hopeless. The longer we stay on the wrong political road, the more difficult it is to correct the error.

If—to take one example out of a hundred—rent conrol has been imposed for only a short time, so that the average of controlled rents is still about 90 percent of what free market rents would be, it is no great political problem to remove the controls. But if, as has sometimes happened, rent controls have been imposed so long in a severe inflation that the controlled rents averaged only 10 percent of free market rates, then any attempt to remove the controls might bring on riots. This has happened frequently in recent years in countries in which, for example, the government has been subsidizing food prices and can no longer afford it.

The wrong road has been the road of government economic intervention. The right road would have been to permit and encourage free markets. There are, it is true, a number of politicians today who praise the free market in speeches, but there are very few people, even among economists, who understand why the free market solves so many intractable problems and performs so many near-miracles.

The market does this because it reflects and responds to everybody's demand and to everybody's supply, and it reflects to some extent everybody's expectations regarding the future. This means that it makes the maximum use of everybody's knowledge, and not merely the knowledge of a handful of officials. It reflects this knowledge by constant daily changes in prices of individual commodities and services. These price changes are daily directing production out of this commodity and into that, reducing surpluses and relieving shortages.

The market does not fulfill this function perfectly, because everyone's knowledge is limited and subject to error; and these errors do not necessarily cancel each other. But the market is constantly and quickly correcting these errors. It works incomparably better in maximizing and properly directing incentives than any other imaginable system. Only when this truth is sufficiently recognized by the public will the free market be restored.

15

The Torrent of Laws

All over the United States, if you are reading this in a daylight hour, there is a ceaseless downpour of new laws. Every day some of us, somewhere, are being encumbered or shackled by still more restrictions. There are just too many laws.

But how do we tell how many laws are too many, and which ones are pernicious?

Let us begin with some elementary considerations. A law may be defined as an edict which either forbids you to do something or compels you to do something. Sometimes, it is true, it may be merely a guiding rule which tells you how to do something, or defines procedures or standards, like weights and measures. But such standard-setting laws are few in number. Most laws are prohibitions or compulsions—in short, commands.

Why are laws necessary? They are necessary, first of all, to prevent people from injuring or aggressing against their neighbors; to prevent theft and fraud, vandalism and violence. On the more positive side, they are necessary to lay down rules of action, so that others may know what to expect of us and we of others, so that we may anticipate each other's actions, keep out of each other's way, and work and act so far as possible in cooperation and harmony.

In a modern society, the traffic laws epitomize law in general. When they instruct us to keep on the right side, to drive within a specified speed limit on a given street or highway, to stop at a red light, to signal our intended turns, they may seem to an impatient driver to be restricting his liberty, to be preventing him from getting to his destination in minimum time. But because these restrictions apply to everyone else, they are, if they are well conceived, helping not only him but all of us to get to our multitudinous destinations in the minimum time in which this can be done smoothly and safely.

How many traffic laws do we need? That is a difficult question to answer numerically. A general traffic code need consist only of a few simple rules, but they could all, it would seem, easily be embodied in

From the January 1979 issue of *The Freeman*.

a single statute. In any case, if the government confined itself to enacting a code of laws simply intended to prevent mutual aggression and to maintain peace and order, it is hard to see how such a code would run into any great number of laws.

England in 1854

Now let us look at the situation we actually face. In order to get an adequate picture, let us begin by comparing it with the situation as it existed more than a century ago in, for example, England. Let us take the year 1854, when the British philosopher Herbert Spencer wrote an essay on "Overlegislation." Some of us are apt to assume that the mid-nineteenth century in England was perhaps the time and place when a great nation came nearest to a laissez-faire regime. Spencer did not find it so. He found the country buried under needless legislation, and piling up more. With the change of a few details, his essay sounds as if it were written yesterday:

> Take up a daily newspaper and you will probably find a leader exposing the corruption, negligence, or mismanagement of some State department. Cast your eye down the next column, and it is not unlikely that you will read proposals for an extension of State supervision. . . . Thus, while every day chronicles a failure, there every day reappears the belief that it needs but an Act of Parliament and a staff of officers, to effect any end desired.

Spencer went on to refer to mid-nineteenth-century England's "20,000 statutes, which it assumes all Englishmen to know, and which not one Englishman does know." He found officialdom systematically slow, stupid, extravagant, unadaptive, and corrupt; and yet given more and more duties to fulfill. Instead of being confined to its primary duty of protecting each individual against others, the State is asked in a hundred ways to protect each individual against himself—"against his own stupidity, his own idleness, his own improvidence, rashness, or other defect."

"It is in the very nature of things," he continued, "that an agency employed for two purposes must fulfill both imperfectly."

> . . . And if an institution undertakes, not two functions, but a score—if a government, whose office it is to defend citizens against aggressors, foreign and domestic, engages also to disseminate Christianity, to administer charity, to teach children their lessons, to adjust prices of food, to inspect coal mines, to regulate railways, to superintend housebuilding, to arrange cab-fares, to look into people's stink-traps, to vaccinate their children, to send out emigrants, to prescribe hours of labor, to examine lodging-houses, to test the knowledge of mercantile captains, to provide public libraries, to read and authorize dramas, to inspect passenger-ships, to see that small dwellings are supplied with water, to regulate endless things from a banker's issues down to the boat fares on the Serpentine—is it not manifest that its primary duty must be ill discharged in proportion to the multiplicity of affairs it busies itself with?

Let us now pass over a century and a quarter, and see how our situation today compares with England's then.

It is the individual states that enact the laws that affect their citizens most often and most intimately in their daily living. A figure averaging the number of laws passed each year in each of the 50 states would be hard to compile on a continuing basis and perhaps mean less than particular examples. Let us take our two most populous states, New York and California. During 1975, 1976, and 1977, the New York state legislature passed, respectively, 870, 966, and 982 public laws. ("Private laws" are not included here, as these individually affect only a handful of people.) During these same three years the California state legislature passed 1280, 1487, and 1261 public laws.

Prohibitions or Rule-Changes

Now let us look at the implications of this. What does a new law do? It either puts a new prohibition or a new compulsion on each of us (or a large number of us), or it changes the rules under which we have hitherto been acting. So on the basis of these figures the citizens of individual states are being subjected to an average of about a thousand new prohibitions or rule-changes every year. No one is excused from not knowing what every one of these new laws commands. I leave it to the reader to picture what all this means in terms of human liberty.

But we have not even got to Federal laws. Supposedly, these are only needed to cover such matters as interstate commerce and are subject to severe limitations by the Constitution, so an innocent reader of that document might not see the need for many such laws. Though the Federal books were presumably blank when it started, the First Congress, which began on March 1789, did not see the need for many Federal laws. It enacted only 94.

But then, as more and more laws were piled up, succeeding Congresses were convinced that more and more additional laws were necessary. The 85th Congress, which opened in January 1957, enacted 1,009 laws; the 94th, which began in January 1975, enacted 588. The ten Congresses during that period enacted an average of 735 laws each, which means an average of 367 new Federal laws a year—or one new law every day. The reader should be reminded that individually many of these laws ran to well over 100 pages each.

Congressional Promises

The mania for piling up additional laws—new compulsions or prohibitions or changes of the rules—seems to be endemic in our democratic process. Every two years, when a new Congress is chosen, the rival candidates are eager to convince the voters that they can shower more blessings upon them than their respective competitors. "There ought to be a law," they tell the voters, to forbid this or that, or to give you this or that. "If I am elected, I will introduce a bill"—to guarantee you this or that. So almost every Congressman introduces at least one bill with his name attached to it.

In the 94th Congress, which began in January, 1975, 3,899 bills were introduced in the Senate and 15,863 in the House—an average of 37 bills per member. These are by no means unusual figures. In the 93rd Congress, 4,260 bills were introduced in the Senate and 17,690 bills in the House. It is at least one stroke of luck for the country that only about one in every 30 or more such bills survives to enactment. But the individual Congressman who introduces it has made his point. He has "carried out his promise" to the voters.

It has been estimated that American legislative bodies ranging from city councils to Congress pass 150,000 new laws every year.[1] This total does not mean too much, because only a small section of the total applies to the residents of any given town or state. But a very meaningful figure would be the total number of live laws that still do apply to American residents of any given city or state.

Since its beginning Congress has enacted more than 40,000 laws. It is a fair assumption that most of these are still operative in some form.

When we come to the individual states we get to some really formidable figures. For Connecticut I am officially informed that: "We do not have information on the 'live' laws now on the books, but it is our understanding that there are about 3,500,000 words in the eleven volumes of the General Statutes."[2] The legislative authorities of California regret that so far as the number of "presently operative statutes" of that state are concerned, "no such enumeration is readily obtainable," though "most (but not all) enactments of the California legislature are codified in one of twenty-eight codes." And the Department of State of New York informs me that so far as the total of live laws on the state's books are concerned, "unfortunately, we don't have the answer to this question." So far as the "consolidated" (as distinguished from the "unconsolidated") laws are concerned, however, these can be found in "six volumes covering 891 pages." No one is allowed to plead ignorance of any of these state laws, of course, if he happens to violate one.

Local Ordinances

When we come to the number of town and city ordinances to which each of us is subject, it is difficult to say precisely what would be an average figure. But in Boston, for example, the Building Code alone contains about 500 pages; in addition, the City of Boston code consists of approximately 300 pages of ordinances and 300 pages of statutes. The Administrative Code of New York City consists of ten volumes running to a total of 8,000 pages. There are also 23 thick volumes of ringbinder notebooks containing the rules and regulations of city agencies published since 1967.

But on top of all of these laws—Federal, state, and local —is piled the greatest mountain of all—the endless orders, regulations, and edicts issued by the Federal and state "independent agencies." There are 89 separate Federal independent agencies listed in the Congressional Directory for 1977. These are in addition to the innumerable commissions, "offices," "services," and "administrations" listed under the 12 cabinet departments. As long ago as 1954 the Hoover Commission found that the Federal government embraced no fewer than 2,133 different functioning agencies, bureaus, departments, and divisions. And practically all of them were running "programs."

It was 10 years ago that Delaware Congressman William V. Roth and his staff made an eight-month statistical study and came up with the finding that "no one, anywhere, knows exactly how many Federal programs there are"—or who is spending how much on what. According to the 1968 Roth study, the Federal government at that time had 1,571 identifiable programs. Questionnaires sent to various agencies drew spotty responses. Inquiries were made as to the purpose of some 478 programs in Health, Education and Welfare; only 21 responded.

In August 1978, Congressman Gene Taylor from Missouri, going through stacks of the Code of Federal Regulations, found that the Code ran to 19,789 pages in 1938, to 20,643 in 1958, to 73,149 in 1976, and calculated it would top 120,000 pages by the end of 1978.

Adding the Costs

How can we add up the countless costs, penalties, discouragements, delays, hazards, impediments, obstructions, that these orders place in the way of production and commerce?

Even if we give up the futile attempt to add up the government regulations numerically, we can still point to some of the costs and hardships that they impose on the taxpayer, the motorist, the businessman, the homeowner, the consumer, the worker, the investor, and the nation as a whole. In the July Tax Review of 1978, published by the Tax Foundation of New York, Murray L. Weidenbaum, a former Assistant Secretary of the Treasury, has detailed some of these costs:

- The outlays of 41 regulator agencies are esimated to have increased from $2.2 billion in the fiscal year 1974 to $4.8 billion in fiscal 1979, a growth of 115 percent over the five-year period.
- Federally mandated safety and environmental features increased the price of the average passenger automobile by $666 in 1978.
- There are over 4,400 different Federal forms that the private sector must fill out each year. That takes 143 million man hours. The Federal Paperwork Commission recently estimated that the total cost

of Federal paperwork imposed on private industry ranges from $25 billion to $32 billion a year, and that "a substantial portion of this cost is unnecessary."

• Regulatory requirements imposed by Federal, state, and local governments are adding between $1,500 and $2,500 to the cost of a typical new house.

• On the basis of a conservative estimating procedure, the aggregate cost of complying with Federal regulation came to $62.9 billion in 1976, or over $300 for each man, woman, and child in the United States. On the same basis, these costs may have reached $96.7 billion in the fiscal year ending September 30, 1978.

• The minimum-wage law has priced hundreds of thousands of people out of the labor markets. One increase alone has been shown, on the basis of careful research, to have reduced teen-age employment by 225,000.

• Approximately $10 billion of new private capital spending is devoted each year to meeting governmentally-mandated environmental, safety, and similar regulations rather than being invested in profit-making projects. Edward Denison of the Brookings Institution has estimated that in recent years these deflections of private investment from productive uses have resulted in a loss of approximately one-fourth of the potential annual increase in productivity.

• The nation as a whole feels the effect of government regulation in a reduced rate of innovation and in many other ways. The adverse consequences of government intervention in business decision-making range from a slowdown in the availability of new pharmaceutical products to the cancellation of numerous small pension plans.

Congressman Gene Taylor, whose figures on the extent of the Code of Federal Regulations I have previously cited, declares: "The cost imposed on the American economy by federal regulatory activity is now more than $60 billion per year. This serves to drive up the cost of consumer items, harasses small businessmen, fuels inflation, and increases the tax burden on the individual citizen."

An Ominous Trend

Suppose we turn back from our survey of the present enormous power and control now exercised by government, to a look at its growth since 1854 in England when Herbert Spencer was already expressing his alarm at the extent of that control. If the reader will glance down the list of the interferences that Spencer was then deploring, he will see that our own government is still engaged in all of them, or their equivalent (with the exception only of disseminating Christianity and sending out emigrants), but has added literally hundreds more.

In 1977 The Conference Board of New York was referring to some of that year's economic interventions: price and income controls; limitations on profits; growing representation of workers and government on company boards of directors; statutory wage hikes; credit limitations; foreign exchange and import controls; limitations on foreign ownership; rent controls and subsidies; regulations on land-use planning; environmental, safety, and consumer protection regulations; antitrust laws; direct and indirect taxes; and government ownership. But the list could have been indefinitely extended.

There are two or three ways of trying to measure the size or growth of government quantitatively. One index is the number of people that it wholly or partly supports. In 1940 all American governments, Federal, state, and local, were employing 4,474,000 people. In 1977, the number was 14,624,000. The Federal government alone, in 1978, employed 2,066,000 persons in its armed forces and 1,930,100 in full-time permanent civilian employment. In addition, it was making Social Security payments to some 33 million persons, and the Congressional Budget Office was estimating that about 44 million were receiving some form of welfare aid.

The annual expenditures of the Federal government tell a succinct story. If we take them at ten-year intervals since 1929, we get the following result:

Year	**Expenditures**
1929	$ 3.1 billion
1939	8.8 "
1949	38.8 "
1959	92.1 "
1969	184.5 "
1979	487.5 "

If any forecaster had dared to predict in 1929 that 50 years later the Federal government would be spending nearly 160 times as much in dollars in a single year (or 43 times as much in "real" terms), nobody would have believed him. By such a comparison, we have had a 4,200 percent growth in the Federal government since 1929.

A Bewildering Mass of Government Interventions

Some readers may object that it is meaningless to complain about the mere number of laws; that we should carefully separate the "good" laws from the "bad," and deplore only the latter. What this objection overlooks is that the mere multiplication and proliferation of laws is itself a major evil. Every unnecessary law is itself bound to be pernicious. And almost all laws that interfere with the functioning of the free market tend to delay or prevent necessary readjustments in the balance of production and consumption and to have other consequences opposite to those that the framers intended. When the rules of the game are being changed every day, when the totality of laws and regulations reaches the tens of thousands and the hundreds of thousands, the number of legislative blunders must multiply far more than proportionately. How is it possible to talk of retaining our liberties, for example, when collectively we are subjected not only to thousands of prohibitions and compulsions but to daily increasing prohibitions and compulsions?

More than 40 years ago the Swedish economist Gustav Cassell was warning: "The leadership of the state in economic affairs . . . is necessarily connected with a bewildering mass of governmental interferences of a steadily cumulative nature. The arbitrariness, the mistakes and the inevitable contradictions of such a polity will, as daily experience shows, only strengthen the demand for a more rational coordination of the different measures and, therefore, for unified leadership. For this reason planned economy will always tend to develop into dictatorship."

Whatever the outcome may be, the future seems ominous. By whatever standard we measure it—the number of laws, the rate at which new ones are enacted, the multiplication of bureaus and agencies, the number of officeholders, pensioners, and relief-recipients the taxpayer is forced to support, the total or relative tax load, the total or per-capita expenditures—there has been an accelerative growth in the size, arbitrary power, and incursion of government, and in the new prohibitions, compulsions, and costs it keeps imposing upon us all.

---

1. *Newsweek,* January 10, 1977.

2. Letter, June 7, 1978, from Agnes L. Kerr, Director, Administrstive-Legislative Division, Office of the Secretary of State, State of Connecticut.

16

From Spencer's 1884 to Orwell's 1984

In 1884, Herbert Spencer wrote what quickly became a celebrated book, *The Man Versus the State.* The book is seldom referred to now, and gathers dust on library shelves—if, in fact, it is still stocked by many libraries. Spencer's political views are regarded by most present-day writers, who bother to mention him at all, as "extreme *laissez faire,*" and hence "discredited."

But any open-minded person who takes the trouble today to read or reread *The Man Versus the State* will probably be startled by two things. The first is the uncanny clairvoyance with which Spencer foresaw what the future encroachments of the State were likely to be on individual liberty, above all in the economic realm. The second is the extent to which these encroachments had already occurred in 1884, the year in which he was writing.

The present generation has been brought up to believe that government concern for "social justice" and for the plight of the needy was something that did not even exist until the New Deal came along in 1933. The ages prior to that have been pictured as periods when no one "cared," when laissez faire was rampant, when everybody who did not succeed in the cutthroat competition that was euphemistically called free enterprise—but was simply a system of dog-eat-dog and the devil-take-the-hindmost—was allowed to starve. And if the present generation thinks this is true even of the 1920s, it is absolutely sure that it was so in the 1880s, which it would probably regard as the very peak of the prevalence of *laissez faire.*

The Seeds of Change

Yet the new reader's initial astonishment when he starts Spencer's book may begin to wear off before he is halfway through, because one cause for surprise explains the other. All that Spencer was doing was to project or extrapolate the legislative tendencies existing in the 1880s into the future. It was because he was so clear-sightedly appalled by

From the February 1969 issue of *The Freeman.*

these tendencies that he recognized them so much more sharply than his contemporaries, and saw so much more clearly where they would lead if left unchecked.

Even in his Preface to *The Man Versus the State* he pointed out how "increase in freedom on form" was being followed by "decrease of freedom in fact. . . ."

> Regulations have been made in yearly growing numbers, restraining the citizen in directions where his actions were previously unchecked, and compelling actions which previously he might perform or not as he liked; and at the same time heavier public burdens . . . have further restricted his freedom, by lessening that portion of his earnings which he can spend as he pleases, and augmenting the portion taken from him to be spent as public agents please.

In his first chapter, "The New Toryism," Spencer contends that "most of those who now pass as Liberals, are Tories of a new type." The Liberals of his own day, he points out, had already "lost sight of the truth that in past times Liberalism habitually stood for individual freedom versus State-coercion."

So the complete Anglo-American switch of reference, by which a "liberal" today has come to mean primarily a State-interventionist, had already begun in 1884. Already "plausible proposals" were being made "that there should be organized a system of compulsory insurance, by which men during their early lives shall be forced to provide for the time when they will be incapacitated." Here is already the seed of the American Social Security Act of 1935.

Spencer also pays his respects to the anti-libertarian implications of an increasing tax burden. Those who impose additional taxes are saying in effect: "Hitherto you have been free to spend this portion of your earnings in any way which pleased you; hereafter you shall not be free to spend it, but we will spend it for the general benefit."

Spencer next turns to the compulsions that labor unions were even then imposing on their members, and asks: "If men use their liberty in such a way as to surrender their liberty, are they there after any the less slaves?"

In his second chapter, "The Coming Slavery," Spencer draws attention to the existence of what he calls "political momentum"—the tendency of State interventions and similar political measures to increase and accelerate in the direction in which they have already been set going. Americans have become only too familiar with this momentum in the last few years.

Spencer illustrates: "The blank form of an inquiry daily made is—'We have already done this; why should we not do that?'" "The buying and working of telegraphs by the State" [which already existed in England when he wrote], he continued, "is made a reason for urging that the State should buy and work the railways." And he went on to quote the demands of one group that the State should take possession of the railways, "with or without compensation."

The British State did not buy and work the railways until 64 years later, in 1948, but it did get around to it, precisely as Spencer feared.

It is not only precedent that prompts the constant spread of interventionist measures, Spencer points out, "but also the necessity which arises for supplementing ineffective measures, and for dealing with the artificial evils continually caused. Failure does not destroy faith in the agencies employed, but merely suggests more stringent use of such agencies or wider ramifications of them." One illustration he gives is how "the evils produced by compulsory charity are now proposed to be met by compulsory insurance." Today, in America, one could point to scores of examples (from measures to cure "the deficit in the balance of payments" to the constant multiplication of measures to fight the government's "war on poverty") of interventions mainly designed to remove the artificial evils brought about by previous interventions.

One Turn Deserves Another

Everywhere, Spencer goes on, the tacit assumption is that "government should step in whenever anything is not going right. . . . The more numerous governmental interventions become . . . the more loud and perpetual the demands for intervention." Every additional relief measure raises hopes of further ones:

> The more numerous public instrumentalities become, the more is there generated in citizens the notion that everything is to be done for them, and nothing by them. Every generation is made less familiar with the attainment of desired ends by individual actions or private agencies; until, eventually, gov-

ernmental agencies come to be thought of as the only available agencies.

Forms of Slavery

"All socialism," Spencer concludes, "involves slavery. . . . That which fundamentally distinguishes the slave is that he labors under coercion to satisfy another's desires." The relation admits of many gradations. Oppressive taxation is a form of slavery of the individual to the community as a whole. "The essential question is—How much is he compelled to labor for other benefit than his own, and how much can he labor for his own benefit?"

Even Spencer would probably have regarded with incredulity a prediction that in less than two generations England would have rates of income tax rising above 90 per cent, and that many an energetic and ambitious man, in England and the United States, would be forced to spend more than half his time and labor working for the support of the community, and allowed less than half his time and labor to provide for his family and himself.

Today's progressive income tax provides a quantitative measurement of the relative extent of a man's economic liberty and servitude.

Those who think that public housing is an entirely new development will be startled to hear that the beginnings of it—as well as some of its harmful consequences—were already present in 1884:

> Where municipal bodies turn housebuilders [wrote Spencer], they inevitably lower the values of houses otherwise built, and check the supply of more. . . . The multiplication of houses, and especially small houses being increasingly checked, there must come an increasing demand upon the local authority to make up for the deficient supply. . . . And then when in towns this process has gone so far as to make the local authority the chief owner of houses, there will be a good precedent for publicly providing houses for the rural population, as proposed in the Radical program, and as urged by the Democratic Federation [which insists on] the compulsory construction of healthy artisans' and agricultural laborers' dwellings in proportion to the population.

One State intervention Spencer did not foresee was the future imposition of rent controls, which make it unprofitable for private persons to own, repair, or renovate old rental housing or to put up new. The consequences of rent control provoke the indignant charge that "private enterprise is simply not doing the job" of providing enough housing. The conclusion is that therefore the government must step in and take over that job.

What Spencer did expressly fear, in another field, was that public education, providing gratis what private schools had to charge for, would in time destroy the private schools. What, of course, he did not foresee was that eventually the government would provide free tuition even in tax-supported colleges and universities, thus more and more threatening the continuance of private colleges and universities—and so tending more and more to produce a uniform conformist education, with college faculties ultimately dependent for their jobs on the government, and so developing an economic interest in professing and teaching a statist, pro-government and socialist ideology. The tendency of government-supported education must be finally to achieve a government monopoly of education.

Ancient Roots of Tyranny

As the "liberal" readers of 1969 may be shocked to learn that the recent State interventions which they regard as the latest expressions of advanced and compassionate thought were anticipated in 1884, so the statist readers of Spencer's day must have been shocked to learn from him how many of the latest State interventions of 1884 were anticipated in Roman times and in the Middle Ages. For Spencer reminded them, quoting an historian, that in Gaul, during the decline of the Roman Empire, "so numerous were the receivers in comparison with the payers, and so enormous the weight of taxation, that the laborer broke down, the plains became deserts, and woods grew where the plough had been."

Spencer reminded his readers also of the usury laws under Louis XV in France, which raised the rate of interest "from five to six when intending to reduce it to four." He reminded them of the laws against "forestalling" (buying up goods in advance for later resale), also in early France. The effect of such laws was to prevent anyone from buying "more than two bushels of wheat at market," which prevented traders and dealers from equalizing supplies over time, thereby intensifying scarcities. He reminded his readers also of the measure which, in 1315, to diminish the pressure of famine, prescribed the prices of foods, but which was later repealed after it had caused the entire disappearance of various foods from the markets. He reminded them, again, of the many endeavors to fix wages, beginning with the Statute of Laborers under Edward III (1327–77). And still again, of statute 35 of Edward III, which aimed to keep down the price of herrings (but was soon repealed because it raised the price). And yet again, of the law of Edward III, under which innkeepers at seaports were sworn to search their guests "to prevent the exportation of money or plate."

This last example will uneasily remind Americans of the present prohibition of private gold holdings and gold export, and of the Johnson Administration's attempt to put a punitive tax on foreign travel, as well as the actual punitive tax that it did put on foreign investment. Let us add the still existing prohibitions even by allegedly advanced European nations against taking more than a tiny amount of their local *paper* currency out of the country!

The Federal Bulldozer Then

I come to one last specific parallel between 1884 and the present. This concerns slum clearance and urban renewal. The British government of Spencer's day responded to the existence of wretched and overcrowded housing by enacting the Artisans' Dwellings Acts. These gave to local authorities powers to pull down bad houses and provide for the building of good ones:

> What have been the results? A summary of the operations of the Metropolitan Board of Works, dated December 21, 1883, shows that up to last September it had, at a cost of a million and a quarter to ratepayers, unhoused 21,000 persons and provided houses for 12,000—the remaining 9,000 to be hereafter provided for being, meanwhile, left houseless. This is not all. . . . Those displaced . . . form a total of nearly 11,000 artificially made homeless, who have had to find corners for themselves in miserable places that were already overflowing.

Those who are interested in a thorough study of the present-day parallel to this are referred to Professor Martin Anderson's *The Federal Bulldozer* (M.I.T. Press, 1964; McGraw-Hill paperback, 1967). I quote just one short paragraph from his findings:

> The federal urban renewal program has actually aggravated the housing shortage for low-income groups. From 1950 to 1960, 126,000 dwelling units, most of them low-rent ones, were destroyed. This study estimates that the number of new dwelling units constructed is less than one-fourth of the number demolished, and that most of the new units are high-rent ones. Contrast the net addition of millions of standard dwelling units to the housing supply by private enterprise with the minute construction effort of the federal urban renewal program. (p. 229)

There is an eloquent paragraph in Spencer's book reminding his readers of the '80s of what they did *not* owe to the State:

> It is not to the State that we owe the multitudinous useful inventions from the spade to the telephone; it is not the State which made possible extended navigation by a developed astronomy; it was not the State which made the discoveries in physics, chemistry, and the rest, which guide modern manufacturers, it was not the State which devised the machinery for producing fabrics of every kind, for transferring men and things from place to place, and for ministering in a thousand ways to our comforts. The world-wide transactions conducted in merchants' offices, the rush of traffic filling our streets, the retail distributing system which brings everything within easy reach and delivers the necessaries of life daily at our doors, are not of governmental origin. All these are results of the spontaneous activities of citizens, separate or grouped.

Aggravated Waste

Our present-day statists are busily trying to change all this. They are seizing billions of additional dollars from the taxpayers to turn them over for "scientific research." By this compulsorily subsidized government competition they are discouraging and draining away the funds for private scientific research; and they threaten to make such research, in time, a government monopoly. But whether this will result in more scientific progress in the long run is doubtful. True, enormously more money is being spent on "research," but it is being diverted in questionable directions—in military research; in developing greater and greater superbombs and other weapons of mass destruction and mass annihilation; in planning supersonic passenger airplanes developed on the assumption that civilians must get to their European or Caribbean vacation spots at 1,200 or 1,800 miles an hour, instead of a mere 600, no matter how many eardrums or windows of groundlings are shattered in the process; and finally, in such Buck Rogers stunts as landing men on the moon or on Mars.

It is fairly obvious that all this will involve enormous waste; that government bureaucrats will be able to dictate who gets the research funds and who doesn't, and that this choice will either depend upon fixed arbitrary qualifications like those determined by Civil Service examinations (hardly the way to find the most original minds), or upon the grantees keeping in the good graces of the particular government appointee in charge of the distribution of grants.

But our Welfare Statists seem determined to put us in a position where we will be dependent on government even for our future scientific and industrial progress—or in a position where they can at least plausibly argue that we are so dependent.

A Denial of Private Property

Spencer next goes on to show that the kind of State intervention he is deploring amounts to not merely an abridgment but a basic rejection of private property: A "confusion of ideas, caused by looking at one face only of the transaction, may be traced throughout all the legislation which forcibly takes the property of this man for the purpose of giving gratis benefits to that man." The tacit assumption underlying all these acts of redistribution is that:

> No man has any claim to his property, not even to that which he has earned by the sweat of his brow, save by the permission of the community; and that the community may cancel the claim to any extent it thinks fit. No defense can be

> made for this appropriation of A's possessions for the benefit of B, save one which sets out with the postulate that society as a whole has an absolute right over the possessions of each member.

In the final chapter (just preceding a Postscript) Spencer concluded: "The function of Liberalism in the past was that of putting a limit to the powers of kings. The function of true Liberalism in the future will be that of putting a limit to the power of Parliaments."

In endorsing some of the arguments in Spencer's *The Man Versus the State,* and in recognizing the penetration of many of his insights and the remarkable accuracy of his predictions of the political future, we need not necessarily subscribe to every position that he took. The very title of Spencer's book was in one respect unfortunate. To speak of "the man versus the State" is to imply that the State, *as such,* is unnecessary and evil. The State, of course, is absolutely indispensable to the preservation of law and order, and the promotion of peace and social cooperation. What is unnecessary and evil, what abridges the liberty and threatens the true welfare of the individual, is the State that has usurped excessive powers and grown beyond its legitimate functions—the Superstate, the socialist State, the redistributive State in brief, the ironically misnamed "Welfare State."

But Spencer was certainly right in the main thrust of his argument, which was essentially that of Adam Smith and other classical liberals, that the two indispensable functions of government are first, to protect the nation against aggression from any other nation, and second, to protect the individual citizen from the aggression, injustice, or oppression of any other citizen—and that every extension of the functions of government beyond these two primary duties should be scrutinized with jealous vigilance.

We are deeply indebted to Herbert Spencer for recognizing with a sharper eye than any of his contemporaries, and warning them against, "the coming slavery" toward which the State of their own time was drifting, and toward which we are more swiftly drifting today.

It is more than a grim coincidence that Spencer was warning of the coming slavery in 1884, and that George Orwell, in our time, has predicted that the full consummation of this slavery will be reached in 1984, exactly one century later.

17

"Planning" vs. the Free Market

When we discuss "economic planning," we must be clear concerning what it is we are talking about. The real question being raised is not: plan or no plan? but *whose* plan?

Each of us, in his private capacity, is constantly planning for the future: what he will do the rest of today, the rest of the week, or on the weekend; what he will do this month or next year. Some of us are planning, though in a more general way, ten or 20 years ahead.

We are making these plans both in our capacity as consumers and as producers. Employees are either planning to stay where they are, or to shift from one job to another, or from one company to another, or from one city to another, or even from one career to another. Entrepreneurs are either planning to stay in one location or to move to another, to expand or contract their operations, to stop making a product for which they think demand is dying and to start making one for which they think demand is going to grow.

Now the people who call themselves "Economic Planners" either ignore or by implication deny all this. They talk as if the world of private enterprise, the free market, supply, demand, and competition, were a world of chaos and anarchy, in which nobody ever planned ahead or looked ahead, but merely drifted or staggered along. I once engaged in a television debate with an eminent Planner in a high official position who implied that without his forecasts and guidance American business would be "flying blind." At best, the Planners imply, the world of private enterprise is one in which everybody works or plans at cross purposes or makes his plans solely in his "private" interest rather than in the "public" interest.

Now the Planner wants to substitute his *own* plan for the plans of everybody else. At best, he wants the government to lay down a Master Plan to which everybody else's plan must be subordinated.

This article was reprinted in the December 1962 issue of *The Freeman* from an address at the 1962 meeting of the Mont Pelerin Society in Knokke, Belgium.

It Involves Compulsion

It is this aspect of Planning to which our attention should be directed: Planning always involves *compulsion*. This may be disguised in various ways. The government Planners will, of course, try to persuade people that the Master Plan has been drawn up for their own good, and that the only persons who are going to be coerced are those whose plans are "not in the public interest."

The Planners will say, in the newly fashionable phraseology, that their plans are not "imperative," but merely "indicative." They will make a great parade of "democracy," freedom, cooperation, and non-compulsion by "consulting all groups"—"Labor," "Industry," the Government, even "Consumers Representatives"—in drawing up the Master Plan and the specific "goals" or "targets." Of course, if they could really succeed in giving everybody his proportionate weight and voice and freedom of choice, if everybody were allowed to pursue the plan of production or consumption of specific goods and services that he had intended to pursue or would have pursued anyway, then the whole Plan would be useless and pointless, a complete waste of energy and time. The Plan would be meaningful only if it forced the production and consumption of *different* things or different quantities of things than a free market would have provided. In short, it would be meaningful only insofar as it put compulsion on *somebody* and forced some change in the pattern of production and consumption.

There are two excuses for this coercion. One is that the free market produces the *wrong* goods, and that only government Planning and direction could assure the production of the "right" ones. This is the thesis popularized by J. K. Galbraith. The other excuse is that the free market does not produce *enough* goods, and that only government Planning could speed things up. This is the thesis of the apostles of "economic growth."

The "Five-Year Plans"

Let us take up the "Galbraith" thesis first. I put his name in quotation marks because the thesis long antedates his presentation of it. It is the basis of all the communist "Five-Year Plans" which are now aped by a score of socialist nations. While these Plans may consist in setting out some general "overall" percentage of production increase, their characteristic feature is rather a whole network of specific "targets" for specific industries: there is to be a 25 percent increase in steel capacity, a 15 percent increase in cement production, a 12 percent increase in butter and milk output, and so forth.

There is always a strong bias in these Plans, especially in the communist countries, in favor of heavy industry, because it gives increased power to make war. In all the Plans, however, even in noncommunist countries, there is a strong bias in favor of industrialization, of heavy industry as against agriculture, in the belief that this necessarily increases real income faster and leads to greater national self-sufficiency. It is not an accident that such countries are constantly running into agricultural crises and food famines.

But the Plans also reflect either the implied or explicit moral judgments of the government Planners. The latter seldom plan for an increased production of cigarettes or whisky, or, in fact, for any so-called "luxury" item. The standards are always grim and puritanical. The word "austerity" makes a chronic appearance. Consumers are told that they must "tighten their belts" for a little longer. Sometimes, if the last Plan has not been too unsuccessful, there is a little relaxation: consumers can, perhaps, have a few more motor cars and hospitals and playgrounds. But there is almost never any provision for, say, more golf courses or even bowling alleys. In general, no form of expenditure is approved that cannot be universalized, or at least "majoritized." And such so-called luxury expenditure is discouraged, even in a so-called "indicative" Plan, by not allowing access by promoters of such projects to bank credit or to the capital markets. At some point government coercion or compulsion comes into play.

"The Nation" Cannot Afford It

This disapproval and coercion may rest on several grounds. Nearly all "austerity" programs stem from the belief, not that the person who wants to make a "luxury" expenditure cannot afford it, but that "the nation" cannot afford it. This involves the assumption that, if I set up a bowling alley or patronize one, I am somehow depriving my fellow citizens of more necessary goods or services. This would be true only on the assumption that the proper thing to do is to tax my so-called surplus income away from me and turn it over to others in the form of money, goods, or services. But if I am allowed to keep my "surplus" income, and am forbidden to spend it on bowling alleys or on imported wine and cheese, I will spend it on something else that is not forbidden. Thus when the British austerity program after World War II prevented an Englishman from consuming imported luxuries, on the ground that "the nation" could not afford the "foreign exchange" or the "unfavorable balance of payments," officials were shocked to find that the money was being squandered on football pools or dog races. And there is no reason to suppose, in any case, that the "dollar shortage" or the "unfavorable balance of payments" was helped in the least. The austerity program, insofar as it was not enforced by higher income taxes, probably cut down potential exports as much as it did potential imports; and insofar as it was enforced by higher income taxes, it discouraged exports by restricting and discouraging production.

But we come now to the specific Galbraith thesis, growing out of the agelong bureaucratic suspicion of luxury spending, that consumers generally do not know how to spend the income they have earned; that they buy whatever advertisers tell them to buy; that consumers are, in short, boobs and suckers, chronically wasting their money on trivialities, if not on absolute junk. The bulk of consumers also, if left to themselves, show atrocious taste, and crave cerise automobiles with ridiculous tailfins.

Bureaucratic Choice

The natural conclusion from all this—and Galbraith does not hesitate to draw it—is that consumers ought to be deprived of freedom of choice, and that government bureaucrats, full of wisdom—of course, of a very unconventional wisdom—should make their consumptive choices for them. The consumers should be supplied, not with what they themselves want, but with what bureaucrats of exquisite taste and culture think is good for them. And the way to do this is to tax away from people all the income they have been foolish enough to earn above that required to meet their bare necessities, and turn it over to the bureaucrats to be spent in ways in which the latter think would really do people the most good—more and better roads and parks and playgrounds and schools and television programs—all supplied, of course, by government.

And here Galbraith resorts to a neat semantic trick. The goods and services for which people voluntarily spend their own money make up, in his vocabulary, the "private sector" of the economy, while the goods and services supplied to them by the government, out of the income it has seized from them in taxes, make up the "public sector." Now the adjective "private" carries an aura of the selfish and exclusive, the inward looking, whereas the adjective "public" carries an aura of the democratic, the shared, the generous, the patriotic, the outward looking—in brief, the public-spirited. And as the tendency of the expanding welfare state has been, in fact, to take out of private hands and more and more take in to its own hands provision of the goods and services that are considered to be most essential and most edifying—roads and water supply, schools and hospitals and scientific research, education, old-age insurance, and medical care—the tendency must be increasingly to associate the word "public" with everything that is really necessary and laudable, leaving the "private sector" to be associated merely with the superfluities and capricious wants that are left over after everything that is really important has been taken care of.

If the distinction between the two "sectors" were put in more neutral terms—say, the "private sector" versus the "governmental sector," the scales would not be so heavily weighted in favor of the latter. In fact, this more neutral vocabulary would raise in the mind of the hearer the question whether certain activities now assumed by the modern welfare state do legitimately or appropriately come within the governmental province. For Galbraith's use of the word "sector," "private" or "public," cleverly carries the implication that the public "sector" is legitimately not only whatever the government has already taken over but a great deal besides. Galbraith's whole point is that the "public sector" is "starved" in favor of a "private sector" overstuffed with superfluities and trash.

Voluntary versus Coercive

The true distinction, and the appropriate vocabulary, however, would throw an entirely different light on the matter. What Galbraith calls the "private sector" of the economy is, in fact, the *voluntary* sector; and what he calls the "public sector" is, in fact, the *coercive* sector. The voluntary sector is made up of the goods and services for which people voluntarily spend the money they have earned. The coercive sector is made up of the goods and services that are provided, regardless of the wishes of the individual, out of the taxes that are seized from him. And as this sector grows at the expense of the voluntary sector, we come to the essence of the welfare state. In this state nobody pays for the education of his own children but everybody pays for the education of everybody else's children. Nobody pays his own medical bills, but everybody pays everybody else's medical bills. Nobody helps his own old parents, but everybody else's old parents. Nobody provides for the contingency of his own unemployment, his own sickness, his own old age, but everybody provides for the unemployment, sickness, or old age of everybody else. The welfare state, as Bastiat put it with uncanny clairvoyance more than a century ago, is the great fiction by which everybody tries to live at the expense of everybody else.

This is not only a fiction; it is bound to be a failure. This is sure to be the outcome whenever effort is separated from reward. When people who earn more than the average have their "surplus," or the greater part of it, seized from them in taxes, and when people who earn less than the average have the deficiency, or the greater part of it, turned over to them in hand-outs and doles, the production of all must sharply decline; for the energetic and able lose their incentive to produce more than the average, and the slothful and unskilled lose their incentive to improve their condition.

The Growth Planners

I have spent so much time in analyzing the fallacies of the Galbraithian school of economic Planners that I have left myself little in which to analyze the fallacies of the Growth Planners. Many of their fallacies are the same; but there are some important differences.

The chief difference is that the Galbraithians believe that a free market economy produces too much (though, of course, they are the "wrong" goods), whereas the Growthmen believe that a free market economy does not produce nearly enough. I will not here deal with all the statistical errors, gaps, and fallacies in their arguments, though an analysis of these alone could occupy a fat book. I want to concentrate on their idea that some form of government direction or coercion can by some strange magic increase production above the level that can be achieved when everybody enjoys economic freedom.

For it seems to me self-evident that when people are free, production tends to be, if not maximized, at least optimized. This is because, in a system of free markets and private property, everybody's reward tends to equal the value of his production. What he gets for his production (and is allowed to keep) is in fact what it is worth in the market. If he wants to double his income in a single year, he is free to try—and may succeed if he is able to double his production in a single year. If he is content with the income he has—or if he feels that he can only get more by excessive effort or risk—he is under no pressure to increase his output. In a free market everyone is free to maximize his satisfactions, whether these consist in more leisure or in more goods.

But along comes the Growth Planner. He finds by statistics (whose trustworthiness and accuracy he never doubts) that the economy has been growing, say, only .8 percent a year. He concludes, in a flash of genius, that a growth rate of 5 percent a year would be faster. How does he propose to achieve this?

What Rate of Growth?

There is among the Growth Planners a profound mystical belief in the power of words. They declare that they "are not satisfied" with a growth rate of a mere 2.8 percent a year; they demand a growth rate of 5 percent a year. And once having spoken, they act as if half the job had already been done. If they did not assume this, it would be impossible to explain the deep earnestness with which they argue among themselves whether the growth rate "ought" to be 4 or 5 or 6 percent. (The only thing they always agree on is that it ought to be greater than whatever it actually is.) Having decided on this magic overall figure, they then proceed either to set specific targets for specific goods (and here they are at one with the Russian Five-Year Planners) or to announce some general recipe for reaching the overall rate.

But why do they assume that setting their magic target rate will increase the rate of production over the existing one? And how is their growth rate supposed to apply as far as the individual is concerned? Is the man who is already making $50,000 year to be coerced into working for an income of $52,500 next year? Is the man who is making only $5,000 a year to be forbidden to make more than $5,250 next year? If not, what is gained by making a specific "annual growth rate" a governmental "target"? Why not just permit or encourage everybody to do his best, or make his own decision, and let the average "growth" be whatever it turns out to be?

The way to get a maximum rate of "economic growth"—assuming this to be our aim—is to give maximum encouragement to production, employment, saving, and investment. And the way to do this is to maintain a free market and a sound currency. It is to encourage profits, which must in turn encourage both investment and employment. It is to refrain from oppressive taxation that siphons away the funds that would otherwise be available for investment. It is to allow free wage rates that permit and encourage full employment. It is to allow free interest rates, which would tend to maximize saving and investment.

The Wrong Policies

The way to *slow down* the rate of economic growth is, of course, precisely the opposite of this. It is to discourage production, employment, saving, and investment by incessant interventions, controls, threats, and harassment. It is to frown upon profits, to declare that they are excessive, to file constant antitrust suits, to control prices by law or by threats, to levy confiscatory taxes that discourage new investment and siphon off the funds that make investment possible, to hold down interest rates artificially to the point where real saving is discouraged and malinvestment encouraged, to deprive employers of genuine freedom of bargaining, to grant excessive immunities and privileges to labor unions so that their demands are chronically excessive and chronically threaten unemployment—and then to try to offset all these policies by government spending, deficits, and monetary inflation. But I have just described precisely the policies that most of the fanatical Growthmen advocate.

Their recipe for inducing growth always turns out to be—inflation. This does lead to the *illusion* of growth, which is measured in their statistics in monetary terms. What the Growthmen do not realize is that the magic of inflation is always a short-run magic, and quickly played out. It can work temporarily and under special conditions—when it causes prices to rise faster than wages and so restores or expands profit margins. But this can happen only in the early stages of an inflation which is not expected to continue. And it can happen even then only because of the temporary acquiescence or passivity of the labor union leaders. The consequences of this short-lived paradise are malinvestment, waste, a wanton redistribution of wealth and income, the growth of speculation and gambling, immorality and corruption, social resentment, discontent and upheaval, disillusion, bankruptcy, increased governmental controls, and eventual collapse. This year's euphoria becomes next year's hangover. Sound long-run growth is always retarded.

In Spite of "The Plan"

Before closing, I should like to deal with at least one statistical argument in favor of government Planning. This is that Planning has actually succeeded in promoting growth, and that this can be statistically proved. In reply I should like to quote from an article on economic planning in the Survey published by the Morgan Guaranty Trust Company of New York in its issue of June 1962:

> There is no way to be sure how much credit is due the French plans in themselves for that country's impressive 4½ percent average annual growth rate over the past decade. Other factors were working in favor of growth: a relatively low starting level after the wartime destruction, Marshall Plan funds in the early years, later an ample labor supply siphonable from agriculture and from obsolete or inefficient industries, most recently the bracing air of foreign competition let in by liberalization of import restrictions, the general dynamism of the Common Market, the breakthrough of the consumer as a source of demand. For the fact that France today has a high degree of stability and a strong currency along with its growth, the stern fiscal discipline applied after the devaluation of late 1958 must be held principally responsible. That a plan is fulfilled, in other words, does not prove that the same or better results could not have been achieved with a lesser degree of central guidance. Any judgment as to cause and effect, of course, must also consider the cases of West Germany and Italy, which have sustained high growth rates without national planning of the economy.

In brief, statistical estimates of growth rates, even if we could accept them as meaningful and accurate, are the result of so many factors that it is never possible to ascribe them with confidence to any single cause. Ultimately we must fall back upon an a priori conclusion, yet a conclusion that is confirmed by the whole range of human experience: that when each of us is free to work out his own economic destiny, within the framework of the market economy, the institution of private property, and the general rule of law, we will all improve our economic condition much faster than when we are ordered around by bureaucrats.

18

Private Property, Public Purpose

The socialists and communists propose to cure poverty by seizing private property, particularly property in the means of production, and turning it over to be operated by the government.

What the advocates of all expropriation schemes fail to realize is that property in private hands used for the production of goods and services for the market is already for all practical purposes public wealth. It is serving the public just as much as—in fact, far more effectively than—if it were owned and operated by the government.

Suppose that a single rich man were to invest his capital in a railroad owned by himself alone. He could not use this merely to transport his own family and their personal goods. That would be ruinously wasteful. If he wished to make a profit on his investment, he would have to use his railroad to transport the public and their goods. He would have to devote his railroad to a public use.

And unlike a government agency, the private owner is obliged by self-preservation to try to avoid losses, which means that he is forced to run his railroad economically and efficiently. And also unlike a government agency, the private capitalist is nearly always obliged to face competition—which means to make the services he provides or the goods he sells superior or at least equal to those provided by his competitors. Therefore the private capitalist normally serves the public far better than the government could if it took over his property. Looked at from the standpoint of the service they provide, the private railroads today are worth vastly more to the public than to their owners.

Though socialists chronically fail to understand it, there is nothing original in the theme just stated. It was hinted at in Adam Smith: "Every individual is continually exerting himself to find out the most advantageous employment for whatever capital he can command. It is his own advantage, indeed, and not that of the society, which he has in view. But the study of his own advantage naturally, or rather neces-

---

From the December 1970 issue of *The Freeman*.

sarily leads him to prefer that employment which is most advantageous to the society."[1]

At another point Adam Smith was even more explicit:

> Every prodigal appears to be a public enemy, and every frugal man a public benefactor.... The principle which prompts to save, is the desire of bettering our condition.... An augmentation of fortune is the means by which the greater part of men propose and wish to better their condition.... [A]nd the most likely way of augmenting their fortune, is to save and accumulate some part of what they acquire .... [The funds they accumulate] are destined for the maintenance of productive labor.... The productive powers of the same number of laborers cannot be increased, but in consequence either of some addition and improvement to those machines and instruments which facilitate and abridge labor; or of a more proper division and distribution of employment. In either case an additional capital is almost always required.[2]

In the history of economic thought, however, it is astonishing how much this truth was neglected or forgotten, even by some of Smith's most eminent successors. But the theorem has been revived, and some of its corollaries more explicitly examined, by several writers in the present century.

How Henry Ford Profitably Served the Public

One of them was George E. Roberts, director of the U. S. Mint under three Presidents, who was responsible for the *Monthly Economic Letter* of the National City Bank of New York from 1914 until 1940.

An example often cited by Roberts was Henry Ford and his automobile plant. Roberts pointed out in the July letter of 1918 that the portion of the profits of Henry Ford's automobile business that he had invested in the development and manufacture of a farm tractor was not devoted to Ford's private wants; nor was that portion which he invested in furnaces for making steel; nor that portion invested in workingmen's houses. "If Henry Ford had exceptional talent for the direction of large productive enterprises the public had no reason to regret that he had an income of $50,000,000 a year with which to enlarge his operations. If that income came to him because he had a genius for industrial management, the results to the public were probably larger than they would have been if the $50,000,000 had been arbitrarily distributed at 50 cents per head to all the [then, 1918] population of the country."

In brief, only that portion of his income which the owner spends upon himself and his dependents is devoted to him or to them. All the rest is devoted to the public as completely as though the title of ownership was in the state. The individual may toil, study, contrive, and save, but all that he saves inures to others.

But the Ford Motor Company, from the profits of which the original owner drew so little for his own personal needs, is not a unique example in American business. Perhaps the greater part of private profits are today reinvested in industry to pay for increased production and service for the public.

Profits After Taxes Average 4 Percent of Sales

Let us see what happened, for example, to all the corporate profits in the United States in 1968, 50 years after George Roberts was writing about the Ford Company. These aggregate net profits amounted before taxes to a total of $88.7 billion (or one-eighth of the total national income in that year of $712.7 billion).

Out of these profits the corporations had to pay 46 percent, or $40.6 billion, to the government in taxes. The public, of course, got directly whatever benefit these provided. Corporate profits after taxes then amounted to $48.2 billion, or less than 7 percent of the national income.

These profits after taxes, moreover, averaged only 4 cents for every dollar of sales. This meant that for every dollar that the corporations took in from sales, they paid out 96 cents—partly for taxes, but mainly for wages and for supplies from others.

But by no means all of the $48.2 billion earned after taxes went to the stockholders of the corporations in dividends. More than half—$24.9 billion—was retained or reinvested in the business. Only $23.3 billion went to the stockholders in dividends.

There is nothing untypical in these 1968 corporate reinvestment figures. In every one of the six years preceding 1968 the amount of funds retained for reinvestment exceeded the total amount paid out in dividends.

Moreover, even the $25 billion figure understates corporate reinvestment in 1968. For in that year the corporations suffered $46.5 billion depreciation on their old plant and equipment. Nearly all of this was reinvested in repairs to old equipment or to complete replacement. The $24.9 billion represented reinvestment of profits in *additional* or greatly improved equipment.

And even the $23.3 billion that finally went to stockholders was not all retained by them to be spent on their personal consumption. A great deal of it was reinvested in new enterprises. The amount is not precisely ascertainable; but the U. S. Department of Commerce estimates that total personal savings in 1968 exceeded $40 billion.

Thus because of both corporate and personal saving, an ever-increasing supply is produced of finished goods and services to be shared by the American masses.

In a modern economy, in brief, those who save and invest can hardly help but serve the public. As Mises has put it: "In the market society the proprietors of capital and land can enjoy their property only by employing it for the satisfaction of other people's wants. They must serve the consumers in order to have any advantage from what is their own. The very fact that they own means of production forces them to submit to the wishes of the public. Ownership is an asset only for those who know how to employ it in the best possible way for the benefit of the consumers. It is a social function."[3]

It follows from this that the rich can do the most good for the poor if they refrain from ostentation and extravagance, and if instead they save and invest their savings in industries producing goods for the masses.

F. A. Harper has gone so far as to write: "Both fact and logic seem to me to support the view that savings invested in privately owned economic tools of production amount to an act of charity. And further, I believe it to be—as a type—the greatest economic charity of all."[4]

Professor Harper supports this view by quoting, among others, from Samuel Johnson, who once said: "You are much surer that you are doing good when you *pay* money to those who work, as a recompense of their labor, than when you *give* money merely in charity."[5]

So, saving and sound investment are by far the most important means by which the rich can confer benefits on the poor.

Saving and Investment

This theme has found expression in this century by a deplorably small number of writers. One of the most persuasive was Hartley Withers, a former editor of the famous London *Economist,* who published an ingratiating little book in 1914, a few weeks before the outbreak of the First World War, called *Poverty and Waste.*[6] The contention of his book is that when a wealthy man spends money on luxuries he causes the production of luxuries and so diverts capital, energy, and labor from the production of necessaries, and so makes necessaries scarce and dear for the poor. Withers does not ask him

> . . . to give his money away, for he would probably do more harm than good thereby, unless he did it very carefully and skilfully; but only to invest part of what he now spends on luxuries so that more capital may be available on luxuries so that more capital may be available for the output of necessaries. So that by the simultaneous process of increasing the supply of capital and diminishing the demand for luxuries the wages of the poor may be increased and the supply of their needs may be cheapened; and he himself may feel more comfortable in the enjoyment of his income.[7]

Yet in spite of the authority of the classical economists and the inherent strength of the arguments for saving and investment, the gospel of spending has an even older history. One of the chief tenets of the "new economics" of our time is that saving is not only ridiculous but the chief cause of depressions and unemployment.

Adam Smith's arguments for saving and investment were at least partly a refutation of some of the mercantilist doctrines thriving in the century before he wrote. Professor Eli Heckscher, in his *Mercantilism* (2 vol., 1935), quotes a number of examples of what he calls "the deep-rooted belief in the utility of luxury and the evil of thrift. Thrift, in fact, was regarded as the cause of unemployment, and for two reasons: in the first place, because real income was believed to diminish by the amount of money which did not enter into exchange, and secondly, because saving was believed to withdraw money from circulation."[8]

An example of how persistent these fallacies were, long after Adam Smith's refutation, is found in the words that the sailor-turned-novelist, Captain Marryat, put into the mouth of his hero, Mr. Midshipman Easy, in his novel by that name published in 1836: "The luxury, the pampered state, the idleness—if you please, the wickedness—of the rich, all contribute to the support, the comfort, and the employment of the poor. You may behold extravagance—it is a vice; but that very extravagance circulates money, and the vice of one contributes to the happiness of many. The only vice which is not redeemed by producing commensurate good, is avarice."

Mr. Midshipman Easy is supposed to have learned this wisdom in the navy, but it is almost an exact summary of the doctrine preached in Bernard Mandeville's *Fable of the Bees* in 1714.

Luxury Spending

Now though this doctrine is false in its attack on thrift, there is an important germ of truth in it. The rich can hardly prevent themselves from helping the poor to some extent, almost regardless of how they spend or save their money. So far from the wealth of the rich being the cause of the poverty of the poor, as the immemorial popular fallacy has it, the poor are made less poor by their economic relations with the rich. Even if the rich spend their money foolishly and wastefully, they give employment to the poor as servants, as suppliers, even as panders to their vices. But what is too often forgotten is that if the rich saved and invested their money they would not only give employment to just as many people producing capital goods, but that as a result of the reduced costs of production and the increased supply of consumer goods which this investment brought about, the real wages of the workers and the supply of goods and services available to them would greatly increase.

What is also forgotten by the defenders of luxury spending is that, though it improves the condition of the poor who cater to it, it also increases their dissatisfaction, unrest, and resentment. The result is increased envy of, and sullenness toward, those who are making them better off.

The first eminent economist who attempted to refute Adam Smith's proposition that "every prodigal appears to be a public enemy, and every frugal man a public benefactor" was Thomas R. Malthus. Malthus's objections were partly well taken and partly fallacious. I have examined them rather fully in another place;[9] and I shall content myself here with quoting a few lines from the answer that a greater economist than Malthus, David Ricardo, made at the time (circa 1814–21): "Mr. Malthus never appears to remember that to save is to spend, as surely as what he exclusively calls spending. . . . I deny that the wants of consumers generally are diminished by parsimony—they are transferred with the power to consume to another set of consumers."[10]

John Maynard Keynes

We have yet to discuss the views of the most influential opponent of saving in our time—John Maynard Keynes.

It is widely believed, especially by his disciples, that Lord Keynes did not condemn saving until, in a sudden vision on his road to Damascus, the truth flashed upon him and he published it in *The General Theory of Employment, Interest, and Money* in 1936. All this is apocryphal. Keynes disparaged saving almost from the beginning of his career. He was warning his countrymen in a broadcast address in January, 1931, that "whenever you save five shillings, you put a man out of work for a day." And long before that, in his *Economic Consequences of the Peace,* published in 1920, he was writing passages like this:

> The railways of the world which [the nineteenth century] built as a monument to posterity, were, not less than the Pyramids of Egypt, the work of labor which was not free to consume in immediate enjoyment the full equivalent of its efforts.
>
> Thus this remarkable system depended for its growth on a double bluff or deception. On the one hand the laboring classes accepted from ignorance or powerlessness, or were compelled, persuaded, or cajoled by custom, convention, authority, and the well-established order of Society into accepting, a situation in which they could call their own very little of the cake that they and Nature and the capitalists were cooperating to produce. And on the other hand the capitalist

> classes were allowed to call the best part of the cake theirs and were theoretically free to consume it, on the tacit underlying condition that they consumed very little of it in practice. The duty of "saving" became nine-tenths of virtue and the growth of the cake the object of true religion. There grew round the nonconsumption of the cake all those instincts of puritanism which in other ages has withdrawn itself from the world and has neglected the arts of production as well as those of enjoyment. And so the cake increased; but to what end was not clearly contemplated. Individuals would be exhorted not so much to abstain as to defer, and to cultivate the pleasures of security and anticipation. Saving was for old age or for your children; but this was only in theory—the virtue of the cake was that it was never to be consumed, neither by you nor by your children after you. (pp. 19–20)

This passage illustrates the irresponsible flippancy that runs through so much of Keynes's work. It was clearly written tongue-in-cheek. In the very next sentences Keynes made a left-handed retraction: "In writing thus I do not necessarily disparage the practices of that generation. In the unconscious recesses of its being Society knew what it was about," etc.

Yet he let his derision stand to do its harm.

If we accepted Keynes's original passage as sincerely written, we would have to point out in reply: (1) The railways of the world cannot be seriously compared with the pyramids of Egypt, because the railways enormously improved the production, transportation, and availability of goods and services for the masses. (2) There was no bluff and no deception. The workers who built the railroads were perfectly "free" to consume in immediate enjoyment the full equivalent of their efforts. It was the *capitalist* classes that did nearly all the saving, not the workers. (3) Even the capitalist classes did consume *most* of their slice of the cake; they were simply wise enough to refrain from consuming *all* of it in the same year as they baked it.

This point is so fundamental, and both Keynes and his disciples have so confused themselves and others with their mockery and intellectual somersaults, that it is worth making the matter plain by constructing an illustrative table.

Results in Ruritania: A Larger "Cake"

Let us assume that in Ruritania, as a result of net annual saving and investment of 10 percent of output, there is over the long run an average increase in real production of 3 percent a year. Then the picture of economic growth we get over a ten-year period runs like this in terms of index numbers:

Year	Total Production	Consumers' Goods	Capital Goods
First	100.0	90.0	10.0
Second	103.0	92.7	10.3
Third	106.1	95.5	10.6
Fifth	112.5	101.3	11.2
Tenth	130.5	117.5	13.0

(These results do not differ too widely from what has been happening in recent years in the United States.)

What this table illustrates is that total production in Ruritania increases each year *because of the net saving* (and consequent investment), and would not increase without it. The saving is used year after year to increase the quantity and improve the quality of existing machinery or other capital equipment, and so to increase the output of *both* consumption and capital goods.

Each year there is a larger and larger "cake." Each year, it is true, not all of the currently produced cake is consumed. But there is no irrational or cumulative consumer restraint. For each year a larger and larger cake is in fact consumed; until even at the end of five years (in our illustration), the annual consumers' cake alone is equal to the combined producers' and consumers' cakes of the first year. Moreover, the capital equipment, the ability to produce goods, is now 12 percent greater than in the first year. And by the tenth year the ability to produce goods is 30 percent greater than in the first year; the total cake produced is 30 percent greater than in the first year, and the consumers' cake alone is more than 17 percent greater than the combined consumers' and producers' cakes in the first year.

No Allowances for Depreciation

There is a further point to be taken into account. Our table is built on the assumption that there has been a *net* annual saving and investment of 10 percent a year; but in order to achieve this Ruritania will probably have to have a *gross* annual saving and investment of, say, twice as much, or 20 percent, to cover the repairs, depreciation and deterioration taking place every year in housing, roads, trucks, factories, equipment. This is a consideration for which no room can be found in Keynes's simplistic and mocking cake analogy. The same kind of reasoning which would make it seem silly to save for new capital would also make it seem silly to save enough even to replace old capital.

In a Keynesian world, in which saving was a sin, production would go lower and lower, and the world would get poorer and poorer.

In the illustrative table I have by implication assumed the long run equality of saving and investment. Keynes himself shifted his concepts and definitions of both saving and investment repeatedly. In his *General Theory* the discussion of their relation is hopelessly confused. At one point (p. 74) he tells us that saving and investment are "necessarily equal" and "merely different aspects of the same thing." At another point (p. 21) he is telling us that they are "two essentially different activities" without even a "nexus."

Produce, Save, Invest

Let us, putting all this aside, try to look at the matter both simply and realistically. Let us define saving as an excess of production over consumption; and let us define investment as the employment of this unconsumed excess to create additional means of production. Then, though saving and investment are not always *necessarily equal,* over the long run they tend to equality.

New capital is formed by production combined with saving. Before there can be a given amount of investment, there must be a preceding equal amount of saving. Saving is the first half of the action necessary for more investment. "To complete the act of forming capital it is of course necessary to complement the negative factor of saving with the positive factor of devoting the thing saved to a productive service. . . . [But] saving is an indispensable condition precedent of the formation of capital."[11]

Keynes constantly deplored saving while praising investment, persistently forgetting that the second was impossible without the first.

Of course it is most desirable economically that whatever is saved should also be invested, and in addition invested prudently and wisely. But in the modern world, investment follows or accompanies saving almost automatically. Few people in the Western world today keep their money under the floor boards. Even the poorer savers put their money out at interest in savings banks; and those banks act as intermediaries to take care of the more direct forms of investment. Even if a man keeps a relatively large sum in an inactive checking deposit, the bank in which he keeps it, trying always to maximize its profits or to minimize losses, seeks to keep itself "fully loaned up"—that is, with close to the minimum necessary cash reserves. If there is insufficient demand at the time for commercial loans, the bank will buy Treasury bills or notes. The result in the United States, for example, is that a bank in New York or Chicago would normally lend out five-sixths of the "hoarder's" deposit; and a "country bank" would lend out even more of it.

Of course, to repeat, a saver can do the most economic good, both for himself and his community, if he invests most of his savings, and invests them prudently and wisely. But—contrary to the theories of the mercantilists and the Keynesians—even if he "hoards" his savings he may often benefit both himself and the community and at least under normal conditions do no harm.

To understand more clearly why this is so it may be instructive to begin by distinguishing between three kinds of (or motives for) saving, and three groups of savers—roughly the poor, the middle class, and the wealthy.

Rent-Day Saving

Let us call the most necessary kind, which even the poorest must practice, "rent-day saving." Men buy and pay for things over different time periods. They buy and pay for food, for the most part, daily. They pay rent weekly or monthly. They buy major articles of clothing once or twice a year. A man who earns $10 a day cannot afford to spend $10 a day on food and drink. He can spend on them, say, not more than $6 a day, and must put aside $4 a day from which to pay out part at the end of the month for rent, light, and heat, and another part for a winter overcoat at the end of six months, and so on. This is the kind of saving necessary to ensure one's ability to spend throughout the year. "Rent-day saving" can symbolize all the saving necessary to pay for regularly recurrent and unavoidable living expenses. Obviously this kind of saving, sustained only for weeks or a season, is not cumulative and can in no circumstances be held responsible for business depressions. It is utter irresponsibility to ridicule it.

Rainy-Day Saving Can't Cause Depression

The next kind of saving, which applies especially to the middle classes, or moderately well off, is what we may call "rainy-day saving." This is saving against such possible contingencies as loss of a job, illness in the family, death of the breadwinner, or the like.

It is this "rainy-day saving" that the Keynesians most deplore, and from which they fear the direst consequences. Yet even in extreme cases it does not, except in very special cyclical circumstances, tend to bring about any depression or economic slowdown.

Let us consider, for example, a society consisting entirely of "hoarders" and "misers." They are hoarders and misers in this sense: that they all assume they are going to live till 70 but will be forced to retire at 60; and they want to have as much to spend in each of their last ten years as in their 40 working years from 20 to 60. This means that each family will save one-fifth of its annual income over 40 years in order to have the same amount to spend in each of its final ten years.

We are deliberately assuming the extreme case, so let us assume that the money saved is not invested in a business or in stocks or bonds, is not even put in a savings bank, earns no interest, but is simply "hoarded."

This of course would permit no economic improvement whatever, but if it were the regular permanent way of life in that community, at least *it would not lead to a depression.* The people who refrained from buying a certain amount of consumers' goods and services would not be bidding up their prices; they would simply be leaving them for others to buy. If this saving for old age were the regular and expected way of life, and not some sudden unanticipated mania for saving, the manufacturers of consumers' goods would not have produced an oversupply to be left on their hands; the older people in their seventh decade would in fact be spending more than similarly aged people in a "spending" society, and the unspent savings of those who died would revert to the spending stream. Over a long period, year by year, there would be just as much spent as in a "spending" society.

Let us remember that money saved, in an evenly-rotating economy, where there is neither monetary inflation nor deflation, does not go out of existence. Savings, even when they are not invested in production goods, are merely *deferred or postponed* spending. The money stays somewhere and is always finally spent. In the long run, in a society with a relatively stable ratio between hoarders and spenders, savings are constantly coming back into the spending stream, through old-age spending or through deaths, keeping the stream at an even flow.

What we are trying to understand is merely the effect of saving *per se,* and not of sudden and unanticipated *changes* in spending and saving. Therefore we are *abstracting* from the effects produced by unexpected changes in spending and saving or changes in the stock of money. If even a heavy amount of saving were the regular way of life in a community, the relative production and prices of consumers' and producers' goods would already be adjusted to this. Of course, if a depression sets in from some other cause, and the prices of securities and of goods begin to fall, and people suddenly fear the loss of their jobs, or a further fall in prices, this may lead to a massive and unanticipated *increase* in saving (or more exactly in nonspending) and this may of course intensify a depression already begun from other causes. But depressions cannot be blamed on regular, predictable, anticipated saving.

Some readers may contend that I have not yet imagined the most extreme case of saving—a society, say, all the members of which perpetually save more than half as much as they earn, and keep saving, not for old age, or for any reasonable contingency, but simply because of a "religion" of saving. In brief, these would be the cake nonconsumers of Keynes's satire. But such an imaginary society involves a contradiction of assumptions. If the members of that society intended always to live at their existing modest or even mean level, why would they keep exerting themselves to produce more than they ever expected to consume? That would be pathologic to the point of insanity. Keynes's allegory of the extent of supposed nineteenth-century thrift was surely his own hallucination.

Capitalistic Saving for Investment in Industry

We come finally to the third type of saving—what we may call "capitalistic" saving. This is saving that is put aside for investment in industry—either directly, or indirectly in the form of savings bank deposits. It is saving that yields interest or profits. The saver hopes, in his old age or even earlier, to live on the income yielded by his investments rather than by consuming his saved capital.

This type of "capitalistic" saving was until recently confined to the very rich. Indeed, even the very rich were not able to take advantage of this type of saving until the modern development of banks and corporations. As late as the beginning of the eighteenth century we hear of London merchants on their retirement taking a chest of gold coin with them to the country with the intention of gradually drawing on that hoard for the rest of their lives.[12] Today the greater part even of the American middle classes, however, enjoy the advantage of capitalistic saving.

To sum up. Contrary to age-old prejudices, the wealth of the rich is not the cause of the poverty of the poor, but helps to alleviate that poverty. No matter whether it is their intention or not, almost anything that the rich can legally do tends to help the poor. The spending of the rich gives employment to the poor. But the saving of the rich, and their investment of these savings in the means of production, gives just as much employment, and in addition makes that employment constantly more productive and more highly paid, while it also constantly increases and cheapens the production of necessities and amenities for the masses.

The rich should of course be directly charitable in the conventional sense, to people who because of illness, disability, or other misfortune cannot take employment or earn enough. Conventional forms of private charity should constantly be extended. But the most effective charity on the part of the rich is to live simply, to avoid extravagance and ostentatious display, and to save and invest so as to provide more people with increasingly productive jobs, and to provide the masses with an ever-greater abundance of the necessities and amenities of life.

---

1. *Wealth of Nations* (1776), Bk. IV, Ch. II.
2. *Ibid.*, Bk. II, Ch. III.
3. Ludwig von Mises, *Human Action* (Third Revised Edition, Chicago: Henry Regnery Co., 1966), p. 648.

4. "The Greatest Economic Charity." Essay in symposium *On Freedom and Free Enterprise,* Mary Sennholz, ed. (Van Nostrand, 1956), p. 99.

5. James Boswell, *The Life of Samuel Johnson* (Boston: Charles E. Lauriat Co., 1925), Vol. II, p. 636.

6. (London: Smith, Elder, 1914; Second, Revised Edition. John Murray, 1931.)

7. *Poverty and Waste,* p. 139.

8. Vol. II, p. 208.

9. *The Failure of the "New Economics"* (Princeton: Van Nostrand, 1959), pp. 40–43 and 355–362.

10. *Notes on Malthus* (Sraffa edition) p. 449 and p. 309.

11. Eugen von Böhm-Bawerk, *Positive Theory of Capital,* 1891 (South Holland Ill.: Libertarian Press, 1959), pp. 104–118.

12. F. A. Hayek, *Profits, Interest and Investment* (London: George Routledge, 1939), pp. 162–163. See also the numerous cases mentioned in G. M. Trevelyan's *English Social History* (David McCay, 1942).

19

Keynesianism in a Nutshell

John Maynard Keynes was, basically, an inflationist. This has not been clearly recognized because he never spelled out, step by step, the consequences of his proposed remedy for unemployment and depression. That remedy was deficit spending by the government. He recognized that increased government spending paid for by equally increased taxation would not "add purchasing power." The increased taxation would offset any "stimulus" that the increased government spending would provide. What counted, he confessed, was the government deficit. But he failed to take his readers beyond this step. How would that deficit be financed? Either the money would have to be borrowed, or new (paper) money or credit would have to be created. But if the money were borrowed, then the previous spending stimulus would be reversed by a deflation when the borrowing was repaid. The only thing to prevent this reversal would be to allow the new spending to remain outstanding. In other words, the Keynesian solution to every slow-down in business or rise in unemployment was still another dose of inflation.

I may point out (if that is still deemed necessary in this inflationary era) that no inflation of which we have historical knowledge resulted in sound and continued business expansion but only in currency depreciation, a wanton redistribution of profits and losses, disorganized output, and economic demoralization. This has been true whether we begin with the coinage debasement of ancient Rome or the paper money scheme of John Law in 1716.

The lessons of inflation are soon forgotten. They apparently must be relearned in every generation.

From the November 1982 issue of *The Freeman*.

OF POVERTY AND WELFARE

20

Defining Poverty

Any study of poverty should logically begin with a definition of the problem we are trying to solve. Precisely what *is* poverty?

Of the thousands of books and articles on the subject that have appeared over the last two centuries, it is astonishing how few have troubled to ask this question. Their writers have taken it for granted that both they and their readers knew precisely what was being discussed. Yet popularly the term is very vague. It is nearly always employed in a relative rather than an absolute sense. In Victorian England it became the fashion for some politicians to say that "the Rich and the Poor form Two Nations." But as every family's income, if arranged on a scale according to its dollar amount, would probably form a dot on a continuous smooth curve, the dividing line between the poor and the not-poor would be an arbitrary one. Is the poorer half of the population anywhere to be called the Poor, and the richer half the Rich?

The discussion today is conducted dominantly in these comparative terms. Our reformers are constantly telling us that we must improve the condition of the lowest fifth or the lowest third of the population. This way of discussing the subject was made fashionable by President Franklin D. Roosevelt in his Second Inaugural address in January, 1937: "I see one-third of a nation ill-housed, ill-clad, ill-nourished." (The objective standards on which this statement was based were never specified.)

It is obvious, however, that all merely relative definitions of poverty make the problem insoluble. If we were to double the real income of everybody, or triple it, there would still be a lowest third, a lowest fifth, or a lowest tenth. Comparative definitions lead us, in fact, into endless difficulties. If poverty means having less than one wants, nearly all of us are poor. If poverty means being worse off than somebody else, then all but one of us is poor. An enormous number of us are, in fact, *subjectively* deprived. As one writer on poverty succinctly put it

---

From the September 1971 issue of *The Freeman*.

nearly 60 years ago: "It is part of man's nature never to be satisfied as long as he sees other people better off than himself."[1]

Attempt at Definition

A discussion of the role that envy plays in economic and all human affairs can be deferred to another place. In any case we are driven to try to find an absolute or objective definition of poverty. This turns out to be more difficult than it might at first seem. Suppose we say that a man is in poverty when he has less than enough income, or less than enough in nutrition (and shelter and clothing), to maintain himself in normal health and strength. We soon find that the objective determination of this amount is by no means simple.

Let us turn to some of the recent "official" definitions in the United States. In January, 1964, when President Johnson was launching his "war on poverty," the annual report of the Council of Economic Advisers contained a long section on the problem. This offered not one but several definitions of poverty. One was relative: "One fifth of our families and nearly one-fifth of our total population are poor." A second was at least partly subjective: "By the poor we mean those who are not now maintaining a decent standard of living—those whose basic needs exceed their means to satisfy them." Each of us might have his own conception of a "decent" standard, and every family might have its own ideas of its "needs." A third definition was: "Poverty is the inability to satisfy minimum needs."

The Council of Economic Advisers, basing its estimates on "low-cost" food budgets compiled by the Social Security Administration, decided that the poverty "boundary line" was established by "a family whose annual money income from all sources was $3,000 (before taxes and expressed in 1962 prices)." Yet, on the very next page the Council report declared that in 1962 "5.4 million families, containing more than 17 million persons, had total incomes below $2,000." How could these 17 million persons exist and survive if they had so much less than enough "to satisfy minimum needs"?

In a 50-page study published in 1965,[2] Rose D. Friedman subjected these Council estimates to a thorough analysis. Using precisely the same data and the same concept of "nutritive adequacy" as the Council, she found that the dividing line between the poor and the not poor would be not $3,000, but a figure around $2,200 as the relevant income for a nonfarm family of four. Where the Council on the basis of its figure estimated that 20 percent of all American families in 1962 were poor, Mrs. Friedman found that on her adjusted calculation only about 10 percent were poor.

I must refer the interested reader to the full text of her study for the details of her excellent analysis, but two of her disclosures will be enough to illustrate the carelessness of the Council's own estimates.

One astonishing error by the Council was to use its $3,000 a year estimate as the "poverty boundary" for all families of any size. Mrs. Friedman's estimates ranged from $1,295 for two-person households, to $2,195 for four-person households, to $3,155 for households of seven persons or more. (The official "poverty line" estimates now also specify a similar range of differences for families of different sizes.)

A second error of the Council was equally astonishing. Based on a previous official estimate that a poor family of four needed about $1,000 a year in 1962 for adequate nutrition, the Council multiplied this amount arbitrarily by three to get what the family needed for all purposes. But it is notorious that poorer families spend a larger proportion of their income on food than do richer families. Mrs. Friedman found that this multiple of three was much higher than the level at which three-fourths of the families concerned did get along on and still get an adequate diet. She found that the amount actually spent for food, on the average, by a family of four with an income of $2,200 was about $1,250 a year. In other words, the fraction of income spent on food at this level was about 60 percent and not 33 percent. Yet the official "poverty line" estimates, at this writing, are still kept unrealistically high by continuing to be implicitly based on this arbitrary multiple of three times adequate diet costs.

One of the great problems involved in arriving at any objective standard of poverty is the constantly changing concept of what constitutes "adequate" nutrition. This was once measured in calories. As time has gone on, and scientific research has continued, it has been insisted that adequacy also requires certain amounts of protein, calcium, iron, Vitamin A, thiamine, riboflavin, niacin, ascorbic acid, etc. The newest insistence has been on the need for a multitude of amino acids. Recently a nutrition survey done at Pennsylvania State College concluded that "only one person in a thousand escapes malnutrition!"[3] On this basis even affluence is no assurance of nutritional adequacy.

Yet compare this scientific ideal not only with the historic situation before the present century, when getting enough to eat was the major problem of the great majority of the populace of the world, but with the conditions that still prevail among that majority. Compared with a supposed subsistence minimum of 3,500 calories, half the people of the world today still get less than 2,250 calories per day, and live on a diet primarily of cereal in the form of millet, wheat, or rice. Another 20 percent get less than 2,750 calories per person per day. Only the well-to-do three-tenths of the human race today get more than 2,750 calories as well as a varied diet which provides the calories that not only satisfy hunger but also maintain health.[4]

Official estimates of "poverty threshold" income by Federal bureaus are still unrealistically high. I quote from a recent official bulletin:

> The decade of the sixties has witnessed a sizable reduction in the number of persons living in poverty. Since 1959, the first year for which data on poverty are available, there has been an average annual decline of 4.9 percent in the number of poor persons. However, between 1969 and 1970, the number of poor persons increased by about 1.2 million, or 5.1 percent. This is the first time that there has been a significant increase in the poverty population. In 1970, about 25.5 million persons, or 13 percent of the population, were below the poverty level, according to the results of the Current Population Survey conducted in March, 1971 by the Bureau of the Census.

Yet though the estimate of the poor was then only 13 percent of the population compared with about 20 percent in 1962, the government statisticians were still using their old high estimate for 1962—and writing up the dollar amount year by year to correspond with increases in the Consumer Price Index. The same bulletin quoted above informs us: "The poverty threshold for a nonfarm family of four was $3,968 in 1970 and $2,973 in 1959.[5] If Mrs. Friedman's more careful calculations had been used, the "poverty threshold" for a nonfarm family of four would have been closer to $2,900 than to $3,968 in 1970 and the percentage of "the poor" would have been closer to 7 percent than to 12.6. In fact, an earlier bulletin of the Bureau of the Census,[6] which had estimated that "about 1 out of 10 families were poor in 1969, compared with about 1 out of 5 in 1959," informs us that if the Bureau's various "poverty thresholds" for families of different sizes were decreased to 75 percent of its existing estimates (i.e. to approximately the levels suggested by Mrs. Friedman's calculations), then "the number of poor persons would drop by 40 percent in 1969, and the poverty rate for persons would drop from 12 percent to 7 percent."

It is clear from all this that government bureaucrats can make the numbers and percentage of "the poor," and hence the dimensions of the problem of poverty, almost whatever they wish, simply by shifting the definition.

Changing the Answer

And some of our American bureaucrats have been doing just that. On December 20, 1970, for example, the Bureau of Labor Statistics announced that, as of the spring of that year, it took a gross income of $12,134 to maintain a family of four on a "moderate" standard of living in the New York-northeastern New Jersey area. The implication was that any family of four with a smaller income than that was less than "moderately" well off and presumably the taxpayers should be forced to do something about it.

Yet the *median* income of a typical American family[7] was estimated by the Bureau of the Census to be only $9,433 in 1969. This means that half of the number of American families were receiving less than that. Clearly a good deal less than half of American families were lucky enough to be receiving the "moderate" income of $12,134.

Most of those who try to frame a definition of poverty no doubt have in mind some practical purpose to be served by such a definition. The purpose of the Federal bureaucracy is to suggest that any income below its definition constitutes a problem requiring government relief, presumably by taxing the families who earn higher incomes to supplement or subsidize the lower. If the present official U. S. definitions of poverty were applied to a country like India, we would have to label as poverty stricken the overwhelming majority of its population. But we do not have to go to India for such an example. If we go back only a little more than forty years ago in our own country, we find that in the so-called prosperous year 1929, more than half of the people in the United States would have been labeled "poor" if the "poverty-threshold" income since developed by the Council of Economic Advisers had then been applied. (This is based on statistical comparisons that fully allow for the changes in the price level in the meantime.)[8]

Let us look at one more example of the consequences of establishing an excessive or merely relative definition of poverty:

"The term poverty may connote hunger, but this is not what is usually meant in discussions about poverty in America. Consider, for example, the facilities available to the poor. Tunica County, Mississippi, is the poorest county in our poorest state. About eight out of every ten families in this county had incomes under $3,000 in 1960 [i.e., under the official "poverty-threshold" level] and most of them were poor by national standards; yet 52 percent owned television sets, 46 percent owned automobiles, and 37 percent owned washing machines. These families might have been deprived of hope and poor in spirit, but their material possessions, though low by American standards, would be the envy of the majority of mankind today.[9]

Preserving the Incentive

To sum up: It is difficult, and perhaps impossible, to frame a completely objective definition of poverty. Our conception of poverty necessarily involves a value judgment. People in different ages, in different countries, in different personal circumstances, will have different ideas of what constitutes poverty, depending on the range of conditions to which they themselves are accustomed. But while the conception of poverty will necessarily be to some extent relative and even individual, we should make every effort to keep it as objective as we can. Otherwise if, for example, our national income in real terms continues to rise as much in the next forty years as in the past forty years, our social reformers will tend to raise correspondingly their standard of what constitutes "poverty." And if this happens, the paradoxical result will be that the problem of poverty will seem to them to be getting larger all the time when it is really getting smaller all the time.

One writer has seriously suggested that we "define as poor any family with an income less than one-half that of the median family."[10] But on this definition, if the income of all groups increased more or less proportionately, as in the past, and by no matter what rate or what multiple, the percentage of "the poor" would never go down, while the implied absolute amount of relief required would keep soaring.

Our definition obviously should not be such as to make our problem perpetual and insoluble. We must avoid any definition that implies the need of a level of help or any method of help that would tempt the recipient to become permanently dependent on it, and undermine his incentives to self support. This is likely to happen whenever we offer an able-bodied adult in charity or relief more than or even as much as he could earn by working. What he needs is a level of subsistence sufficient to maintain reasonable health and strength. This subsistence level must constitute our working definition of the poverty line. Any relief program that tries to provide more than this for idle able-bodied adults will in the end do more harm than good to the whole community.

---

1. Hartley Withers, *Poverty and Waste* (1914), p. 4.
2. *Poverty Definition and Perspective,* American Enterprise Institute, Washington, D.C.
3. Foundation for Nutrition and Stress Research, Redwood City, Calif. Bulletin No. 1, July, 1968.
4. Rose D. Friedman. *op. cit.,* and M. K. Bennett. *The World's Food* (New York: Harper & Bros. 1954).
5. May 7, 1971, U. S. Department of Commerce, Bureau of the Census. *Consumer Income,* Series P-60, No. 77.
6. Series P-60, No. 76, December 16, 1970.
7. Not necessarily a family of four. The term "family" as used by the Bureau for this calculation "refers to a group of two or more persons related by blood, marriage, or adoption and residing together; all such persons are considered members of the same family." *Economic Report of the President,* February, 1971, Table C-20 p. 220.
8. Source: Jeanette M. Fitzwilliams, "Size Distribution of Income in 1962," *Survey of Current Business,* April, 1963 Table 3; Herman P. Miller, *Rich Man, Poor Man* (New American Library, 1964), p. 47.
9. Herman P. Miller, *Rich Man, Poor Man* (New York: Thomas Y. Crowell Co. 1971), pp. 110–111.
10. Victor Fuchs, "Toward a Theory of Poverty," in U.S. Chamber of Commerce, *The Concept of Poverty,* Washington, D. C., 1965, p. 74.

21

Why Some Are Poorer

Throughout history, until about the middle of the eighteenth century, mass poverty was nearly everywhere the normal condition of man. Then capital accumulation and a series of major inventions ushered in the Industrial Revolution. In spite of occasional setbacks, economic progress became accelerative. Today, in the United States, in Canada, in nearly all of Europe, in Australia, New Zealand, and Japan, mass poverty has been practically eliminated. It has either been conquered or is in process of being conquered by a progressive capitalism. Mass poverty is still found in most of Latin America, most of Asia, and most of Africa.

Yet even the United States, the most affluent of all countries, continues to be plagued by "pockets" of poverty and by individual poverty.

Temporary pockets of poverty, or of distress, are an almost necessary result of a free competitive enterprise system. In such a system some firms and industries are growing or being born, others are shrinking or dying; and many entrepreneurs and workers in the dying industries are unwilling or unable to change their residence or their occupation. Pockets of poverty may be the result of a failure to meet domestic or foreign competition, of a shrinkage or disappearance of demand for some product, of mines or wells that have been exhausted, of land that has become a dust bowl, and of droughts, floods, earthquakes, and other natural disasters. There is no way of preventing most of these contingencies, and no all-encompassing cure for them. Each is likely to call for its own special measures of alleviation or adjustment. Whatever general measures may be advisable can best be considered as part of the broader problem of individual poverty.

This problem is nearly always referred to by socialists as "the paradox of poverty in the midst of plenty." The implication of the phrase is not only that such poverty is inexcusable, but that its existence must be the fault of those who have the "plenty." We are most likely to see

From the January 1972 issue of *The Freeman*.

the problem clearly, however, if we stop blaming "society" in advance and seek an unemotional analysis.

Diverse and International

When we start seriously to itemize the causes of individual poverty, absolute or relative, they seem too diverse and numerous even to classify. Yet in most discussion we do find the causes of individual poverty tacitly divided into two distinct groups—those that are the fault of the individual pauper and those that are not. Historically, many so-called "conservatives" have tended to blame poverty entirely on the poor: they are shiftless, or drunks or bums: "Let them go to work." Most so-called "liberals," on the other hand, have tended to blame poverty on everybody but the poor: they are at best the "unfortunate," the "underprivileged," if not actually the "exploited," the "victims" of the "maldistribution of wealth," or of "heartless *laissez faire*."

The truth, of course, is not that simple, either way. We may, occasionally, come upon an individual who seems to be poor through no fault whatever of his own (or rich through no merit of his own). And we may occasionally find one who seems to be poor entirely through his own fault (or rich entirely through his own merit). But most often we find an inextricable mixture of causes for any given person's relative poverty or wealth. And any quantitative estimate of fault versus misfortune seems purely arbitrary. Are we entitled to say, for example, that any given individual's poverty is only 1 percent his own fault, or 99 percent his own fault—or fix any definite percentage whatever? Can we make any reasonably accurate quantitative estimate of the percentage even of those who are poor *mainly* through their own fault, as compared with those whose poverty is mainly the result of circumstances beyond their control? Do we, in fact, have any *objective* standards for making the separation?

A good idea of some of the older ways of approaching the problem can be obtained from the article on "Poverty" in *The Encyclopedia of Social Reform,* published in 1897.[1] This refers to a table compiled by a Professor A. G. Warner in his book, *American Charities.* This table brought together the results of investigations in 1890 to 1892 by the charity organization societies of Baltimore, Buffalo, and New York City, the associated charities of Boston and Cincinnati; the studies of Charles Booth in Stepney and St. Pancras parishes in London, and the statements of Böhmert for 76 German cities published in 1886. Each of these studies tried to determine the "chief cause" of poverty for each of the paupers or poor families it listed. Twenty such "chief causes" were listed altogether.

Professor Warner converted the number of cases listed under each cause in each study into percentages, wherever this had not already been done; then took an unweighted average of the results obtained in the fifteen studies for each of these "Causes of Poverty as Determined by Case Counting," and came up with the following percentages. First came six "Causes Indicating Misconduct": Drink 11.0 percent, Immorality 4.7 Laziness 6.2, Inefficiency and Shiftlessness 7.4, Crime and Dishonesty 1.2, and Roving Disposition 2.2—making a total of causes due to misconduct of 32.7 percent.

Professor Warner next itemized fourteen "Causes Indicating Misfortune": Imprisonment of Bread Winner 1.5 percent, Orphans and Abandoned 1.4, Neglect by Relatives 1.0, No Male Support 8.0, Lack of Employment 17.4, Insufficient Employment 6.7, Poorly Paid Employment 4.4, Unhealthy or Dangerous Employment 0.4, Ignorance of English 0.6, Accident 3.5, Sickness or Death in Family 23.6, Physical Defect 4.1, Insanity 1.2, and Old Age 9.6—making a total of causes indicating misfortune of 84.4 percent.

No Objective Standards

Let me say at once that as a statistical exercise this table is close to worthless, full of more confusions and discrepancies than it seems worth analyzing here. Weighted and unweighted averages are hopelessly mixed. And certainly it seems strange, for example, to list all cases of unemployment or poorly paid employment under "misfortune" and none under personal shortcomings.

Even Professor Warner points out how arbitrary most of the figures are: "A man has been shiftless all his life, and is now old; is the cause of poverty shiftlessness or old age? . . . Perhaps there is hardly a single case in the whole 7,000 where destitution has resulted from a single cause."

But though the table has little value as an effort in quantification, any attempt to name and classify the causes of poverty does call attention to how many and varied such causes there can be, and to the difficulty of separating those that are an individual's own fault from those that are not.

An effort to apply objective standards is now made by the Social Security Administration and other Federal agencies by classifying poor families under "conditions associated with poverty." Thus we get comparative tabulations of incomes of farm and nonfarm families, of white and Negro families, families classified by age of "head," male head or female head, size of family, number of members under 18, educational attainment of head (years in elementary schools, high school, or college), employment status of head, work experience of head (how many weeks worked or idle), "main reason for not working: ill or disabled, keeping house, going to school, unable to find work, other, 65 years and over"; occupation of longest job of head, number of earners in family; and so on.

These classifications, and their relative numbers and comparative incomes, do throw objective light on the problem, but much still depends on how the results are interpreted.

Oriented Toward the Future

A provocative thesis has been put forward by Professor Edward C. Banfield of Harvard in his book, *The Unheavenly City*."[2] He divides American society into four "class cultures": upper, middle, working, and lower classes. These "subcultures," he warns, are not necessarily determined by present economic status, but by the distinctive psychological orientation of each toward providing for a more or less distant future.

At the most future-oriented end of this scale, the upper-class individual expects long life, looks forward to the future of his children, grandchildren, even great grandchildren, and is concerned also for the future of such abstract entities as the community, nation, or mankind. He is confident that within rather wide limits he can, if he exerts himself to do so, shape the future to accord with his purposes. He therefore has strong incentives to "invest" in the improvement of the future situation—i.e., to sacrifice some present satisfaction in the expectation of enabling someone (himself, his children, mankind, etc.) to enjoy greater satisfactions at some future time. As contrasted with this:

> The lower-class individual lives from moment to moment. If he has any awareness of a future, it is of something fixed, fated, beyond his control: things happen to him, he does not *make* them happen. Impulse governs his behavior, either because he cannot discipline himself to sacrifice a present for a future satisfaction or because he has no sense of the future. He is therefore radically improvident: whatever he cannot consume immediately he considers valueless. His bodily needs (especially for sex) and his taste for "action" take precedence over everything else—and certainly over any work routine. He works only as he must to stay alive, and drifts from one unskilled job to another, taking no interest in the work.[3]

Professor Banfield does not attempt to offer precise estimates of the number of such lower-class individuals, though he does tell us at one point that "such ['multiproblem'] families constitute a small proportion both of all families in the city (perhaps 5 percent at most) and of those with incomes below the poverty line (perhaps 10 to 20 percent). The problems that they present are out of proportion to their numbers, however; in St. Paul, Minnesota, for example, a survey showed that 6 percent of the city's families absorbed 77 percent of its public assistance, 51 percent of its health services, and 56 percent of its mental health and correction casework services."[4]

Obviously if the "lower class culture" in our cities is as persistent and intractable as Professor Banfield contends (and no one can doubt the fidelity of his portrait of a sizable group), it sets a limit on what government policy makers can accomplish.

By Merit, or by Luck

In judging any program of relief, our forefathers usually thought it necessary to distinguish sharply between the "deserving" and the "undeserving" poor. But this, as we have seen, is extremely difficult to do in practice. And it raises troublesome philosophic problems. We commonly think of two main factors as determining any particular individual's state of poverty or wealth—personal merit, and "luck." "Luck" we tacitly define as anything that causes a person's economic (or other) status to be better or worse than his personal merits or efforts would have earned for him.

Few of us are objective in measuring this in our own case. If we are relatively successful, most of us tend to attribute our success wholly to our own intellectual gifts or hard work; if we have fallen short in our worldly expectations, we attribute the outcome to some stroke of hard luck, perhaps even chronic hard luck. If our enemies (or even some of our friends) have done better than we have, our temptation is to attribute their superior success mainly to good luck.

But even if we could be strictly objective in both cases, is it always possible to distinguish between the results of "merit" and "luck"? Isn't it luck to have been born of rich parents rather than poor ones? Or to have received good nurture in childhood and a good education rather than to have been brought up in deprivation and ignorance? How wide shall we make the concept of luck? Isn't it merely a man's bad luck if he is born with bodily defects—crippled, blind, deaf, or susceptible to some special disease? Isn't it also merely bad luck if he is born with a poor intellectual inheritance—stupid, feeble-minded, an imbecile? But then, by the same logic, isn't it merely a matter of good luck if a man is born talented, brilliant, or a genius? And if so, is he to be denied any credit or merit for being brilliant?

We commonly praise people for being energetic or hardworking, and blame them for being lazy or shiftless. But may not these qualities themselves, these differences in degrees of energy, be just as much inborn as differences in physical or mental strength or weakness? In that case, are we justified in praising industriousness or censuring laziness?

However difficult such questions may be to answer philosophically, we do give definite answers to them in practice. We do not criticize people for bodily defects (though some of us are not above deriding them), nor do we (except when we are irritated) blame them for being hopelessly stupid. But we do blame them for laziness or shiftlessness, or penalize them for it, because we have found in practice that people do usually respond to blame and punishment, or praise and reward, by putting forth more effort than otherwise. This is really what we have in mind when we try to distinguish between the "deserving" and the "undeserving" poor.

What Happens to Incentive

The important question always is the effect of outside aid on incentives. We must remember, on the one hand, that extreme weakness or despair is not conducive to incentive. If we feed a man who has actually been starving, we for the time being probably increase rather than decrease his incentives. But as soon as we give an idle able-bodied man more than enough to maintain reasonable health and strength, and especially if we continue to do this over a prolonged period, we risk undermining his incentive to work and support himself. There are unfortunately many people who prefer near-destitution to taking a steady job. The higher we make any guaranteed floor under incomes the larger the number of people who will see no reason either to work or to save. The cost to even a wealthy community could ultimately become ruinous.

An "ideal" assistance program, whether private or governmental, would (1) supply everyone in dire need, through no fault of his own, enough to maintain him in reasonable health; (2) would give nothing to anybody not in such need; and (3) would not diminish or undermine anybody's incentive to work or save or improve his skills and earning power, but would hopefully even increase such incentives.

But these three aims are extremely difficult to reconcile. The nearer we come to achieving any one of them fully, the less likely we are to achieve one of the others. Society has found no perfect solution of this problem in the past, and seems unlikely to find one in the future. The best we can look forward to, I suspect, is some never-quite-satisfactory compromise.

Fortunately, in the United States the problem of relief is now merely a residual problem, likely to be of constantly diminishing importance as, under free enterprise, we constantly increase total production. The real problem of poverty is not a problem of "distribution" but of production. The poor are poor not because something is being withheld from them but because, for whatever reason, they are not producing enough. The only permanent way to cure their poverty is to increase their earning power.

---

1. Ed. by Wm. D. P. Bliss (New York: Funk & Wagnalls).
2. Boston: Little Brown, 1970.
3. *Ibid.,* p. 53.
4. *Ibid.,* p 127.

22

Should We Divide the Wealth?

From time immemorial there have been reformers who demanded that wealth and income should be "divided equally"—or at least divided with less glaring inequalities than the reformers saw around them.

These demands have never been more insistent than they are today. Yet most of them are based, in the first place, on a completely erroneous idea of the extent to which present wealth or income in the United States is "maldistributed." An American socialist, Daniel De Leon, announced in a celebrated speech in 1905 that, on the average, the owners of American industry grabbed off 80 percent of the wealth produced in their factories, while the workers got only 20 percent.[1] His contention was widely accepted and exerted great influence.

Yet the truth, as we have seen in the article on "The Distribution of Income" (*The Freeman,* October 1971), is exactly the opposite. Labor in America is getting the lion's share of the nation's output. In recent years the employees of the country's corporations have been getting more than seven-eighths of the corporate income available for division, and the shareowners less than an eighth. More than 70 percent of the personal income in the nation in 1970 was received in the form of wages and salaries. Business and professional income totaled less than 7 percent, interest payments only 8 percent, and dividends only 3 percent.

The truth seems to be that personal income in this country is already distributed roughly in proportion to each person's current contribution to output as measured by its market value. Some people, of course, inherit more wealth than others, and this affects their total personal income. How large a role this plays is statistically difficult to determine, but the income distribution figures just cited would indicate that the role is minor. As a percentage of the total population, there are today very few "idle rich," however conspicuous a few playboys may make themselves at the night clubs and gaudy playgrounds of the world.

From the February 1972 issue of *The Freeman.*

Moreover, the "surplus" money simply doesn't exist to raise mass incomes very much. In 1968, out of a total of 61 million income taxpayers, 383,000, or six-tenths of 1 percent, paid taxes on incomes of $50,000 or more. Their total adjusted gross income came to some $37 billion, or 6.6 percent of total gross incomes reported. Out of this amount they paid a little more than $13 billion, or 36 percent of their income, in taxes. This left them with about $24 billion for themselves.

Suppose the government had seized the whole of this and distributed it among the 200 million total population. This would have come to $120, or $10 more a month, per person. As the disposable personal per capita income in 1968 was $2,939, this expropriation would have raised the average income of the recipients by 4 percent to $3,059. (Per capita income actually rose anyway to $3,108 in 1969 and to $3,333 in 1970.) Of course if the government resorted to any such violent expropriation, it could not repeat it after the first year, for the simple reason that people would cease earning incomes of $50,000 a year or more to be seized.

A Destructive Process

Any attempt to equalize wealth and income by forced redistribution must destroy wealth and income. We can recognize this most clearly if we begin with the extreme case. If the median income per family has been $10,000 a year, and we decide that every family must be guaranteed exactly that and no family can be allowed to retain more than that, then we will destroy all economic incentives to work, earn, improve one's skills, or save. Those who had been getting less than that would no longer need to work for it; those who had been getting more would no longer see the point in working for the surplus to be seized, or even in working at all, since their income would be "guaranteed" in any case. People could be got to work only by coercion; most labor would be forced labor, and very little of it would be skilled or efficient.

The so-called "instinct of workmanship," without economic rewards, would have nothing to guide it into one channel rather than another, and nothing to hold it beyond the point of fatigue. Useful and profitable work would be black-market work. Those who survived would do so at a near-subsistence level.

But the same kind of results, less extreme in degree, would follow from less extreme redistribution measures. The most fashionable of these at the moment is the Guaranteed Annual Income, I have already analyzed this at length, together with its most popular variant, the Negative Income Tax, in my book, *Man vs. the Welfare State,*[2] and will only briefly indicate the objections to it here.

A guaranteed minimum income would not have quite the universal destructive effect on incentives as would an attempt to impose a compulsorily equal income, with the ceiling made identical with the floor. At least people earning incomes above the minimum guarantee, though they would be oppressively taxed, would still have some incentive to continue earning whatever surplus they were allowed to retain. But all those guaranteed a minimum income, whether they worked or not, would have no incentive to work at all if the guaranteed minimum were above what they had previously been earning, or were capable of earning, only a moderate amount above the guarantee.

It is clearly wrong in principle to allow the government forcibly to seize money from the people who work and to give it unconditionally to other able-bodied people where they accept work or not. It is wrong in principle to give money to people solely because they say they haven't any—and especially to support such people on a permanent and not merely on a temporary emergency basis. It is wrong in principle to force the workers and earners indefinitely to support the nonworkers and nonearners.

This must undermine the incentives of both the workers and the nonworkers. It puts a premium on idleness. It is an elementary requirement of economic incentive as well as justice that the man who works for a living should always be better off because of this, other things equal, than the man who refuses to work for a living.

We have to face the fact that there are a substantial number of people who would rather live in near-destitution without working than to live comfortably at the cost of accepting the disciplines of a steady job. The higher we raise the income guarantee (and once we adopted it, the political pressures would be for raising it constantly), the greater the number of people who would see no reason to work.

Nor would a so-called "Negative Income Tax" do much to solve the problem. The Negative Income Tax is merely a misleading euphemism for a tapered-off guaranteed minimum income. The proposal is that for every dollar that a man earns for himself, his government income subsidy would be reduced, say, only 50 cents, instead of being reduced by the whole amount that he earns. In this way, it is argued, his incentive for self-support would not be entirely destroyed: for every dollar he earned for himself he would be able to retain at least half.

This proposal has a certain surface plausibility; in fact, the present writer put it forward himself more than thirty years ago,[3] but abandoned it shortly thereafter when its flaws became evident. Let us look at some of these:

1. The NIT (negative income tax), by neglecting the careful applicant-by-applicant investigation of needs and resources made by the traditional relief system, would, like a flat guaranteed income, open the government to massive fraud. It would also, like the flat guaranteed income, force the government to support a family whether or not it was making any effort to support itself.

2. It is true that the NIT would not destroy incentives quite as completely as the flat guaranteed income, but it would seriously undermine them nonetheless. It would still give millions of people a guaranteed income whether they worked or not. Once more we must keep in mind that there are a substantial number of people who prefer near-destitution in idleness to a comfortable living at the cost of working. It is true that under the NIT scheme they would be allowed to keep half of anything they earned for themselves up to nearly twice the amount of the basic NIT benefit, but they would tend to look upon this as the equivalent of a tax of 50 percent on these earnings, and many would not think such earnings worth the trouble.

3. The NIT might prove even more expensive for the taxpayers than the flat guaranteed income. The sponsors of NIT, in their original monetary illustrations, proposed that the "break-off point" of their scheme would be something like the official "poverty threshold" income—which is now (1972) about $4,320 for a nonfarm family of four. At this point no NIT benefits would be paid. If the family's income was only $3,320, falling short of the poverty-line income by $1,000, then a $500 NIT benefit would be paid. And if the family's earned income was zero, then a benefit of $2,160 would be paid.

But, of course, if no other government subsidy were paid to the family (and the original NIT sponsors proposed that their plan be a complete *substitute* for all other welfare payments) then the government would be paying the poorest families only *half* of what its own administrators officially declared to be the *minimum* on which such families could reasonably be expected to live. How could such a program be politically defended?

As soon as the NIT program gets into practical politics, therefore, the pressure will be irresistible to make the payment to a family with zero income at least equal to the official poverty-line income. If this means $4,320 for a family of four, say, then *some* NIT payment must be made to each family until its income reaches *twice* the official poverty-line income, or $8,640 for every family of four. And this means that even if a family were already earning much more than the official poverty-line income—say, $8,000 a year—it would still have to be subsidized by the government. "Everybody must be treated alike."

4. This would be ruinously expensive, but it is still not the end. The subsidized families would object to paying a 50 percent income tax (as their spokesmen would put it) on everything they earned for themselves. So they would be allowed to earn a certain amount entirely exempted from such a deduction. (Such an exemption has already been granted on self-earnings of Social Security recipients, and it is proposed in a pending Congressional bill to enact an NIT.) This would make the NIT still more crushingly expensive for the remaining taxpayers.

5. There would be political pressures every year for increasing the amount of these exempted earnings. In fact, a 50 percent "income tax on the poor" would be denounced as an outrage. In time the proposal would be certain to be made that *all* the self-earnings of the NIT subsidy recipients be exempted from any offsetting deductions whatever. But this would mean that once a family had been granted the initial minimum income guarantee of, say, $4,320 a year, it would still be getting that full sum in addition to whatever it earned for itself. But "everybody must be treated alike." Therefore there would be no break-off point, or even any tapering off. Every family—including the Rockefellers, the Fords, the Gettys, and all other millionaires—would get the full guaranteed income.

This end-result cannot be dismissed as mere fantasy. The principle of a government subsidy to any family, no matter how rich, is already accepted in our own Social Security scheme and in Great Britain under the name of "family allowances." It is merely that the amounts are smaller. So the Negative Income Tax, as a social measure, turns out to be only a halfway house. Carried to its logical conclusion, it becomes a uniform guaranteed handout to industrious and idle, thrifty and improvident, poor and rich alike.

6. It is an anticlimax to point out, but it needs to be done, that there is no political possibility that a flat guaranteed income or a "negative income tax" would be enacted as a complete *substitute* for the existing mosaic of welfare and relief measures. Can we seriously imagine that the specific pressure groups now getting veterans' allowances, farm subsidies, rent subsidies, relief payments, Social Security benefits, food stamps, Medicare, Medicaid, old age assistance, unemployment insurance, and so on and so on, would quietly give them up, with out protests, demonstrations, or riots? The overwhelming probability is that a guaranteed income or NIT program would simply be thrown on top of the whole present rag-bag of welfare measures piled up over the last 30 to 40 years.

We may put it down as a political law that all State handout schemes tend to grow and grow until they bring on a hyper-inflation and finally bankrupt the State.

Land Reform

Perhaps I should devote at least one or two paragraphs here to so-called "land reform." This appears to be the most ancient of schemes for forcibly dividing the wealth. In 133 B. C., for example, Tiberius Gracchus succeeded in getting a law passed in Rome severely limiting the number of acres that any one person could possess. The typical "land reform" since his day, repeatedly adopted in backward agricultural countries, has consisted in confiscating the big estates and either "collectivizing" them or breaking them up into small plots and redistributing these among the peasants. Because there are always fewer such workable parcels than families, and because, though each parcel of land may be of the same nominal acreage, each has a different nature, fertility, location, and degree of development (with or without clearance, grading, irrigation, roads, buildings, and the like), each must have a different market value. The distribution of land can never be universal and can never be "fair"; it must necessarily favor a selected group, and some more than others within that group.

But apart from all this, such a measure always reduces efficiency and production. From the moment it is proposed that property be seized, its owners "mine" its fertility and refuse to invest another dollar in it, and some may not even raise another crop. It does not pay to use modern equipment on small farms, and in any case the owners are unlikely to have the necessary capital. "Land reform" of this type is an impoverishment measure.

The Henry George scheme of a 100 percent "single tax" on ground rent would also discourage the most productive utilization of land and sites, and adversely affect general economic development. But to explain adequately why this is so would require so lengthy an exposition that I must refer the interested reader to the excellent analyses that have already been made by Rothbard, Knight, and others.[4]

Progressive Taxation

Among the "advanced" nations of the West, however, the most frequent contemporary method of redistributing income and wealth is through progressive income and inheritance taxes. These now commonly rise to near-confiscatory levels. A recent compilation[5] comparing the highest marginal income-tax rates in fifteen countries yielded the following results: Switzerland 8 percent, Norway 50, Denmark 53, West Germany 55, Sweden 65, Belgium 66, Australia 68, Austria 69, Netherlands 71, Japan 75, France 76, United States 77, Canada 82, United Kingdom 91, and Italy 95 percent.

Two main points may be made about these hyper-rates: (1) they are counter-productive even in raising revenues, and (2) they do hurt not only the rich but the poor, and tend to make them poorer.

All the revenues yielded by the U. S. personal income tax of 1968, with its rates ranging from 14 to 70 percent, plus a 10 percent surcharge, would have been yielded, with the same exemptions and deductions, by a flat income tax of 21.8 percent. If all the tax rates above 50 percent had been reduced to that level, the loss would not have been as much as it took to run the government for a full day. In Great Britain, in the fiscal year 1964–65, the revenue from all the surtax rates (ranging above the standard rate of 41¼ percent up to 96¼ percent) yielded less than 6 percent of all the revenue from the income tax, and barely more than 2 percent of Britain's total revenues. In Sweden, in 1963, the rates between 45 and 65 percent brought in only 1 percent of the total national income-tax revenue. And so it goes. The great masses of the people are accepting far higher rates of income tax than they would tolerate if it were not for their *illusion* that the very rich are footing the greater part of the bill.

One effect of seizing so high a percentage of high earnings is to diminish or remove the incentive to bring such earnings into existence in the first place. It is very difficult to estimate this effect in quantitative terms, because we are comparing actualities merely with might-be's and might-have-been's. In March, 1947, the National City Bank, based on reports of the Bureau of Internal Revenue, presented the illuminating table below. (The dollar figures stand for millions of dollars.)

	1926–28 average	**1942**
National Income	$77,000	$122,000
Incomes over $300,000:		
Total amount	$ 1,669	$ 376
Taxes paid	$ 281	$ 292
Top tax rate	25%	88%
No. of returns	2,276	654

In other words, during the same period in which the total national income *increased* 58 percent, total incomes over $300,000 *fell* 77 percent. If the aggregate of such $300,000 incomes had risen proportionately to the whole national income, the total would have reached $2,644 million—seven times greater than it actually was.

A great deal more statistical analysis of this sort could instructively be undertaken not only from U.S. but many foreign income-tax returns.

It is not merely the effect of personal and corporate income taxes in reducing the incentives to bring high earnings into existence that needs to be considered, but their total effect in soaking up the sources of capital funds. Most of the funds that the present tax structure now seizes for current government expenditures are precisely those that would have gone principally into investment—i. e., into improved machines and new plants to provide the increased per capita productivity which is the only permanent and continuous means of increasing wages and total national wealth and income. In the long run, the high rates of personal and corporate income taxes hurt the poor more than the rich.

Equality, Once for All

A socialist proposal that used to be aired frequently a generation or two ago, but is not much heard now (when the emphasis is on trying to legislate permanent equalization of incomes), is that the wealth of the country ought to be distributed equally "once for all," so as to give everybody an even start. But Irving Fisher pointed out in answer that this equality could not long endure.[6] It is not merely that everybody would continue to earn different incomes as the result of differences in ability, industry, and luck, but differences in thrift alone would soon re-establish inequality. Society would still be divided into "spenders" and "savers." One man would quickly go into debt to spend his money on luxuries and immediate pleasures; another would save and invest present income for the sake of future income. "It requires only a very small degree of saving or spending to lead to comparative wealth or poverty, even in one generation."

Even communists have now learned that wealth and income cannot be created merely by alluring slogans and utopian dreams. As no less a figure than Leonid I. Brezhnev, First Secretary of the Soviet Communist party, recently put it at a party congress in Moscow: "One can only distribute and consume what has been produced, this is an elementary truth."[7] What the communists have still to learn, however, is that the institution of capitalism, of private property and free markets, tends to maximize production, while economic dictatorship and forced redistribution only discourage, reduce, and disrupt it.

---

1. See Howard E. Kershner, *Dividing the Wealth* (Devin-Adair, 1971), pp. 17–24.
2. (New Rochelle, N.Y.: Arlington House, 1969), pp. 62–100.
3. In *The Annalist* (published by *The New York Times*), Jan. 4. 1939.
4. Murray N. Rothbard, *Power and Market: Government and the Economy (* Institute for Humane Studies, Inc., 1970), pp. 91–100. Frank H. Knight, "The Fallacies in the 'Single Tax'," *The Freeman,* August 10, 1953.
5. First National City Bank of New York.
6. *Elementary Principles of Economics* (New York: Macmillan, 1921), pp. 478–483.
7. *The New York Times,* May 29, 1971.

23

False Remedies for Poverty

From the beginning of history sincere reformers as well as demagogues have sought to abolish or at least to alleviate poverty through state action. In most cases their proposed remedies have only served to make the problem worse.

The most frequent and popular of these proposed remedies has been the simple one of seizing from the rich to give to the poor. This remedy has taken a thousand different forms, but they all come down to this. The wealth is to be "shared," to be "redistributed," to be "equalized." In fact, in the minds of many reformers it is not poverty that is the chief evil but inequality.

These direct redistribution schemes (including "land reform" and "the guaranteed income") are so immediately relevant to the problem of poverty that they warrant separate treatment. Here I must content myself with reminding the reader that all schemes for redistributing or equalizing incomes or wealth must undermine or destroy incentives at both ends of the economic scale. They must reduce or abolish the incentives of the unskilled and shiftless to improve their condition by their own efforts, and even the able and industrious will see little point in earning anything beyond what they are allowed to keep. These redistribution schemes must inevitably reduce the size of the pie to be redistributed. They can only level down. Their long-run effect must be to reduce production and lead toward national impoverishment.

The problem we face here is that the false remedies for poverty are almost infinite in number. An attempt at a thorough refutation of any single one of them would run to disproportionate length. But some of these false remedies are so widely regarded as real cures or mitigations of poverty that if I do not refer to them, I may be accused of having undertaken a comprehensive analysis of the remedies for poverty while ignoring some of the most obvious.

What I shall do, as a compromise, is to take up some of the more popular of the alleged remedies for poverty and indicate briefly in each

---

From the February 1971 issue of *The Freeman*

case the nature of their shortcomings or the chief fallacies involved in them.[1]

Unions and Strikes

The most widely practiced "remedy" for low incomes in the last two centuries has been the formation of monopolistic labor unions and the use of the strike threat. In nearly every country today this has been made possible to its present extent by government policies that permit and encourage coercive union tactics and inhibit or restrict counteractions by employers. As a result of union exclusiveness, of deliberate inefficiency, of featherbedding, of disruptive strikes and strike-threats, the long-run effect of customary union policies has been to discourage capital investment and to make the average real wage of the whole body of workers lower, and not higher, than it would otherwise have been.

Nearly all of these customary union policies have been dishearteningly shortsighted. When unions insist on the employment of men that are not necessary to do a job (requiring unneeded firemen on Diesel locomotives; forbidding the gang size of dock workers to be reduced below, say, 20 men no matter what the size of the task; demanding that a newspaper's own printers must duplicate advertising copy that comes in already set in type, etc.) the result may be to preserve or create a few more jobs for specific men in the short run, but only at the cost of making impossible the creation of an equivalent or greater number of more productive jobs for others.

The same criticism applies to the age-old union policy of opposing the use of labor-saving machinery. Labor-saving machinery is only installed when it promises to reduce production costs. When it does that, it either reduces prices and leads to increased production and sales of the commodity being produced, or it makes more profits available for increased reinvestment in other production. In either case its long run effect is to substitute more productive jobs for the less productive jobs it eliminates. Yet as late as 1970, a book appeared by a writer who enjoys an exalted reputation as an economist in some quarters, opposing the introduction of labor-saving machines in the underdeveloped countries on the ground that they "decrease the demand for labor"[2] The natural conclusion from this would be that the way to maximize jobs is to make all labor as inefficient and unproductive as possible.

Overtime Rates

A similar judgment must be passed on all "spread-the-work" schemes. The existing Federal Wage-Hour Law has been on the books for many years. It provides that the employer must pay a 50 percent penalty overtime rate for all hours that an employee works in excess of 40 a week, no matter how high the employee's regular hourly rate of pay.

This provision was inserted at the insistence of the unions. Its purpose was to make it so costly for the employer to work men overtime that he would be obliged to take on additional workers.

Experience shows that the provision has in fact had the effect of narrowly restricting the length of the working week. In the ten year period, 1960 to 1969 inclusive, the average annual work week in manufacturing varied only between a low of 39.7 hours in 1960 and a high of 41.3 hours in 1966. Even monthly changes do not show much variation. The lowest average working week in manufacturing in the fourteen months from June, 1969 to July, 1970 was 39.7 hours and the highest was 41 hours.

But it does not follow that the hour-restriction either created more long-term jobs or yielded higher total payrolls than would have existed without the compulsory 50 percent overtime rate. No doubt in isolated cases more men have been employed than would otherwise have been. But the chief effect of the over time law has been to raise production costs. Firms already working full standard time often have to refuse new orders because they cannot afford to pay the penalty overtime necessary to fill those orders. They cannot afford to take on new employees to meet what may be only a temporarily higher demand because they may also have to install an equivalent number of additional machines.

Higher production costs mean higher prices. They must therefore mean narrowed markets and smaller sales. They mean that fewer goods and services are produced. In the long run the interests of the whole body of workers must be adversely affected by compulsory overtime penalties.

All this is not to argue that there ought to be a longer work week, but rather that the length of the work week, and the scale of overtime rates, ought to be left to voluntary agreement between individual workers or unions and their employers. In any case, legal restrictions on the length of the working week cannot in the long run increase the number of jobs. To the extent that they can do that in the short run, it must necessarily be at the expense of production and of the real income of the whole body of workers.

Minimum Wage Laws

This brings us to the subject of minimum-wage laws. It is profoundly discouraging that in the second half of the twentieth century, in what is supposed to be an age of great economic sophistication, the United States should have such laws on its books, and that it should still be necessary to protest against a nostrum so futile and mischievous. It hurts most the very marginal workers it is designed to help.

I can only repeat what I have written in another place.[3] When a law exists that no one is to be paid less than $64 for a 40-hour week, then no one whose services are not worth $64 a week to an employer will be employed at all. We cannot make a man worth a given amount by making it illegal for anyone to offer him less. We merely deprive him of the right to earn the amount that his abilities and opportunities would permit him to earn, while we deprive the community of the moderate services he is capable of rendering. In brief, for a low wage we substitute unemployment.

But I cannot devote more space to this subject here. I refer the reader to the careful reasoning and statistical studies of such eminent economists as Professors Yale Brozen, Arthur Burns, Milton Friedman, Gottfried Haberler, and James Tobin, who have emphasized, for example, how much our continually rising legal minimum wage requirements have increased unemployment in recent years, especially among teen-aged Negroes.

The Mounting Burden of Welfare Plans and Taxes

In the last generation there has been enacted in almost every major country of the world a whole sackful of "social" measures, most of them having the ostensible purpose of "helping the poor" in one respect or another. These include not only direct relief, but unemployment benefits, old-age benefits, sickness benefits, food subsidies, rent subsidies, farm subsidies, veterans' subsidies—in seemingly endless profusion. Many people receive not only one but many of these subsidies. The programs often overlap and duplicate each other.

What is their net effect? All of them must be paid for by that chronically forgotten man, the taxpayer. In perhaps half the cases, Paul is in effect taxed to pay for his own benefits, and gains nothing on net balance (except that he is forced to spend his earned money in other directions than he himself would have chosen). In the remaining cases, Peter is forced to pay for Paul's benefits. When any one of these schemes or a further expansion of it, is being proposed, its political sponsors always dwell on what a generous and compassionate government should pay to Paul; they neglect to mention that this additional money must be seized from Peter. In order that Paul may receive the equivalent of more than he earns, Peter must be allowed to keep less than he earns.

The mounting burden of taxation not only undermines individual incentives to increased work and earnings, but in a score of ways discourages capital accumulation and distorts, unbalances, and shrinks production. Total real wealth and income is made smaller than it would otherwise be. On net balance there is more poverty rather than less.

But increased taxation is so unpopular that most of these "social" handout schemes are originally enacted without enough increased taxation to pay for them. The result is chronic government deficits, paid for by the issuance of additional paper money. And this has led in the last quarter century to the constant depreciation of the purchasing power of practically every currency in the world. All creditors, including the buyers of government bonds, insurance policy holders, and the depositors in savings banks, are systematically cheated. Once more the chief victims are the working and saving families with moderate incomes.

Yet everywhere this monetary inflation, eventually so disruptive and ruinous to orderly balanced production, is rationalized by politicians and even by putative economists as necessary for "full employment" and "economic growth." The truth is that if this monetary inflation is persisted in, it can only lead to economic disaster.

Price and Wage Controls

Many of the very people who originally advocate inflation (or the policies which inevitably lead to it), when they see its consequences of raising prices and money wages, propose to cure the situation, not by halting the inflation, but by having the government impose price and wage controls. But all such attempts to suppress the symptoms enormously increase the harm done. Price and wage controls, to precisely the extent that they can be made temporarily effective, only distort, disrupt, and reduce production—again leading toward impoverishment.

Yet here again, as with the other false remedies for poverty, it would be an unjustifiable digression to spell out in detail all the fallacies and evil consequences of special subsidies, improvident government spending, deficit financing, monetary inflation, and price-and-wage controls. I have myself dealt with these subjects in two previous books: *The Failure of the New Economics*[4] and *What You Should Know About Inflation*[5] and there is, of course, an extensive literature on the subject. The chief point to be reiterated here is that these policies do not help to cure poverty.

Another false remedy for poverty is the progressive income tax, as well as a very heavy burden of capital gains taxes, inheritance taxes, and corporate income taxes. All of these have the effect of discouraging production, investment, and capital accumulation. To that extent they must prolong rather than cure poverty.

Outright Socialism

We come now to the final false remedy for poverty to be considered in this article—outright socialism.

Now the word "socialism" is loosely used to refer to at least two distinct proposals, usually but not necessarily tied together in the minds of the proposers. One of these is the redistribution of wealth or income—if not to make incomes equal, at least to make them much more nearly equal than they are in a market economy. But the majority of those who propose this objective today think that it can be achieved by retaining the mechanisms of private enterprise and then taxing the bigger incomes to subsidize the smaller incomes.

By "outright socialism" I refer to the Marxist proposal for "the public ownership and control of the means of production."

Now one of the most striking differences between the 1970s and the 1950s, or even the 1920s, is the rise in the political popularity of Socialism Two—the redistribution of income—and the decline in the political popularity of Socialism One—government ownership and management. The reason is that the latter, in the last half century, has been so widely tried. Particularly in Europe there is now a long history of government ownership and management of such "public utilities" as the railroads, the electric light and power industries, the telegraph and telephone. And everywhere the history has been much the same—deficits practically always, and in the main poor service compared with what private enterprise supplied. The mail service, a government monopoly nearly everywhere, is also nearly everywhere notorious for its deficits, inefficiency, and inertia. (The contrast with the performance of "private" industry is often blurred, however, in the United States, for example, by the slow strangulation of the railroads, telephone, and power companies by government regulation and harassment.)

As a result of this history, most of the socialist parties in Europe find that they can no longer attract votes by promising to nationalize even more industries. But what is still not recognized by the socialists, by the public, or even by more than a small minority of economists, is that present government ownership and management of industries, not only in "capitalist" Europe but even in Soviet Russia, works only as well as it does because it is parasitic for accounting on the world market prices established by private enterprise.

Too Much Taken for Granted

We are so accustomed to the miracle of private enterprise that we habitually take it for granted. But how does private industry solve the incredibly complex problem of turning out tens of thousands of different goods and services in the proportions in which they are wanted by the public? How does it decide how many loaves of bread to produce and how many overcoats, how many hammers and how many houses, how many pins and how many Pontiacs, how many teaspoons and how many telephones? And how does it decide the no less difficult problem of which are the most economical and efficient methods of producing these goods?

It solves these problems through the institutions of private property, the free market, and the existence of money—through the interrelations of supply and demand, costs and prices, profits and losses.

When shoes are in deficient supply compared with the marginal cost of producing them, their price, and therefore the margin of profit in producing them, will increase in relation to the price and margin of profit in producing other things. Therefore, the existing producers will turn out more shoes, and perhaps new producers will order machinery to make them. When the new supply catches up with existing demand, the price of shoes, and the profit of making them, will fall; the supply will no longer be increased. When hats go out of fashion and fewer are worn, the price will decline, and some may remain unsalable. Fewer hats will be made. Some producers will go out of business, and the previous labor and salvageable capital devoted to producing hats will be forced into other lines. Thus, there will be a constant tendency toward equalization of profit margins (comparative risks considered) in all lines. These yearly, seasonal, or daily changes in supply and demand, cost and price, and comparative profit margins, will tend to maintain a delicate but constantly changing balance in the production of the tens of thousands of different services and commodities in the proportions in which consumers demand them.

The Competitive Role

The same guide of comparative money prices and profits will also decide the kinds and proportions of capital goods that are turned out, as well as which one of hundreds of different possible methods of production is adopted in each case.

In addition, within each industry as well as between industries, competition will be taking place. Each producer will not only be trying to turn out a better product than his competitors, a product more likely to appeal to buyers, but he will also be trying to reduce his cost of production as low as he possibly can in order to increase his margin of profit—or perhaps even, if his costs are already higher than average, to meet his competition and stay in business. This means that competition always tends to bring about the least-cost method of production—in other words, the most economical and efficient method of production.

Those who are most successful in this competition will acquire more capital to increase their production still further; those who are least successful will be forced out of the field. So capitalist production tends constantly to be drawn into the hands of the most efficient.

But how can this appallingly complex problem of supplying goods in the proportions in which consumers want them, and with the most economical production methods, be solved if the institutions of capitalism—private ownership, competition, free markets, money, prices, profits and losses—do not exist?

The Baffling Problem of Economic Calculation

Suppose that all property—at least in the means of production—is taken over by the state, and that banks and money and credit are abolished as vicious capitalist institutions; how is the government to solve the problem of what goods and services to produce, of what qualities, in what proportions, in what localities, and by what technological methods?

There cannot, let us keep in mind, be a hundred or a thousand different decisions by as many different bureaucrats, with each allowed to decide independently how much of one given product must be made. The available amount of land, capital, and labor is always limited. The factors of production needed to make A are therefore not available for B or C; and so on. So there must be a single unified over-all decision, with the relative amounts and proportions to be made of each commodity all planned in advance in relation to all the others, and with the factors of production all allocated in the corresponding proportions.

So there must be only one Master Production Plan. This could conceivably be adopted by a series of majority votes in a parliament, but in practice, to stop interminable debate and to get anything done, the broad decisions would be made by a small handful of men, and the detailed execution would probably be turned over to one Master Director who had the final word.

How would he go about solving his problem?

We must keep in mind that without free competitive markets, money, and money-prices, he would be helpless. He would know, of course (if the seizure of the means of production has only recently occurred), that people under a capitalist system lived in a certain number of houses of various qualities, wore a certain amount of clothing consisting of such and such items and qualities, ate a certain amount of food consisting of such and such meats, dairy products, grains, vegetables, nuts, fruits, and beverages. The director could simply try to continue this pre-existing mix indefinitely. But then his decisions would be completely parasitic on the previous capitalism, and he would produce and perpetuate a completely stationary or stagnant economy. If such an imitative socialism had been put into effect in, say, the France of 1870, or even of 1770, or 1670, and France had been cut off from foreign contacts, the economy of France would still be producing the same type and per capita quantity of goods and services, and by the same antiquated methods, as those that had existed in 1870, or even in 1770, or 1670, or whatever the initial year of socialization.

It is altogether probable that even if such a slavishly imitative production schedule were deliberately adopted it would overlook thousands of miscellaneous small items, many of them essential, because some bureaucrat had neglected to put them into the schedule. This has happened time and again in Soviet Russia.

What Shall Be Produced?

But let us assume that all these problems are somehow solved. How would the socialist Planners go about trying to improve on capitalist production? Suppose they decided to increase the quantity and quality of family housing. As total production is necessarily limited by existing technological knowledge and capital equipment, they could transfer land, capital, and labor to the production of more such housing only at the cost of producing less food, or less clothing, or fewer hospitals, or schools, or cars, or roads, or less of something else. How could they decide what was to be sacrificed? How would they fix the new commodity proportions?

But putting aside even this formidable problem, how would the Planners decide what machines to design, what capital goods to make, what technological methods to use, and at what localities, to produce the consumers' goods they wanted and in the proportions they wanted them?

This is not primarily a technological question, but an economic one. The purpose of economic life, the purpose of producing any thing, is to increase human satisfactions, to increase human well-being.

In a capitalist system, if people are not willing to pay at least as much for the consumer goods that have been produced as was paid for the labor, land, capital equipment, and raw materials that were used to produce them, it is a sign that production has been misdirected and that some of these productive factors have been wasted. There has been a net decrease in economic well-being instead of an increase.

There are many feasible methods—crucible, Bessemer, open hearth, electric furnace, basic oxygen process—of making steel from iron. In fact, there are today a thousand technically feasible ways of making almost anything out of almost anything. In a private enterprise system, what decides which method will be used at a given place and time is a comparison of prospective costs.

And this necessarily means costs in terms of money. In order to compare the economic efficiency of one productive method with another the methods must be reduced to some common denominator. Otherwise numerical comparison and calculation are impossible. In a market system this common denominator is achieved by comparisons in terms of money and of prices stated in money. It is only by this means that society can determine whether a given commodity is being produced at a profit or a loss, or at what comparative profits or losses any number of different commodities are being produced.

"Playing" Capitalism

In recent years even the most doctrinaire communist countries have become aware of this. They are going to be guided hereafter, they say, by profit and loss. An industry must be profitable to justify itself. So they fix money prices for everything and measure profit and loss in monetary terms.

But this is merely "playing" free markets. This is "playing" capitalism. This imitation is the unintended flattery that the communists now pay to the system they still ostensibly reject and denounce.

But the reason why this mock market system has so far proved so disappointing is that the communist governments do not know how to fix prices. They have achieved whatever success they have had when they have simply used the quotations they found already existing for international commodities in the speculative markets —i.e., in the capitalist markets—in the Western world. But there are a limited number of such grains and raw materials with international markets. In any case, their prices change daily, and are always for specific grades at specific locations.

In trying to fix prices for commodities and the multitudinous objects not quoted on these international markets the communist countries are at sea. The Marxist labor theory of value is false and therefore useless to them. We can not measure the value of anything by the number of hours of "labor time" put into it. There are enormous differences in the skill, quality, and productivity of different people's labor. Nor can we, as suggested by some Soviet economists, base prices on "actual costs of production." Costs of production are themselves prices—the prices of raw materials, of factories and machinery, rent, interest, the wages of labor, and so on.

Our Differences Guide Us

And nowhere, in a free market, are prices for long exactly equal to costs of production. It is precisely the differences between prices and costs of production that are constantly, in a free market economy, redirecting and changing the balance of production as among thousands of different commodities and services. In industries where prices are well above marginal costs of production, there will be a great incentive to increase output, as well as in creased means to do it. In industries where prices fall below marginal costs of production, output must shrink. Everywhere supply will keep adjusting itself to demand.

Where prices have been set arbitrarily, real profits and losses cannot be determined. If I am a commissar in charge of an automobile factory, and do not own the money I pay out, and you are a commissar in charge of a steel plant, and do not own the steel you sell or retain the money you sell it for, and we are each ordered to show a profit, the first thing each of us will do is to appeal to the Central Planning Board to set an advantageous price (to him) for steel and for automobiles. As an automobile commissar, I will want the price of the cars I sell to be set as high as possible, and the price of the steel I buy to be set as low as possible, so that my own "profit" record will look good or my bonus will be fixed high. But as a steel commissar, you will want the selling price of your steel to be fixed as high as possible, and your own cost prices to be fixed low, for the same reason. But when prices are thus fixed blindly, politically, and arbitrarily, who will know what any industry's real profits or losses (as distinguished from its nominal bookkeeping profits or losses) have been?

Decentralized Chaos

The problems of centralized direction of an economy are so insuperable that in socialist countries there are periodically experiments in decentralization. But in an economy only half free —that is, in an economy in which every factory is free to decide how much to produce of what, but in which the basic prices, wages, rents, and interest rates are blindly fixed or guessed at by the sole ultimate owner of the means of production, the state—a decentralized system could quickly become even more chaotic than a centralized one. If finished products *m, n, o, p,* and so on are made from raw materials *a, b, c, d,* and so on in various combinations and proportions, how can the individual producers of the raw materials know how much of each to produce, and at what rate, unless they know how much the producers of the finished products plan to produce of the latter, how much raw materials they are going to need, and just when they are going to need them? And how can the individual producer of raw material *a* or of finished product *m* know how much of it to produce unless he knows how much of that raw material or finished product others in his line are planning to produce, as well as relatively how much ultimate consumers are going to want or demand?

An economic system without private property and free-market price guides must be chaotic. In a communistic system, centralized or decentralized, there will always be unbalanced and unmatched production, shortages of this and unusable surpluses of that, duplications, bottlenecks, time lags, inefficiency, and appalling waste.

In brief, socialism is incapable of solving the incredibly complicated problem of economic calculation. That problem can be solved only by capitalism.[6]

---

1. I have examined most of these schemes in more detail elsewhere (chiefly in my *Economics in One Lesson* and in *Man vs. the Welfare State*) and must refer the interested reader to these and other sources for more extended discussion.

2. Gunnar Myrdal, *The Challenge of World Poverty* (Pantheon Books, 1970), pp. 400–401 and *passim*.

3. *Man vs. the Welfare State* (Arlington House, 1969), 23–25.

4. (Princeton: D. Van Nostrand, 1959).
5. (Princeton: D. Van Nostrand, 1960).
6. For a fuller discussion of the problem of economic calculation, see my novel, *Time Will Run Back* (originally published by Appleton-Century-Crofts in 1951 as *The Great Idea,* and republished under the new title by Arlington House in 1966). And see especially the discussion by the great seminal thinker who has done more than any other to make other economists aware of the existence, nature, and extent of the problem, Ludwig von Mises, in his *Socialism: An Analysis* (London: Jonathan Cape, 1936, 1951, 1953, 1969), and in his *Human Action* (Chicago: Henry Regnery, third revised edition, 1963), pp 200–231 and 698–715. See also *Collectivist Economic Planning,* edited by F. A Hayek (London: George Routledge, 1935), and *Economic Calculation in the Socialist Society* by T. J. B. Hoff (London: William Hodge, 1949).

24

Income Without Work

A group of social reformers, impatient with the present "rag bag" of measures to combat poverty, propose to wipe it out in a single swoop. The government would simply guarantee to everybody, regardless of whether or not he worked, could work, or was willing to work, a minimum income. This guaranteed income would be sufficient for his needs, "enough to enable him to live with dignity."

The reformers estimate that the guaranteed income ought to range somewhere between $3,000 and $6,000 a year for a family of four.

This is not merely the proposal of a few starry-eyed private individuals. The National Commission on Technology, Automation, and Economic Progress, established by Congress in 1964, brought in a 115-page report to the President on February 4 of this year recommending guaranteed incomes for all. And in January the President's Council of Economic Advisers indicated approval of "uniformly determined payments to families based only on the amount by which their incomes fall short of minimum subsistence levels." This plan, they declared, "could be administered on a universal basis for all the poor and would be the most direct approach to reducing poverty."

The plan is spelled out and argued in detail in a book called *The Guaranteed Income,* a symposium of articles by ten contributors, edited by Robert Theobald, who calls himself a "socio-economist." Mr. Theobald has contributed three of the articles, including his preface.

Of the following three paragraphs, Mr. Theobald prints the first two entirely in italics:

> *This book proposes the establishment of new principles specifically designed to break the link between jobs and income. Implementation of these principles must necessarily be carried out by the government. . . .*
>
> *We will need to adopt the concept of an absolute constitutional right to an income. This would guarantee to every citizen of the United States, and to every person who has resided within the*

From the July 1966 issue of *The Freeman.*

> *United States for a period of five consecutive years, the right to an income from the federal government to enable him to live with dignity. No government agency, judicial body, or other organization whatsoever should have the power to suspend or limit any payments assured by these guarantees. . . .*
>
> If the right to these incomes should be withdrawn under *any* circumstances, government would have the power to deprive the individual not only of the pursuit of happiness, but also of liberty and even, in effect, of life itself. This *absolute right* to a due-income would be essentially a new principle of jurisprudence.

The contributors to this volume have arrived at these extraordinary conclusions not only because they share a number of strange ideas of jurisprudence, of "rights," of government, and of the true meaning of liberty and tyranny, but because they share a number of major economic misconceptions.

Nearly all of them seem to share the belief, for example, that the growth of automation and "cybernation" is eliminating jobs so fast (or soon will be) that there soon just won't be jobs for even the most industrious. "The continuing impact of technical change will make it impossible to provide jobs for all who seek them." The goal of "jobs for all" is "no longer valid." And so on.

Ancient Fears of Automation

The fears of permanent unemployment as a result of technological progress are as old as the Industrial Revolution in the late eighteenth and early nineteenth century. They have been constantly reiterated in the last 35 years and as often completely refuted. It is sufficient to point out here that not only has the average unemployment of slightly less than 5 percent in the last 20 years not been growing, and that two-thirds of the jobless have usually remained so for periods of not more than ten weeks, but that the total volume of *employment* in the United States has reached a new high record in nearly every one of these years.

Even if it were true, as the authors of the guaranteed income proposal contend, that the American free enterprise system will soon become so productive that more than anybody really wants can be produced in half the time as now, why would that mean the disappearance of jobs? And how could that justify half the population's, say, being forced to work 40 hours a week to support the other half in complete idleness? Why couldn't everybody work only in the mornings? Or half in the mornings and the other half in the afternoons at the same machines? Or why could not some people come in on Mondays, others on Tuesdays, and so on? It is difficult to understand the logic or the sense of fairness of those who contend that as soon as there is less to be done some people must be supported in idleness by all the rest.

"An Absolute Right"

But that is precisely the contention of the advocates of the guaranteed annual income. These handout incomes are to be given as "an absolute constitutional right," and not to be withheld "under *any* circumstances." (Theobald's italics.) This means that the recipients are to continue to get this income not only if they absolutely refuse to seek or take a job, but if they throw the handout money away at the races, or spend it on prostitutes, on whiskey, cigarettes, marijuana, heroin, or what not. They are to be given "sufficient to live in dignity," and it is apparently to be no business of the taxpayers if a recipient chooses nonetheless to live without dignity, and to devote his guaranteed leisure to gambling, dissipation, drunkenness, debauchery, dope addiction, or a life of crime. "No government agency, judicial body, or other organization whatsoever should have the power to suspend or limit any payments assured by these guarantees." This is surely a "new principle of jurisprudence."

Unrealistic Cost Estimates

How much income do the guaranteed-income advocates propose to guarantee? They differ regarding this, but practically all of them think the government should guarantee at least what they and government officials call the "minimum maintenance level" or the "poverty-income line." The Social Security Administration calculated that the 1964 poverty-income line for nonfarm individuals was $1,540 a year. A nonfarm family of four was defined as poor if its money income was below $3,130. The Council of Economic Advisers has calculated that by this standard 34 million out of our 190 million 1964 population, or 18 percent, were living in poverty. This is in spite of the $40 billion total spent in welfare payments, of which it estimated that $20 billion (in the fiscal year 1965) went to persons who were, or would otherwise have been, below the poverty income line.

How much would a guaranteed income program cost the taxpayers? This would depend, of course, on how big an income was being guaranteed. Many of the income guarantee advocates think that a guarantee merely of the poverty line income would be totally inadequate. They appeal to other "minimum" budgets put together by the Social Security Administration or the Bureau of Labor Statistics, some of which run up to nearly $6,000 for a family of four.

One of the contributors to the Theobald symposium makes the following estimates of the cost to the taxpayers of different guarantees:

For a "minimum maintenance" level of $3,000 a year: total cost, $11 billion a year.

For an "economy" level of $4,000: $23 billion a year.

For a "modest-but-adequate" level of $5,000: $38 billion a year.

These figures are huge, yet they are clearly an underestimate. For the calculations take it for granted that those who could get government checks of $3,000 to $5,000 a year, as an absolute guarantee, without conditions, would continue to go on earning just as much as before. But as even one of the contributors to the Theobald symposium, William Vogt, remarks: "Those who believe that men will want to work whether they have to or not seem to have lived sheltered lives."

Who Would Do the Work?

He goes on to point out, with refreshing realism, how hard it is even today, before any guaranteed income, to get people to shine shoes, wash cars, cut brush, mow lawns, act as porters at railroad or bus stations, or do any number of other necessary jobs. "Millions of service jobs are unfilled in the United States, and it is obvious that men and women will often prefer to exist on small welfare payments rather than take the jobs.... If this situation exists before the guaranteed income is made available, who is going to take care of services when everyone can live without working—as a right?"

Who is, in fact, going to take the smelly jobs, or any low-paid job, once the guaranteed income program is in effect? Suppose, as a married man with two children, your present income from some nasty and irregular work is $2,500 a year. Comes the income guarantee, and you get a check in the mail from the government for $630. This is accompanied by a letter telling you that you are entitled as a matter of unconditional right to the poverty-line income of $3,130, and this $630 is for the difference between that and your earned income of $2,500. You are happy—for just a day. Then it occurs to you that you are a fool to go on working at your nasty job or series of odd jobs for $2, 500 when you can stop work entirely and get the full $3,130 from the government.

So the government would, in fact, have to pay out a tremendous sum. In addition, it would create idleness on a huge scale. To predict this result is not to take a cynical view, but merely to recognize realities. The beneficiaries of the guaranteed income would merely be acting sensibly from their own point of view. But the result would be that the fifth of the population now judged to be below the poverty line would stop producing even most of the necessary goods and services it is producing now. The unpleasant jobs would not get done. There would be less total production, or total real income, to be shared by everybody.

The Shifting "Poverty Line"

But so far we have been talking only about the effect of the guaranteed income on the recipients whose previous incomes have been below the poverty line. What about the other four-fifths of the population, whose incomes have previously been above it? What would be the effect on *their* incentives and actions?

Suppose a married man with two children found at the end of a year that he had earned $3,500? And suppose he found that his neighbor, with the same-sized family, had simply watched television, hung around a bar, or gone fishing during the year and had got a guaranteed income from the government of $3,130? Wouldn't the worker begin to think that he had been something of a sap to work so hard for a mere $370 net, and that it would be much better to lead a pleasantly idle life for just that much less? And wouldn't the same thing occur to all others whose earned incomes were only slightly above the guarantee?

It is not easy to say how far above the guarantee any man's income would have to be for this consideration not to occur to him. But we would do well to remember the following figures: The ***median or*** "middle" income for all families in 1964 was $6,569. The median income for "unrelated" individuals was $1,983. People with these incomes or less—i.e, half the population—would be near enough to the guarantee to wonder why they weren't getting any of it.

Someone Must Pay

If "*everybody* should receive a guaranteed income as a matter of right" (and the italics are Mr. Theobald's), who is to pay him that income? On this point the advocates of the guaranteed income are either beautifully vague or completely silent. The money, they tell us, will be paid by the "government" or by the "State." "The State would acknowledge the duty to maintain the individual."

The state is a shadowy entity that apparently gets its money out of some fourth dimension. The truth is, of course, that the government has nothing to give to anybody that it doesn't first take from someone else. The whole guaranteed-income proposal is a perfect modern example of the shrewd observation of the French economist Bastiat, more than a century ago: "The State is the great fiction by which everybody tries to live at the expense of everybody else."

Rights vs. Obligations

None of the guaranteed-income advocates explicitly recognizes that real "income" is not paper money that can be printed at will but goods and services, and that somebody has to produce these goods and services by hard work. The proposition of the guaranteed-income advocates, in plain words, is that the people who work must be taxed to support not only the people who can't work but the people who won't work. The workers are to be forced to give up part of the goods and services they have created and turn them over to the people who haven't created them or flatly refuse to create them.

Once this proposition is stated bluntly, the spuriousness in all the rhetoric about "the absolute constitutional 'right' to an income" becomes clear. A true legal or moral right of one man always implies an *obligation* on the part of others to do something or refrain from doing something to ensure that right. If a creditor has a right to a sum of money owed to him on a certain day, the debtor has an obligation to pay it. If I have a right to freedom of speech, to privacy, or to the ownership of a house, everyone else has an obligation to respect it. But when I claim a "right" to "an income sufficient to live in dignity," whether I am willing to work for it or not, what I am really claiming is a right to part of *somebody else's* earned income. What I am asserting is that he has a duty to earn more than he needs or wants to live on so that the surplus may be seized from him and turned over to me to live on.

What the guaranteed-income advocates are really saying, behind all their high-sounding phrases and humanitarian rhetoric, is something like this: "Look, we find ourselves with this wonderful apparatus of coercion, the government and its police forces. Why not use it to force the workers to pay part of their earnings over to the nonworkers?"

Lack of Understanding

We can still believe in the sincerity and good intentions of these people, but only by assuming an appalling lack of understanding on their part of the most elementary economic principles. "This book," writes Robert Theobald, "proposes the establishment of new principles specifically designed to break the link between jobs and income." But we cannot break the link between jobs and income. True income is not money, but the goods and services that a money will buy. These goods and services have to be produced. They can only be produced by work, by jobs. We may, of course, break the link between the job and the income *of a particular person,* say Paul, by giving him an income whether he consents to take a job or not. But we can do this only by seizing part of the income of some other person, say Peter, from *his* job. To believe we can break the link between jobs and income is to believe we can break the link between production and consumption. Goods have to be produced by somebody before they can be consumed by anybody.

Claimants to Be Trusted, Taxpayers to Be Examined

One reason for the agitation for an unconditionally guaranteed income is the dislike of some social reformers for the "means test."

The means test is disliked on two grounds—that it is "humiliating" or "degrading," and that it is administratively troublesome—"a comprehensive examination of means and resources, applicant by applicant." The guaranteed-income advocates think they can do away with all this by using the "simple" mechanism of having everybody fill out an income tax blank, whereupon the government would send a check to everybody for the amount that his income, so reported, fell below the government's set "poverty-line" minimum.

The belief that this income-tax mechanism would be administratively simple is a delusion. Before the introduction of the withholding mechanism, before the reporting requirements for payments made to individuals in excess of $600 in any year, and the still more recent requirements for the reporting of even the smallest interest and dividend payments, the income tax was in large part a self-imposed tax. The government depended heavily on the taxpayer's conscientiousness and honesty. To a substantial extent it still does.

The government can check the honesty of individual returns only by a random or arbitrary sampling process. It is altogether probable that more evasion and cheating go on in the low income-tax returns than in the high ones—not because the big-income earners are more honest, but simply because their chances of being examined and caught are higher. The amount of concealment and falsification that would be practiced by persons trying to get as high a guaranteed income as possible would probably be enormous. To minimize the swindling, the government would have to resort to the same case-by-case and applicant-by-applicant process as it does to administer current relief, unemployment insurance, and social security programs.

Is a means test for relief necessarily any more humiliating than the ordeal that the taxpayer must go through when his income tax is being examined, and when every question he is asked and record he is required to provide implies that he is a potential crook? If the reply is that this inquisition is necessary to protect the government from fraud, then the same reply is valid as applied to applicants for relief or a guaranteed income. It would be a strange double standard to insist that those who were being forced to pay the guaranteed income to others should be subject to an investigation from which those who applied for the guaranteed income would be exempt.

Finally, the income-tax mechanism would be irrelevant to the real problem with which the guaranteed-income advocates profess to be concerned. For the applicants would presumably be reporting *last* year's income, which would have no necessary relation to their present need. An applicant's income in the previous year or other previous period might be either much higher or much lower than it is today. The process would not meet present emergencies, such as illness or temporary loss of employment. The guaranteed-income payment might either come too late or prove unneeded or excessive.

Old Subsidies Never Die

One of the main selling arguments of the guaranteed-income advocates is that its net cost to the taxpayers would not be as great as might appear at first sight because it would be a *substitute* for the present "mosaic" or "rag bag" of measures designed to meet the same goal—Social Security, unemployment compensation, Medicare, direct relief, free school lunches, stamp plans, farm subsidies, housing subsidies, rent subsidies, and all the rest.

Neither the record of the past nor a knowledge of political realities supports such an expectation. One of the main selling arguments in the middle 1930s, first for unemployment insurance and later for Social Security, was that these programs would take the place and eliminate the need for the various relief programs and payments then in existence. But in the last 30 years these programs have continued to grow year by year with only minor interruptions. The result is that public assistance payments (including old-age assistance, aid to dependent children, general assistance, etc.) have risen from a total of $657 million in 1936 to $4,736 million in 1963, an increase of 620 percent. And this cost is *in addition to* the present $30 billion or more that the Federal government now spends annually on Social Security and other welfare programs.

So not only may we expect that the guaranteed-income would be thrown on top of all existing welfare payments (we can expect a tremendous outcry against discontinuing any of them), but that demands would arise for constant enlargement of the guaranteed amount. If the average payment were merely the *difference* between an assumed "poverty-line" income of, say, $3,000 and what the family had earned itself, all heads of families earning less than $3,000 would either quit work or threaten to do so unless they were given the full $3,000, and so allowed to "keep" whatever they earned themselves. And once this demand was granted (in an effort to avoid the wholesale idleness and pauperization that would otherwise occur), the people whose earnings were just above the government minimum, or less than twice as much, would point out how unjustly they were being treated. And the only "logical" and "fair" stopping place, it would be argued, would be to give *everybody* the full minimum of $3,000 no matter how much he was earning or getting from other sources.

Anyone who thinks such a prediction farfetched need merely recall how we got into the present system of paying everybody over 72 Social Security benefits regardless of his current earnings from other sources, and paying benefits to every retired person over 65 regardless of the size of his unearned income from other sources. By the same logic, the British government pays comprehensive unemployment, sickness, maternity, widowhood, funeral and other benefits, and retirement pensions, regardless of need or the size of the recipient's income.

Incentives Undermined

We have seen how the guaranteed-income plan, if adopted in the form that its advocates propose, would lead to wholesale idleness and pauperization among nearly all those earning less than the minimum guarantee, and among many earning just a little more. But it would also undermine the incentives of those much further up in the income scale. For they would not only be deprived of the benefits that they saw millions of others getting. It is *they* who would be expected to pay these benefits, through the imposition upon them of far more burdensome income taxes than they were already paying. If these taxes were steeply progressive in proportion to income, as is probable, they would discourage long hours and unusual effort.

It is difficult to make any precise estimate of the effect of a given income-tax rate in discouraging or reducing work and production. Different individuals will, of course, be differently affected. The activities of a man whose whole income comes in the form of a single salary from a single job will be differently affected than those of a surgeon, a doctor, a writer, an actor, an architect, or anyone whose income varies with the number of assignments he is willing to undertake or clients he is willing to serve.

What we do know is that the higher income-tax rates, contrary to popular belief, just don't raise revenue. In the current 1966 fiscal year, individual income taxes are estimated to be raising $51.4 billion (out of total revenues of $128 billion). Yet the tax rates in excess of 50 percent have been bringing in only about $250 million a year—less than 1 percent of total income tax revenues and not enough to run even the present government for a full day. (In other words, if all the personal income-tax rates above 50 percent were reduced to that level, the loss in revenue would be only about $250 million.) If these rates above 50 percent were raised further, it is more probable that they would raise less revenue than more. Therefore, it is the income tax rates on the lower and middle incomes that would have to be raised most, for the simple reason that 75 percent of the personal income of the country is earned by people with less than $15,000 gross incomes.

Poverty for All

It is certain that high income tax rates discourage and reduce the earning of income, and therefore the total production of wealth, to some extent. Suppose, for illustration, we begin with the extreme proposal that we equalize everybody's income by taxing away all income in excess of the average in order to pay it over to those with incomes below the average. (The guaranteed income proposal isn't too far away from that!)

Let us say that the present per capita average yearly income is about $2,800. Then everybody who was getting less than that (and would get just that whether he worked or not) would, of course, as with the guaranteed-income proposal, not need to work productively at all. And no one who was earning more than $2,800 would find it worthwhile to continue to earn the excess, because it would be seized from him in any case. More, it would soon occur to him that it wasn't worthwhile earning even the $2,800, for it would be given to him in any case; and his income would be that whether he worked or not. So if everybody acted under an income equalization program merely in the way that seemed most rational in his own isolated interest, none of us would work and all of us would starve. We might each get $2,800 cash (if someone could be found to continue to run the printing machines just for the fun of it), but there would be nothing to buy with it.

A less extreme equalization program would, of course, have less extreme results. If only 90 percent of all incomes over $2,800 were seized and people could keep 10 cents of every "excess" dollar they earned, there would of course still be a little incentive to earn a little more. And if everyone could keep 25 cents out of every dollar he earned above the $2,800, the incentive would be slightly higher.

But every tax or expropriation must reduce incentives to a certain extent. The effect of the guaranteed-income proposal would be practically to wipe out incentives for those earning (or even wanting) no more than the guarantee, and greatly to reduce incentives for all those earning or capable of earning more than the guarantee. Therefore the guaranteed income would reduce effort and earning and production. It would violently reduce the national income (measured in real terms). And it would reduce the standard of living for four-fifths of the population. The government might be able to pay out the specified amount of guaranteed dollar "income," but the purchasing power of the dollars would appallingly shrink.

The Negative Income Tax

Recognizing the calamitous erosion of incentives that would be brought about by a straight guaranteed income plan, other reformers have advocated what they call a "negative income tax." This proposal was put forward by the prominent economist Professor Milton Friedman of the University of Chicago, in his book *Capitalism and Freedom,* which appeared in 1962. The system he proposed would be administered along with the current income tax system.

Suppose that the poverty-line income were set at $3,000 per "consumer unit" (families or individuals), and suppose that the negative income tax (which is really a subsidy), were a flat rate of 50 percent. Then every "consumer unit" (this is the statisticians' technical term) whose income fell below $3,000 would be paid a subsidy of, say, 50 percent of the difference. If its earned income were $2,000, for example, it would receive $500; if its earned income were $1,000 it would receive $1,000; if its earned income were zero it would receive $1,500.

Professor Friedman freely concedes that his proposal, "like any other measure to relieve poverty . . . reduces the incentives of those helped to help themselves." But he argues that "it does not eliminate that incentive entirely, as a system of supplementing incomes up to some fixed minimum would. An extra dollar earned always means more money available for expenditure."

It is true that the "negative income tax" would not have quite the destructive effect on incentives that the guaranteed income would. Nevertheless, once the principle of the negative income tax were accepted, the demand would immediately arise that the minimum subsidy to be paid should be at least "adequate" to provide a minimum income to support a family "in decency and dignity." So we would be back to the minimum guaranteed income, *plus* supplemental subsidies for those who already had some earned or private income of their own. If this minimum were set at $3,130 for a married man with two children (to return to the Social Security Administration's "poverty-line" figure), this subsidy would be reduced, say, by 50 cents for every dollar earned, and therefore would not stop entirely until the family's own earned income had reached $6,240.

Not Enough Rich to Soak

How many billions of dollars in subsidies this would involve, and what rate of income tax would be required on all families with incomes *above* $6,240 to raise the revenue necessary to pay these subsidies, if any rate could, I leave to the professional statisticians to calculate.

But it is obvious that this program could not be paid for by "the rich." If we were to subsidize all family incomes below $6,240 it would be hardly consistent to tax them. Yet *net* incomes below $6,000 (after exemptions and deductions) are now taxed at rates up to 22 percent, beginning with 14 percent even on the first $500 of net income. In fact, all personal net income of $6,000 or less is now the source of nearly 80 percent of all personal income tax revenue. Yet, as I have already pointed out, the Census Bureau calculates that the median income for all families in 1964 was only $6,569; and taxpayers with adjusted gross incomes of $15,000 or less receive three-quarters of the total personal income there is to be taxed.

Neither a "negative income tax" nor a guaranteed income plan of the dimensions being suggested could possibly be put into effect with dollars of present purchasing power.

It may be added that the negative income tax would have all the administrative problems that would afflict the guaranteed income proposal—fraud, corruption, necessary applicant-by-applicant investigation, and irrelevance of payment to present need.

And once the main principle of either proposal were accepted, the minimum subsidy or guarantee demanded would be bound constantly to increase. Anyone who doubts this need merely consult the history of unemployment insurance and social security benefits since the plans were initiated in the 1930s. It is significant that several of the advocates of the guaranteed income acknowledge that their idea originated with the more modest negative income tax proposal of Milton Friedman. They just expanded it.

So knowing what we do of political pressures, and of the past history of relief, "social insurance," and other "antipoverty" measures, we are forced to conclude that once the principle of either the negative income tax or the guaranteed income were accepted, it would be made an addition to and not a substitute for the present conglomeration of relief and "antipoverty" programs. And even alone it would drastically reduce the productive incentives of those earning less than the guaranteed amount and seriously reduce the incentives of those earning more, because of the oppressive taxation it would necessarily involve. Its overall effect would be to level real incomes down, not up.

Even at present our large and overlapping assortment of relief and antipoverty measures is seriously reducing incentives to the production that would otherwise be possible. Our social reformers have been everywhere overlooking the two-sided nature of the problem of reducing poverty. The obstinate two-sided problem we face is this: How can we mitigate the penalties of misfortune and failure without undermining the incentives to effort and success?

The Poor Laws of England

Our social reformers—who sometimes talk as if no government ever did anything to relieve the plight of the jobless and the poor until the New Deal came along in 1933—are constantly deploring the alleged indifference, callousness, or niggardliness of our forefathers in dealing with the poor. But wholly apart from private charity, previous generations in their governmental capacity were sharply aware of the problem of poverty and made some effort to alleviate it almost as far back as the records go. There were "poor laws" in England even before the days of Queen Elizabeth. A statute of 1536 provided for the collection of voluntary funds for the relief of those unable to work. Eleven years later the City of London decided that these voluntary collections were insufficient, and imposed a compulsory tax to support the poor.

In 1572 a compulsory tax for this purpose was imposed on a national scale.

But the problem soon proved a very serious one for the people of that age. The upper class was very small numerically and proportionately. The middle class itself was always very close to what we would today call the poverty line. The workhouse and other conditions imposed on those on relief seem very cruel to us today. But our ancestors were in constant fear that if they increased relief or relaxed the stern conditions for it they would pauperize increasing numbers of the population and create an insoluble problem.

At the beginning of the nineteenth century, indeed, the cost of poor relief began to get out of hand. The total cost of the poor law administration increased fourfold in the 32 years between 1785 and 1817, and reached a sixth of the total public expenditure. One Buckinghamshire village reported in 1832 that its expenditure on poor relief was eight times what it had been in 1795, and more than the rental of the whole parish had been in that year.

In face of statistics of this kind, England's Whig government decided to intervene. It appointed a royal commission, and in 1834 a new and more severe poor law was passed in accordance with the commission's recommendations.

The guiding principle of the new law was that poor relief should be granted to able-bodied poor and their dependents only in well-regulated workhouses under conditions inferior to those of the humblest laborers outside. This seemed harsh, but the commissioners had argued that "every penny bestowed that tends to render the condition of the pauper more eligible than that of the independent laborer is a bounty on indolence and vice."

If the pendulum swung too far in the direction of severity and niggardliness in the middle nineteenth century, it may be swinging too far in the direction of laxity and prodigality today. A sweeping subsidization of idleness, such as is proposed by the guaranteed income, would only weaken or destroy all incentive to effort, not only on the part of those who were subsidized and supported, but on the part of those who would be forced to support them out of their own earnings. There could be no faster way to impoverish the nation.

The Cure Is Production

One of the worst features of all the plans for sharing the wealth and equalizing or guaranteeing incomes is that they lose sight of the conditions and institutions that are necessary to create wealth and income in the first place. They take for granted the existing size of the economic pie; and in their impatient effort to see that it is sliced more equally they overlook the forces that have not only created the pie in the first place but have been baking a larger one year by year. Economic progress and justice do not consist in beautifully equalized destitution, but in the constant creation of more and more goods and services, of more and more wealth and income to be shared.

The only real cure for poverty is production.

The way to maximize production is to maximize the incentives to production. And the way to do that, as the modern world has discovered, is through the system known as capitalism—the system of private property, free markets, and free enterprise. This system maximizes production because it allows a man freedom in the choice of his occupation, freedom in his choice of those for whom he works or who work for him, freedom in the choice of those with whom he associates and cooperates, and, above all, freedom to earn and to keep the fruits of his labor. In the capitalist system each of us, with whatever exceptions, tends in the long run to get what he creates or helps to create. When each of us recognizes that his reward depends on his own efforts and output, and tends to be proportionate to his output, then each has the maximum incentive to maximize his effort and output.

No Effective Poverty Programs for Underdeveloped Countries

Capitalism brought the Industrial Revolution, and the enormous increase in productivity which this has made possible. Capitalism has enormously raised the economic level of the masses. It has wiped out whole areas of poverty, and continues to wipe out more. The so-called "pockets of poverty" constantly get smaller and fewer.

The condition of poverty, moreover, is relative rather than absolute. What we call poverty in the United States would be regarded as affluence in most parts of Africa, Asia, or Latin America. If an income sufficient to enable a man "to live with dignity" ought to be "guaranteed" as a matter of "absolute right," why don't the advocates of a guaranteed income insist that this right be enforced first of all in the poor countries, such as India and China, where the need is most widespread and glaring? The reason is simply that even the better off groups in these nations have not produced enough wealth and income to be expropriated and distributed to others.

One of the guaranteed-income advocates, in a footnote, admits naively: "We must also recognize that we still have no strategy for the elimination of poverty in the under-developed countries." Of course they haven't. The "strategy" would be the introduction of free enterprise, and of incentives to work, to save, to accumulate capital, better tools, and equipment, and to produce.

But would-be income guarantors ignore or despise the capitalistic system that makes their dreams dreamable and gives their redistribute-the-income proposals whatever plausibility they have. The capitalist system has made this country the most productive and richest in the world. It has continued to achieve its miracles even in the last generation, and to increase them year by year. It has raised the average weekly factory wage from less than $17 in 1933 to $110 today. Even after the rise in prices is allowed for, it has more than doubled our real per capita disposable income—from $893 in 1933 to $2,200 in 1965.

Allowed to continue to operate with even the relative freedom that it has enjoyed in recent years, the capitalist system will continue to produce these miracles. It will continue to make progress against poverty by a *general* increase in income and wealth. But short-sighted and impatient efforts to wipe out poverty by severing the connection between effort and reward can only lead to the growth of a totalitarian state, and destroy the economic progress that this country has so dearly bought.

25

On Appeasing Envy

Any attempt to equalize wealth or income by forced redistribution must only tend to destroy wealth and income. Historically the best the would-be equalizers have ever succeeded in doing is to equalize downward. This has even been caustically described as their intention. "Your levellers," said Samuel Johnson in the mid-eighteenth century, "wish to level *down* as far as themselves; but they cannot bear levelling *up* to themselves." And in our own day we find even an eminent liberal like the late Mr. Justice Holmes writing: "I have no respect for the passion for equality, which seems to me merely idealizing envy."[1]

At least a handful of writers have begun to recognize explicitly the all-pervasive role played by envy or the fear of envy in life and in contemporary political thought. In 1966, Helmut Schoeck, professor of sociology at the University of Mainz, devoted a penetrating book to the subject.[2]

There can be little doubt that many egalitarians are motivated at least partly by envy, while still others are motivated, not so much by any envy of their own, as by the fear of it in others, and the wish to appease or satisfy it.

But the latter effort is bound to be futile. Almost no one is completely satisfied with his status in relation to his fellows. In the envious the thirst for social advancement is insatiable. As soon as they have risen one rung in the social or economic ladder, their eyes are fixed upon the next. They envy those who are higher up, no matter by how little. In fact, they are more likely to envy their immediate friends or neighbors, who are just a little bit better off, than celebrities or millionaires who are incomparably better off. The position of the latter seems unattainable, but of the neighbor who has just a minimal advantage they are tempted to think: "I might almost be in his place."

Moreover, the envious are more likely to be mollified by seeing others deprived of some advantage than by gaining it for themselves. It is not what they lack that chiefly troubles them, but what others

---

This article, a chapter in Hazlitt's book, *The Conquest of Poverty,* published by Arlington House, appeared in the March 1972 issue of *The Freeman.*

have. The envious are not satisfied with equality; they secretly yearn for superiority and revenge. In the French revolution of 1848, a woman coal-heaver is reported to have remarked to a richly dressed lady: "Yes, madam, everything's going to be equal now; I shall go in silks and you'll carry coal."

Envy is implacable. Concessions merely whet its appetite for more concessions. As Schoeck writes: "Man's envy is at its most intense where all are almost equal; his calls for redistribution are loudest when there is virtually nothing to redistribute."[3]

(We should, of course, always distinguish that merely negative envy which begrudges others their advantage from the positive ambition that leads men to active emulation, competition, and creative effort of their own.)

But the accusation of envy, or even of the fear of others' envy, as the dominant motive for any redistribution proposal, is a serious one to make and a difficult if not impossible one to prove. Moreover, the motives for making a proposal, even if ascertainable, are irrelevant to its inherent merits.

We can, nonetheless, apply certain objective tests. Sometimes the motive of appeasing other people's envy is openly avowed. Socialists will often talk as if some form of superbly equalized destitution were preferable to "maldistributed" plenty. A national income that is rapidly growing in absolute terms for practically every one will be deplored because it is making the rich richer. An implied and sometimes avowed principle of the British Labor Party leaders after World War II was that "Nobody should have what everybody can't have."

Equality, Yes; Abundance, No!

But the main objective test of a social proposal is not merely whether it emphasizes equality more than abundance, but whether it goes further and attempts to promote equality at the expense of abundance. Is the proposed measure intended primarily to help the poor, or to penalize the rich? And would it in fact punish the rich at the cost of also hurting everyone else?

This is the actual effect, as we saw earlier,[4] of steeply progressive income taxes and confiscatory inheritance taxes. These are not only counter-productive fiscally (bringing in less revenue from the higher brackets than lower rates would have brought), but they discourage or confiscate the capital accumulation and investment that would have increased national productivity and real wages. Most of the confiscated funds are then dissipated by the government in current consumption expenditures. The long-run effect of such tax rates, of course, is to leave the working poor worse off than they would otherwise have been.

There are economists who will admit all this, but will answer that it is nonetheless politically necessary to impose such near-confiscatory taxes, or to enact similar redistributive measures, in order to placate the dissatisfied and the envious—in order, even, to prevent actual revolution.

Appeasement Provokes Envy

This argument is the reverse of the truth. The effect of trying to appease envy is to provoke more of it.

The most popular theory of the French Revolution is that it came about because the economic condition of the masses was becoming worse and worse, while the king and the aristocracy remained completely blind to it. But Tocqueville, one of the most penetrating social observers and historians of his or any time, put forward an exactly opposite explanation. Let me state it first as summarized by an eminent French commentator in 1899:

> Here is the theory invented by Tocqueville. . . . The lighter a yoke, the more it seems insupportable; what exasperates is not the crushing burden but the impediment; what inspires to revolt is not oppression but humiliation. The French of 1789 were incensed against the nobles because they were *almost* the equals of the nobles; it is the slight difference that can be appreciated, and what can be appreciated that counts. The eighteenth-century middle class was rich, in a position to fill *almost* any employment, *almost* as powerful as the nobility. It was exasperated by this *"almost"* and stimulated by the proximity of its goal; impatience is always provoked by the final strides.[5]

I have quoted this passage because I do not find the theory stated in quite this condensed form by Tocqueville himself. Yet this is essentially the theme of his *L'Ancien Régime et la Revolution,* and he presented impressive factual documentation to support it.

> As the prosperity which I have just described began to extend in France, the community nevertheless became more unsettled and uneasy; public discontent grew fierce; hatred against all established institutions increased. The nation was visibly advancing toward a revolution. . . .
>
> It might be said that the French found their position the more intolerable precisely where it had become better. Surprising as this fact is, history is full of such contradictions.
>
> It is not always by going from bad to worse that a country falls into revolution. It happens most frequently that a people, which had supported the most crushing laws without complaint, and apparently as if they were unfelt, throws them off with violence as soon as the burden begins to be diminished. The state of things destroyed by a revolution is almost always somewhat better than that which immediately preceded it; and experience has shown that the most dangerous moment for a bad government is usually that when it enters upon the work of reform. Nothing short of great political genius can save a sovereign who undertakes to relieve his subjects after a long period of oppression. The evils which were endured with patience so long as they were inevitable seem intolerable as soon as a hope can be entertained of escaping from them. The abuses which are removed seem to lay bare those which remain, and to render the sense of them more acute; the evil has decreased, it is true, but the perception of the evil is more keen. . . .
>
> No one any longer contended in 1780 that France was in a state of decline; there seemed, on the contrary, to be just then no bounds to her progress. Then it was that the theory of the continual and indefinite perfectibility of man took its origin. Twenty years before nothing was to be hoped of the future: then nothing was to be feared. The imagination, grasping at this near and unheard of felicity, caused men to overlook the advantages they already possessed, and hurried them forward to something new.[6]

Aggravated by Sympathy

The expressions of sympathy that came from the privileged class itself only aggravated the situation:

> The very men who had most to fear from the fury of the people declaimed loudly in their presence on the cruel injustice under which the people had always suffered. They pointed out to each other the monstrous vices of those institutions which had weighed most heavily upon the lower orders: they employed all their powers of rhetoric in depicting the miseries of the common people and their ill-paid labor; and thus they infuriated while they endeavored to relieve them.[7]

Tocqueville went on to quote at length from the mutual recriminations of the king, the nobles, and the parliament in blaming each other for the wrongs of the people. To read them now is to get the uncanny feeling that they are plagiarizing the rhetoric of the limousine liberals of our own day.

All this does not mean that we should refrain from taking any measure truly calculated to relieve hardship and reduce poverty. What it does mean is that we should never take governmental measures merely for the purpose of trying to assuage the envious or appease the agitators, or to buy off a revolution. Such measures, betraying weakness and a guilty conscience, only lead to more far-reaching and even ruinous demands. A government that pays social blackmail will precipitate the very consequences that it fears.

---

1. *The Correspondence of Mr. Justice Holmes and Harold J. Laski* (ed. M. De Wolfe Howe, 2 vol. Cambridge, Mass. 1953). From Holmes to Laski, May 12, 1927, p. 942.
2. Helmut Schoeck, *Envy* (English translation, Harcourt, Brace & World, 1969).
3. *Ibid.*, p. 303.
4. "Should We Divide the Wealth?" in *The Freeman*, February, 1972, p. 100.
5. Emile Faguet, *Politicians and Moralists of the Nineteenth Century* (Boston: Little, Brown; 1928), p. 93.
6. Alexis de Tocqueville, *On the State of Society in France before the Revolution of 1789*. London: John Murray, 1856, pp. 321–324. Also available as *The Old Regime and the French Revolution* in a Doubleday paperback.
7. *Ibid.*, pp. 329–330.

26

The Cure for Poverty

The theme of this study is the conquest of poverty, not its "abolition." Poverty can be alleviated or reduced, and in the Western world in the last two centuries it has been almost miraculously alleviated and reduced; but poverty is ultimately individual, and individual poverty can no more be "abolished" than disease or death can be abolished.

Individual or family poverty results when the "breadwinner" cannot in fact win bread; when he cannot or does not produce enough to support his family or even himself. And there will always be some human beings who will temporarily or permanently lack the ability to provide even for their own self-support. Such is the condition of all of us as young children, of many of us when we fall ill, and of most of us in extreme old age. And such is the permanent condition of some who have been struck by misfortune—the blind, the crippled, the feebleminded. Where there are so many causes there can be no all-embracing cure.

It is fashionable to say today that "society" must solve the problem of poverty. But basically each individual—or at least each family—must solve its own problem of poverty. The overwhelming majority of families must produce more than enough for their own support if there is to be any surplus available for the remaining families that cannot or do not provide enough for their own support. Where the majority of families do not provide enough for their own support—where society as a whole does not provide enough for its own support—no "adequate relief system" is even temporarily possible. Hence "society" cannot solve the problem of poverty until the overwhelming majority of families have already solved (and in fact slightly more than solved) the problem of their own poverty.

All this is merely stating in an other form the Paradox of Relief: *The richer the community, the less the need for relief, but the more it is able to provide; the poorer the community, the greater the need for relief, but the less it is able to provide.*

From the June 1972 issue of *The Freeman*.

And this in turn is merely another way of pointing out that relief, or redistribution of income, voluntary or coerced, is never the true solution of poverty, but at best a makeshift, which may mask the disease and mitigate the pain, but provides no basic cure.

Government Relief Measures Intensify the Disease

Moreover, government relief tends to prolong and intensify the very disease it seeks to cure. Such relief tends constantly to get out of hand. And even when it is kept within reasonable bounds it tends to reduce the incentives to work and to save, both of those who receive it and of those who are forced to pay it. It may be said, in fact, that practically every measure that governments take with the ostensible object of "helping the poor" has the long-run effect of doing the opposite. Economists have again and again been forced to point out that nearly every popular remedy for poverty merely aggravates the problem. I have analyzed in this study such false remedies as "land reform," the guaranteed income, the negative income tax, minimum-wage laws, laws to increase the power of the labor unions, opposition to labor-saving machinery, promotion of "spread-the-work" schemes, special subsidies, increased government spending, increased taxation, steeply graduated income taxes, punitive taxes on capital-gains, inheritances, and corporations, and outright socialism.

But the possible number of false remedies for poverty is infinite. Two central fallacies are common to practically all of them. One is that of looking only at the immediate effect of any proposed reform on a selected group of intended beneficiaries and of overlooking the longer and secondary effect of the reform not only on the intended beneficiaries but on everybody. The other fallacy, akin to this, is to assume that production consists of a fixed amount of goods and services, produced by a fixed amount and quality of capital providing a fixed number of "jobs." This fixed production, it is assumed, goes on more or less automatically, influenced negligibly if at all by the incentives or lack of incentives of specific producers, workers, or consumers. "The problem of production has been solved," we keep hearing, and all that is needed is a fairer "distribution."

What is disheartening about all this is that the popular ideology on all these matters shows no advance—and if anything even a retrogression—compared with what it was more than a hundred years ago.

In the middle of the nineteenth century the English economist Nassau Senior was writing in his journal:

> It requires a long train of reasoning to show that the capital on which the miracles of civilization depend is the slow and painful creation of the economy and enterprise of the few, and of the industry of the many, and is destroyed, or driven away, or prevented from arising, by any causes which diminish or render insecure the profits of the capitalist, or deaden the activity of the laborer; and that the State, by relieving idleness, improvidence, or misconduct from the punishment, and depriving abstinence and foresight of the reward, which have been provided for them by nature, may indeed destroy wealth, but most certainly will aggravate poverty.[1]

Man throughout history has been searching for the cure for poverty, and all that time the cure has been before his eyes. Fortunately, as far at least as it applied to their actions as individuals, the majority of men instinctively recognized it—which was why they survived. That individual cure was Work and Saving. In terms of social organization, there evolved spontaneously from this, as a result of no one's conscious planning, a system of division of labor, freedom of exchange, and economic cooperation, the outlines of which hardly became apparent to our forebears until two centuries ago. That system is now known either as Free Enterprise or as Capitalism, according as men wish to honor or disparage it.

It is this system that has lifted mankind out of mass poverty. It is this system that in the last century, in the last generation, even in the last decade, has acceleratively been changing the face of the world, and has provided the masses of mankind with amenities that even kings did not possess or even imagine a few generations ago.

Because of individual misfortune and individual weaknesses, there will always be some individual poverty and even "pockets" of poverty. But in the more prosperous Western countries today, capitalism has already reduced these to a merely residual problem, which will become increasingly easy to manage, and of constantly diminishing importance, if society continues to abide in the main by capitalist principles. Capitalism in the advanced countries has already, it bears repeating, conquered *mass* poverty, as that was known throughout human history and almost everywhere, until a change began to be noticeable sometime about the middle of the eighteenth century. Capitalism will continue to eliminate mass poverty in more and more places and to an increasingly marked extent if it is merely permitted to do so.

In a previous article ("False Remedies for Poverty," *The Freeman*, February 1971), I explained by contrast how Capitalism performs its miracles. It turns out the tens of thousands of diverse commodities and services in the proportions in which they are socially most wanted, and it solves this incredibly complex problem through the institutions of private property, the free market, and the existence of money—through the interrelations of supply and demand, costs and prices, profits and losses. And, of course, through the force of competition. Competition will tend constantly to bring about the most economical and efficient method of production possible with existing technology—and then it will start devising a still more efficient technology. It will reduce the cost of existing production, it will improve products, it will invent or discover wholly new products, as individual producers try to think what product consumers *would* buy if it existed.

Those who are least successful in this competition will lose their original capital and be forced out of the field; those who are most successful will acquire through profits more capital to increase their production still further. So capitalist production tends constantly to be drawn into the hands of those who have shown that they can best meet the wants of the consumers.

True Help for the Poor

Those who truly want to help the poor will not spend their days in organizing protest marches or relief riots, or even in repeated protestations of sympathy. Nor will their charity consist merely in giving money to the poor to be spent for immediate consumption needs. Rather will they themselves live modestly in relation to their income, save, and constantly invest their savings in sound existing or new enterprises to create not only more jobs but better paying ones ("Private Wealth, Public Purpose," *The Freeman*, December 1970).

The irony is that the very miracles brought about in our age by the capitalist system have given rise to expectations that keep running ahead even of the accelerating progress, and so have led to an incredibly shortsighted impatience that threatens to destroy the very system that has made the expectations possible.

If that destruction is to be prevented, education in the true causes of economic improvement must be intensified beyond anything yet attempted.

---

1. Nassau Senior, *Journal Kept in France and Italy from 1848–52* (London: Henry S. King, 2nd ed. 1871), Vol. I, pp. 4–5.

27

The Story of Negro Gains

The myth still assiduously cultivated in some quarters is that the Negro community has been sunk in hopeless poverty and despair, because it has not been allowed to participate in the general economic prosperity of the last ten or 20 years. The actual record does not support this.

What we find, in fact, is that the Negroes as a whole have not only made great absolute economic gains in this period, but gains at least fully proportional to those made by the white population.

The median income of Negro families in 1949 (calculated in 1969 prices) was $2,538. In 1959 this had risen to $3,661, and in 1969 to $6,191. Thus the median income had risen 44 percent in the ten years from 1949 to 1959, and 144 percent in the 20 years to 1969. This was a real gain in "constant" dollars and therefore owed nothing to the steep rise in prices during the period. The percentage of Negro families with incomes under $3,000 (also calculated in constant 1969 dollars) fell from 58.1 percent in 1949 to 41.9 percent in 1959 and to 20.4 percent in 1969.

Thus the Negroes not only shared proportionately with the whites in the economic improvement of the 20-year period, but somewhat better than proportionately. Compared with the 144 percent increase in Negro family "real" incomes between 1949 and 1969, white family real incomes in the same period increased only 97 percent.[1]

Interpreting the Statistics

I have presented the figures in this way in order to emphasize the real economic progress made by the blacks in this twenty-year period. But these figures standing by themselves could give a misleading impression. They fail to call attention to the big gap still remaining between the incomes of white and black families. In 1949, when the median income of Negro families was $2,538 (in 1969 prices) the

From the November 1971 issue of *The Freeman*.

median income of white families was $4,973. In 1969, when the median income of black families had risen to $6,191, that of white families had risen to $9,794. Thus the median income of black families, which averaged only 51 percent of that of white families in 1949, had advanced to no more than 63 percent in 1969.

This, of course, is still far from satisfactory; but the comparison should not lead us to depreciate the extent of the blacks' real gains. Some writers talk as if the only gain worth talking about that the blacks have made is this gain in comparison with increased white incomes. But this is a captious and confused way of looking at the matter, and leads to some paradoxical results. Suppose in this 20-year period the gains of Negro families had been the same as they were in absolute terms, but that the real incomes of white families had shown no improvement whatever. Then though only 20.4 percent of Negro families would have had incomes under $3,000 in 1969, 23.4 percent of white families would still have had such low incomes, as they did in 1949. And though the median income of Negro families would have been $6,191 in 1969, the median income of white families (in 1969 prices) would have been only $4,973, as it was in 1949. In both respects the Negro families, though with no better incomes in absolute terms than they actually had in 1969, would have been better off than the white families. Could this be seriously regarded as a more desirable all-around situation?

In still other ways the Negro has made great progress in the last ten or twenty years. A leading example is in the field of education. In 1957, the median years of school completed by nonwhite men (who were eighteen years of age and over, and who were in the labor force) stood at 8.0 years; for white men the corresponding figure was 11.5 years, a gap of 3.5 years. By 1967, however, the median years of schooling for nonwhite men increased to 10.2 years, and for white men the figure had increased to 12.3 years, reducing the difference to 2.1 years.

Differences Within Groups

One trouble with all the comparisons I have made so far is that, because they arbitrarily group all whites together on the one hand, and all blacks together on the other (for the sake of making over-all comparisons), they may help to encourage the naive tendency of many people to think of the black community as a homogeneous, undifferentiated group all in the same circumstances and with the same outlook. But as Negro leaders have reminded us, for example: "Young Negroes are at least as hostile toward their elders as white New Leftists are toward their liberal parents."[2] In addition Negroes are separated by great gaps in experience—Northern from Southern, urban from rural—and great differences in income. In 1967, for example, the relative spread in incomes among the nonwhite population was even greater than among the whites. The lowest fifth of white families received 5.8 percent of the total income of such families, the highest fifth received 40.7 percent, and the top 5 percent of families 14.9 percent. But among nonwhite families, the lowest fifth received only 4.4 percent of the total income of such families, the highest fifth 44.7 percent, and the top 5 percent received 17.5 percent.

These differences are emphasized further when we compare selected groups of black families from different regions, with the corresponding white groups. In 1969, for the nation as a whole, black families earned 61 percent as much as their white counterparts (compared with 54 percent in 1960). But in the North and West, black families over-all earned 75 percent as much as white families. More striking, Northern black families with the husband and wife under age 35 both present, averaged an $8,900 annual income in 1969, or 91 percent of the average of their white counterparts, compared with only a 62 percent average in 1960. Still more striking, Northern black families with the husband and wife under age 24 averaged 107 percent of the income of their white counterparts. (The Census Bureau thinks this is probably the result of a sampling error. But that the income of such black families is at least equal to that of their white counterparts is suggested by the result of a similar sampling in 1968; this showed such black family incomes averaging 99 percent of corresponding white incomes.)

It is significant that where we find the Negroes making the least progress comparatively is in the areas where the free market is not allowed to operate. This is particularly striking in labor union membership. In the unionized trades the unwritten rule seems to be that the higher the pay, the harder it is for blacks to get in. They make up 11 percent of the labor force. But at latest count, in such high-paying trades as plumbers, sheet-metal workers, electrical workers, and elevator constructors, less than 1 percent of the workers are black.[3]

Minimum Wage Laws and Other Interventions Cause Unemployment

In one important respect, the position of the Negroes has retrogressed. An increasing gap has developed between the respective rates of unemployment of whites and blacks. In June of 1971, the over-all rate of unemployment among whites was 5.2 percent, among Negroes 9.4 percent. A difference of this sort has long existed. For example, even in the relatively good employment years 1950 to 1954 inclusive, when the white unemployment rate averaged 3.7 percent, the rate for Negroes averaged 6.8 percent. Part of this difference probably reflected discrimination by employers, and part of it the exclusion of Negroes from unions. In those five years unemployment among teenagers (16 to 19) was also higher, as it is now, than in the working force as a whole. But the gap in this respect between white and black teenagers was comparatively small. Unemployment among white teenagers in 1950 to 1954 averaged 10.3 percent, and among black teenagers 11.1 percent.

Since that time the situation has been steadily deteriorating. In June of 1971 the unemployment rate among white teenagers was 13.5 percent, while among black teenagers it reached the appalling level of 33.8 percent.

By far the main cause of this has been the Federal minimum wage law. Minimum wage legislation has been on the books since 1938, but in March 1956 the minimum rate was jacked up from 75 cents to $1 an hour, and it has since been raised by successive jumps to $1.60 an hour in February 1968. But the law cannot make a worker worth a given amount by making it illegal for anyone to offer him less. It can merely make it unprofitable for employers to hire workers of low skills, and therefore forces such workers into unemployment. One of the greatest helps we could give the Negro today would be to repeal the statutory minimum wage.

What our politicians still do not realize is that the greatest counteracting force to racial discrimination is the free market. As the economist W. H. Hutt has put it, "The market is color-blind." If an employer can make a greater profit by employing a Negro than a white man at a given job, he is likely to do it. Even the militant Negro Marcus Garvey recognized this, though in a somewhat cynical manner:

> It seems strange and a paradox, but the only convenient friend the Negro worker or laborer has in America at the present time is the white capitalist. The capitalist being selfish—seeking only the largest profit out of labor—is willing and glad to use Negro labor wherever possible on a scale reasonably below the standard union wage . . . but if the Negro unionizes himself to the level of the white worker, the choice and preference of employment is given to the white worker.[4]

In a free market, however, Negro employment does not necessarily depend on acceptance of a lower wage rate. If a Negro—say an outstanding professional baseball player or musician—is clearly superior to the best white competitor, he is likely to be employed in preference, at an even higher rate, because the employer expects to make a greater profit on him.

Not a Separate "Black Economy," but Full Admission to the Market

The chief hope for the economic progress of the Negroes lies not in some dream-world effort to form a separate "black economy," but in their becoming and being accepted as a more fully integrated part of a great expanding capitalist economy. In spite of the discrimination that still exists, the economic position of the Negro in the United States is not only in comparably higher than in Haiti or in any of the all-black countries of Africa, but higher than most whites even in the industrialized countries of Europe.

For what the best available statistical comparisons are worth, here they are: As compared with a median annual income of $2,138 for Negro unrelated individuals in 1968, the per capita gross national product for that year was $91 in Haiti, $238 in Ghana, $298 in Zambia, and $304 in the Ivory Coast. In Chad, the Congo, Mali, Niger, and Nigeria, it ranged from a low of $63 to a high of $88.[5]

Turning to European comparisons: In the early 1960s, when it was calculated that some 44 percent of America's nonwhite population was below the so-called poverty line of $3,000 a year, it developed that some 75 percent of Britain's entire, predominantly white, population was also below that line.[6] The $2,138 median income for American unrelated Negroes in 1968 compares with a per capita gross national product for that year of $1,544 in Austria, $2,154 in Belgium, $2,206 in West Germany $1.418 in Italy. and $1,861 in the United Kingdom.

What chiefly counts is the productivity of the whole economy; what counts is the maximization of the incentives to that productivity. And those incentives are maximized when opportunities are maximized—when we neither favor nor discriminate against any man because of his color, but treat everyone according to his merits as an individual.

---

1. Source: Department of Commerce, Bureau of the Census; *Economic Report of the President,* February 1971, Table C-20, p. 220.
2. Bayard Rustin in *Harper's Magazine,* January 1970.
3. Author's source: *Time,* April 6, 1970.
4. Quoted by Bayard Rustin, *Harper's Magazine,* January 1970.
5. Source: *Statistical Abstract,* 1970, p. 810.
6. Author's source: M. Stanton Evans in *National Review Bulletin,* February 3, 1970.

28

The Ballooning Welfare State

Most of the self-styled liberals of the present day would be astonished to learn that the father of the welfare state that they so much admire was none other than the fervent antiliberal and advocate of "blood and iron," Otto von Bismarck.

"He was the first statesman in Europe to devise a comprehensive scheme of social security, offering the worker insurance against accident, sickness, and old age. This Bismarckian 'socialism' later became a model for every other country in Europe. It represented in part the paternalistic function of the state which Bismarck, as a conservative, had always held."[1] Bismarck's scheme of compulsory insurance went into effect in 1883, and was soon even baptized by German journalists as *der Wohlfahrtsstaat*.

The example of Germany was followed by Austria in 1888 and by Hungary in 1891.

It was not till 1912 that compulsory health insurance was introduced in Great Britain, under Lloyd George's National Insurance Act of 1911. In 1925 came contributory old-age, widows' and orphans' pensions. Unemployment insurance was put on a fresh basis in the Unemployment Act of 1934, which set up at the same time a national system of unemployment assistance. In 1945 the Family Allowance Act was passed. It provided for payment to every family, rich or poor, of an allowance for each child, other than the eldest. In 1946 came the National Health Service Act, offering free medical services and medicines to everyone.

Then, in 1948, as a result of the report of Sir William Beveridge, the whole system of compulsory contributions for social insurance was immensely extended, with wider unemployment benefits, sickness benefits, maternity benefits, widows' benefits, guardians' allowances, retirement pensions, and death grants.

The continuous expansion of "social security" and welfare services in Great Britain is typical of what has happened in most other countries in the Western world over the last half century. The broad pattern

From the April 1972 issue of *The Freeman*.

has been remarkably similar: a multitude of "insurance" programs, supported in part by compulsory contributions and in part by general tax funds, ostensibly protecting everyone against the hazards of poverty, unemployment, accident, sickness, old age, malnutrition, "substandard" housing, or almost any other imaginable lack; programs expanding year by year in the number of contingencies covered, in the number of beneficiaries under each program, in the size of individual benefits paid, and of course in the total financial burden imposed.

So, year by year, the tendency has been for every working person to pay a higher percentage of his earned income either for his own compulsory "insurance' or for the support of others. Year by year, also, the total burden of taxes tends to go up, both absolutely and proportionately. But direct and acknowledged taxes have tended to go up less than total expenditures. This has led to chronic deficits that are met by printing more irredeemable paper money, and so to the almost universal chronic inflation that marks the present age.

Growth of Welfare Programs in the U.S. since 1935

Let us look at the ballooning welfare state in detail as it has developed in our own country.

We may begin with President Franklin D. Roosevelt's 1935 message to Congress in which he declared: "The Federal Government must and shall quit this business of relief. . . . Continued dependence upon relief induces a spiritual and moral disintegration, fundamentally destructive to the national fiber."

The contention was then made that, if unemployment and old-age "insurance" were put into effect, poverty and distress would be relieved by contributory programs that did not destroy the incentives and self-respect of the recipients. Thus relief could gradually be tapered off to negligible levels .

The Social Security Act became law on August 4, 1935.

Let us see first of all what happened to the old-age provisions of that act. There have been constant additions and expansions of benefits. The act was overhauled as early as 1939. Coverage was broadened substantially in 1950. In 1952, 1954, 1956, 1958, and 1960 (note the correspondence with years of Congressional elections) there were further liberalizations of coverage or benefits. The 1965 amendments added Medicare for some 20 million beneficiaries. The 1967 amendments, among other liberalizations, increased payments to the 24 million beneficiaries by an average of 13 percent and raised minimum benefits 25 percent. In 1969, retirement and survivors benefits were raised again by about 15 percent, effective January 1, 1970.

(It is sometimes argued that these benefit increases from 1950 to 1970 were necessary to keep pace with increases in living costs. Actually, the increases in individual monthly benefits totaled 83 percent, compared with a 51.3 percent increase in consumer prices over the same period.)

From $60 to $936

From 1937 to 1950, Social Security was financed by a combined tax rate of only 2 percent on both employer and employee (1 percent each) on wages up to $3,000 a year. Since then both the rates and the maximum wage base have been increased every few years. In 1972 the combined tax rate is 10.4 percent (5.2 percent on each the employer and the employee) on a maximum wage base that has been raised to $9,000. The result is that whereas the maximum annual payment up to 1950 was only $60, it has risen to $936.

In 1947, payroll tax collections for old-age and survivors insurance amounted to $1.6 billion; by 1970, these taxes had increased to $39.7 billion.

At the beginning, the Social Security program was sold to the American public as a form of old-age "insurance." The taxes were represented as the "premiums" paid for this insurance. Everybody who was getting benefits was assured that he could accept these with no loss of "dignity," because he was "only getting what he had paid for."

This was never true, even at the beginning, and has become less true year by year. The low-wage receivers have always been paid much more in proportion to their "premiums" than the higher-wage receivers. The disparity has been increased with succeeding revisions of the act. The typical beneficiary even today is receiving benefits worth about five times the value of the payroll taxes he and his employer paid in.[2]

A Bad Mixture of Insurance and Handouts

The OASDI program has developed into a mixed system of insurance and welfare handouts, with the welfare element getting constantly larger. It is today a bad system judged either as insurance or as welfare. On the one hand, benefits in excess of the amounts they paid for are being given, in some cases, to persons who are not in need of welfare. On the other hand, persons who are in fact receiving welfare handouts are being taught to believe that they are getting only "earned" insurance. Obviously, welfare programs can be expanded even faster than otherwise if they are masked as "contributory insurance" programs.

Our concern here, however, is not with the defects of the OASDI program but primarily with its rate of growth. In 1947, Social Security benefit payments covered only old-age and survivors insurance and amounted to less than half a billion dollars. In 1956, disability insurance was added, and in 1965, health insurance. In 1970, these payments reached about $39 billion.

Unemployment Insurance

Now, let us look at unemployment insurance. This program was also set up under the Social Security Act of 1935. But whereas old-age insurance was on a strictly national basis, unemployment insurance was instituted on a state-by-state basis within the broad scope of certain Federal criteria.

While provisions have differed in each of the fifty states, unemployment insurance has shown the same chronic growth tendency as old-age benefits. In 1937, the states typically required periods of two or three weeks before any benefits were paid. The theory behind this was that a man just out of employment would have at least some minimum savings; that the state would be given time to determine his benefit rights; and that the benefit funds should be conserved for more serious contingencies by reducing or eliminating payments for short periods of unemployment. Now the waiting period has been reduced to only one week, and in some states does not exist at all.

In contrast with the $15 to $18 weekly benefit ceilings in various states in 1940, the maximums now range between $40 and $86 a week, exclusive of dependents' allowances in some states.

Reflecting both legislated increases and rising wage levels, nationwide average weekly benefit payments increased from $10.56 in 1940 to $57.72 in 1971. Even after allowing for higher consumer prices, the real increase in purchasing power of these average benefits was 63 percent, and they continue to increase much faster than either wages or prices. For example, from its average in 1969, the weekly payment in June, 1971, had increased 25 percent as compared to an 8 percent increase in wages and an 11 percent increase in prices.

Fulltime Benefits

As of 1971, state legislation had increased the maximum duration of unemployment benefits from the predominantly prevailing 16-week level in 1940 to 26 weeks in 41 states—and of longer duration ranging to 39 weeks in the other states. In December, 1971, Congress voted to provide 13 weeks additional benefits in states with sustained unemployment rates of more than 6½ percent. This made it possible for workers in such eligible areas to draw such benefits up to a total of 52 consecutive weeks.

Total annual benefit payments increased from about one-half billion dollars in 1940 to $3.8 billion in 1970—more than a seven-fold increase and the highest payout in history. In 1970 alone, total benefits increased 80 percent ($1.7 billion) over the 1969 level. The combination of legislated increases in maximum weekly benefits and in maximum duration of the benefits has increased nearly *tenfold* the total benefits potentially payable to the individual unemployed worker in a year's period (dollars per week multiplied by the number of weeks).[3]

This is bound to increase still further. On July 8, 1969, President Nixon called upon the states to provide for higher weekly unemployment compensation benefits. He suggested that weekly maximums be set at two-thirds of the average weekly wage in a state so that benefits of 50 percent of wages would be paid to at least 80 percent of insured workers. Only one state—Hawaii—responded promptly with the full raise suggested, but other states have scheduled future increases.

There can be no doubt that unemployment compensation reduces the incentive to hold on to an old job or to find a new one. It helps unions to maintain artificially high wage rates and it prolongs and increases unemployment. One economist has likened it to "a bounty for keeping out of the labor market."[4]

Moreover, it is a complete misnomer to call it unemployment "insurance." In the United States the workers do not even make a direct contribution to it (though in the long run it must tend to reduce the real pay of the steady worker). Like so-called government old-age "insurance," it is in fact a confused mixture of insurance and handout.

Those who are continually urging an increase in the percentage of the previous wage-rate paid, or the extension of the benefit-paying period (to avoid undisguised relief), forget that it violates ordinary welfare standards of equity by paying larger sums to the previously better-paid workers than to the previously lower-paid workers.

But apart from these shortcomings, what we are primarily concerned with here is the tendency of unemployment compensation, once adopted, to keep growing both as a percentage of weekly wages and in the length of idle time for which it is paid.

Just what success, if any, the increasingly costly Social Security and unemployment compensation programs have had in enabling the Federal government to "quit this business of relief" we shall see in a subsequent article.

---

1. *Encyclopedia Britannica,* 1965, article "Bismarck," Vol. 3, p. 719.

2. Colin D. Campbell and Rosemary G. Campbell, "Cost-Benefit Ratios under the Federal Old-age Insurance Program," U. S. Joint Economic Committee, Old-age Income Assurance, Part III (Washington, D.C., U. S. Government Printing Office, December 1967), pp. 72–84.

3. Much of the foregoing material on Social Security and unemployment compensation is derived from studies by the American Enterprise Institute, Washington, D. C.

4. W. H. Hutt, *The Theory of Idle Resources* (London: Jonathan Cape, 1939), p. 129.

29

Welfarism Gone Wild

Both Social Security and unemployment compensation were proposed in large part on the argument of Franklin D. Roosevelt and others in 1935 that they would enable the government to "quit this business of relief."

Though all the social "insurance" programs he asked for were enacted, together with a score of others, and though all of these supplementary or "substitute" programs have been constantly enlarged, direct relief, instead of showing any tendency to diminish, has increased beyond anything dreamed of in 1935.

The number of welfare recipients in New York City alone jumped from 328,000 in 1960 to 1,280,000 in October, 1971 (exceeding the total population of Baltimore) and was still growing. On March 10, 1971, the U. S. Department of Health, Education and Welfare reported that more than 10 percent of the residents of the nation's twenty largest cities were on welfare. In New York City, Baltimore, St. Louis, and San Francisco, it was one person in seven; and in Boston, one in five. The Mayor of Newark, N. J., told Congress on January 22, 1971 that 30 percent of the population in his city was on relief.

For the whole country, the number of people on welfare grew from 6,052,000 in 1950 to 7,098,000 in 1960, to 9,540,000 in 1968, to 12,912,000 in September 1970, and to 14,480,000 in September 1971.

Because payments to individuals kept increasing, total expenditures for relief grew still faster. A condensed record is on the next page.

In the fiscal year 1971, relief expenditures of $18.6 billion were running at more than four times the rate of 1960, more than 16 times the rate of 1940, and more than 53 times the rate of 1936.

To economize on figures, I have not only confined myself to five-year interval comparisons, but I have not shown the division between state and local funds. Yet these comparisons are part of the explanation of the skyrocketing growth of these relief figures. It will be noticed

---

From the May 1972 issue of *The Freeman*.

Fiscal year	All Funds (000)	Federal Funds (000)
1936	$ 349,892	$ 20,202
1940	1,123,660	279,404
1945	1,028,000	417,570
1950	2,488,831	1,095,788
1955	2,939,570	1,440,771
1960	4,039,433	2,055,226
1965	5,868,357	3,178,850
1970	14,433,500	7,594,300
1971	18,631,600	9,932,000

Source: U. S. Department of Health, Education and Welfare, NCSS Report F-5 July 6, 1971 and *Social Security Bulletin,* December, 1971.

that while the Federal contribution to direct relief expenditures was only 5 percent in 1936, it was 25 percent in 1940, 44 percent in 1950, and 53 percent in 1971. Yet relief was actually administered at the state and local level. In fact, it was for the most part administered by the cities and counties. The localities contributed only 26 percent toward the total cost of the relief they handed out in 1940, only 11 percent in 1950, 13 percent in 1960, and 11 percent in 1970. When a city government is contributing only 11 cents of its own for every dollar it pays out to relief recipients, it can distribute its political favors cheaply, and has little incentive to exercise vigilance against overpayment and fraud.

Most of those who discuss the mounting cost of direct relief treat this figure in isolation as if it represented the total cost of "the war against poverty." In fact, it is only a small fraction of that cost, recently running in the neighborhood of not much more than a tenth. The figures on the following page are from an official table of "Social Welfare Expenditures Under Public Programs."

Revenue Sharing?

This gigantic total of $171 billion for "social welfare" is more than triple the figure for 1960 and more than 26 times the figure for 1935. Yet the 29-fold increase in Federal expenditures for welfare in the 35-year period, instead of reducing the burden on the states and cities,

Social Welfare Expenditures
(in millions of dollars)

Year	Total	Federal	State and Local
1935	$ 6,548	$3,207	$3,341
1940	8,795	3,443	5,351
1945	9,205	4,399	4,866
1950	23,508	10,541	12,967
1955	32,640	14,623	18,017
1960	52,293	24,957	27,337
1965	77,121	37,720	39,401
1968	113,839	60,314	53,525
1970	145,350	77,321	68,029
1971 (p.)	170,752	92,411	78,341

as originally promised, has been accompanied by a 23-fold increase even in that local burden.

A similar result is evident if we consider the cost of direct relief alone. Though the Federal government was contributing only 5 percent of that total cost in 1936 compared with 53 percent in 1971, the cost to the States and localities has increased 2.6-fold. So much for the theory that "revenue-sharing," or increased Federal contributions, do anything in the long run to reduce the burden of welfare spending on the states and localities. They lead merely to a total increase in that spending.

So the tendency of welfare spending in the United States has been to increase at an exponential rate. This has also been its tendency elsewhere. Only when the economic and budgetary consequences of this escalation become so grave that they are obvious to the majority of the people—i.e., only when irreparable damage has been done—are the welfare programs likely to be curbed. The chronic inflation of the last 25 to 35 years in nearly every country in the world has been mainly the consequence of welfarism run wild.

The causes of this accelerative increase are hardly mysterious. Once the premise has been accepted that "the poor," as such, have a "right" to share in somebody else's income—regardless of the reasons why they are poor or others are better off—there is no logical stopping place in distributing money and favors to them, short of the point where this brings about equality of income for all. If I have a "right" to a "minimum income sufficient to live in decency," whether I am willing to work for it or not, why don't I also have a "right" to just as much income as you have, regardless of whether you earn it and I don't?

Once the premise is accepted that poverty is never the fault of the poor but the fault of "society" (i.e., of the self-supporting), or of "the capitalist system," then there is no definable limit to be set on relief, and the politicians who want to be elected or re-elected will compete with each other in proposing new "welfare" programs to fill some hitherto "unmet need," or in proposing to increase the benefits or reduce the eligibility requirements of some existing program.

No complete count seems to exist anywhere of the present total number of welfare programs. The $171 billion expenditure for social welfare in the fiscal year 1971 is officially divided into roughly $66 billion for "social insurance," $22 billion for "public aid," $11 billion for "health and medical programs," $10 billion for "veterans' programs," $56 billion for "education," nearly $1 billion for "housing," and $5 billion for "other social welfare." But these sub-totals are in turn made up of 47 different groups of programs, and many of these in turn consist of many separate programs.[2]

A Jungle of Agencies

The weary taxpayer reads about such things as food stamps, job training, public housing, rent supplements, "model cities," community-action projects, legal services for the poor, neighborhood health centers, FAP, Office of Economic Opportunity (OEO), Medicaid, Old-Age Assistance (OAA), Aid to the Blind (AB), Aid to the Permanently and Totally Disabled (APTD), Aid to Families with Dependent Children (AFDC), General Assistance (GA), manpower training programs, Head Start, VISTA, and on and on, and has no idea whether one is included under another, whether they duplicate each other's functions, which, if any, have been discontinued, or which are just about to start. All he knows is that there seems to be a new one every month.

In 1969, Mrs. Edith Green, a Democratic Congresswoman from Oregon, asked the Library of Congress to compile the total amount of funds a family could receive from the Federal government if that family took advantage of all the public assistance programs that were available.

Taking a hypothetical family of a mother with four children —one a pre-schooler, one in elementary school, one in high school, and one in college—the library informed her of the following:

This family could collect $2,800 from public assistance; $618 from medical assistance because of AFDC; $336 in cash value for food stamps; and about $200 from OEO for legal services and health care. The family would also be entitled to public housing or rent supplements ranging in value from $406 to $636.

The preschool child would be entitled to enter Head Start, the average cost being $1,050 for each youngster. The child in high school would be eligible for $1,440 worth of services from Upward Bound and the youngster in college would be eligible for an education opportunity grant that could be worth anywhere from $500 to $1,000. He also would be eligible for a National Defense Education Act loan, and if he took advantage of the forgiveness feature, he could get an outright grant of $520. He would also be eligible for a work study program costing in the neighborhood of $475. If the mother wanted to participate in the job opportunity program, this would be worth $3,000.

So this imaginary family, a mother with four children, would be able to take advantage of grants and services worth $11,513 for the year.

In another hypothetical case, a mother with eight children could total an annual welfare income of $21,093.[3]

In 1968 Congressman William V. Roth, Jr., and his staff were able to identify 1,571 programs, including 478 in the Department of Health, Education and Welfare alone, but concluded that "no one, anywhere, knows exactly how many Federal programs there are."

In February 1972, administration witnesses testified before a Congressional committee that there were 168 separate Federal programs geared in whole or in part to combating poverty. But as the total expenditures of these 168 programs were only $31.5 billion (out of $92 billion of Federal "social welfare expenditures") this must have been an incomplete list.[4]

While the Federal government keeps piling up new welfare programs, under Democratic or Republican administrations, almost every individual program shows a tendency to snowball. One reason is that when Congressmen propose a new program, the expenditure set in the initial year is almost always comparatively moderate, to allay opposition—the "entering wedge" technique; but annual increases in spending are built into the law. Another reason is that when a new welfare program is launched, it takes people a little while to catch on to it; and then the stampede begins. A still further reason is that the bureaucrats who administer the program—eager to demonstrate their own vicarious compassion and liberality, as well as the indispensability of their jobs—not only interpret the eligibility requirements very leniently, but actively campaign to advise potential "clients" of their "legal right" to get on the rolls.

There has been a great deal of discussion in the last few years regarding the extent of fraud and cheating among those on relief. From the very nature of the problem this can never be exactly known; but the evidence indicates that it is substantial.

In January, 1971, after a door-to-door check on welfare cases, the State of Nevada struck about 22 percent of the recipients—3,000 people—from the relief rolls. The State Welfare Director reported that they had been cheating taxpayers out of a million dollars a year through failure to report income from other sources, including unemployment benefits. The director blamed the frauds on a Federal regulation that permitted welfare applicants to obtain aid simply by stating that they met all qualifications.

In Michigan, state welfare officials discovered cases of money being pocketed by welfare clients for dental work which was never performed.

In California, a group of San Francisco Bay area residents—all fully employed—conducted an experiment to prove to county supervisors how easy it is to get on relief. They traveled the circuit of welfare offices, applying for and getting on welfare, usually without even furnishing identification. Governor Reagan said that "one managed to get on welfare four times under four different names in one day—all at the same office."

In his message to the California legislature, Governor Reagan pointed out: "The same government that requires a taxpaying citizen to document every statement on his tax return decrees that questioning a welfare applicant demeans and humiliates him."

A spot check of welfare rolls in New York City by the General Accounting Office, reported in September, 1969, showed that 10.7 percent of all families on relief there did not meet the eligibility requirements, and that 34.1 percent of those who were eligible were being overpaid.[5]

In 1971, New York City Comptroller Abraham Beame revealed that the city was losing $2 million a year as a result of forged checks. More millions were lost because people on relief falsely complained that they had not received their checks; they were mailed duplicates. Simply requiring those on relief to come and pick up their checks, rather than getting them by mail, lowered New York City's welfare lists by about 20 percent.

It is impossible to know how much of the blame for the national and local welfare mess is to be put on relief cheaters and how much on loose administration. It is made so easy to get and stay on relief legally that cheating hardly seems necessary.

On January 12, 1969, *The New York Times* ran a front-page story under the headline: "Millions in City Poverty Funds Lost by Fraud and Inefficiency." It reported that "Multiple investigations of the city's $122-million-a-year anti-poverty program are disclosing chronic corruption and administrative chaos," and quoted an assistant district attorney as saying: "It's so bad that it will take ten years to find out what's really been going on inside the Human Resources Administration." The next day Secretary of Labor W. Willard Wirtz said that New York City had the worst administrative problem of any antipoverty program in any city in the country.

But the New York situation kept getting worse. In January, 1971, a welfare mother and her four children were assigned to the Waldorf Astoria, one of New York's most elegant hotels, at a cost of $152.64 for two days. The City's welfare agency claimed with a straight face that there was no room elsewhere. But many other routine practices of the City were almost as costly, with entire hotels "temporarily" filled with relief families at hotel rates. One family was put up at the Broadway-Central at a cost of $390.50 a week. Another, a welfare family of fifteen, was put up at a Bronx motel at a rental that would add up to $54,080 a year.[6]

Dependent Children

Much the fastest growing relief program has been Aid to Families with Dependent Children (AFDC). In the ten years from 1960 to 1970 the number of people aided by this program increased from

3,023,000 to 9,500,000. Costs soared from $621 million in 1955 to $4.1 billion in 1970.

The nationwide cheating on this is probably higher than on any other welfare program. The reason is that a mother and her children, legitimate or illegitimate, become eligible for AFDC relief if there is no employed father present. The mothers report that the father has "deserted." "The fact is," according to one authority, "that in many cases the father never really deserts. He just stays out of sight so the woman can get on AFDC rolls. In slum areas, everyone knows this goes on. It is widespread in New York City." Governor Reagan reported that he knew there were 250,000 homes in California where the father had run out.

One of the fundamental causes for the huge and growing load of relief cases is that there is no adequate investigation of eligibility. The excuse offered by some welfare workers is: "It's impossible to do adequate eligibility checks. There isn't time. It's a question of helping people who need help—rather than catching people who need catching."

Still another reason why there is no adequate investigation of eligibility is that Federal bureaucratic regulations discourage it. As Governor Reagan has put it: "The regulations are interpreted to mean that no caseworker can challenge or question a welfare applicant's statements."[7]

Instead of trying to reform this situation, the Department of Health, Education and Welfare seems mainly concerned to defend it. It has published and circulated widely a booklet called *Welfare Myths vs. Facts*. This turns legitimate criticisms into "myths" by grossly overstating them, and then produces questionable answers. For example:

"Myth: The welfare rolls are full of able-bodied loafers.

"Fact: Less than 1 percent of welfare recipients are able-bodied unemployed males."

This figure, implying that it would have a negligible effect on welfare to find jobs for these men, is incredibly low. It is apparently achieved by treating any physical impairment, however trivial, as a qualification for family relief; it ignores employable women; and it ignores the fact that the average relief family consists of 3.7 persons, who would move off the rolls if the breadwinner went to work. Another example:

"Myth: Once on welfare, always on welfare.

"Fact: The average welfare family has been on the rolls for 23 months. . . . The number of long-term cases is relatively small."

A 23-month *average* for families on relief is hardly something to be complacent about, even if the figure is accurate. The Department's own charts show that more than a third of those on welfare have been there three years or more. Moreover, the Department's average does not count "repeaters." If a family were on relief for, say, 23 months, off a month, back on for another 23 months, and so on, it would not raise the average. Nor does any figure based on relief at any given point in time count the prospective remaining period each case will be on the rolls. Already families have been found on relief for three generations.[8]

Small wonder that President Nixon, in his State of the Union message of January, 1971, called the existing American relief system "a monstrous, consuming outrage."

---

1. *Statistical Abstract of the United States:* 1971, table no. 430, p. 271, and *Social Security Bulletin,* December 1971.

2. See *Social Security Bulletin,* December 1971.

3. *Human Events,* December 13, 1969.

4. *New York Times,* February 16, 1972.

5. These examples were cited in an article "Welfare Out of Control" in *U. S. News & World Report,* February 8, 1971. By coincidence, *Time* and *Newsweek* also carried long feature stories on welfare in their issues of the same date, covering similar material.

6. *Time,* February 8, 1971.

7. *U. S. News & World Report,* March 1, 1971.

8. An excellent analysis of the HEW *Welfare Myths vs. Facts* pamphlet appeared in *The Wall Street Journal* of January 27, 1972, by Richard A. Snyder, a member of the Pennsvlvania Senate.

30

Uruguay: Welfare State Gone Wild

If there were a Nobel prize for the most extreme or worst example of the welfare state (and if such outright communist states as Russia and China were made ineligible), which country has done most to earn it?

The decision would be a hard one. Among the outstanding candidates would be Britain, France, Sweden, and India. But the British case, though the most familiar, is certainly not the worst; it is the most discussed and most deplored because of the former eminence of Britain in the world.

The tragedy certainly reaches its greatest dimensions in India, with much of its 500 million population always on the verge of famine, and kept there by an incredible mixture of economic controls, planning, welfarism, and socialism, imposed by its central and state governments. Moreover, India has always been a poverty-stricken country, periodically swept by drought or floods resulting in human misery on a catastrophic scale, and it is often difficult to calculate just how much worse off its governmental policies have made it.

Perhaps the most dramatic example of a country needlessly ruined by "welfare" policies is Uruguay. Here is a country only about a third larger than the state of Wisconsin, with a population of just under 3 million. Yet that population is predominantly of European origin, with a literacy rate estimated at 90 percent. This country once was distinguished among the nations of Latin America for its high living standards and good management.

Uruguay adopted an elaborate state pension system as early as 1919. But its major troubles seem to have begun after March 1952, when the office of president was abolished, and Uruguay was governed by a nine-man national council elected for a four-year term, six members of which belonged to the majority party and three to the leading minority party. All nine were given equal power.

What is so discouraging about the example of Uruguay is not only that its welfare programs persisted, but that they became more extreme

From the April 1969 issue of *The Freeman*.

in spite of the successive disasters to which they led. The story seems so incredible that instead of telling it in my own words, I prefer to present it as a series of snapshots taken by different firsthand observers at intervals over the years.

* * *

The first snapshot I present is one taken by Karel Norsky in *The Manchester Guardian Weekly* of July 12, 1956:

"Uruguay today offers the sad spectacle of a sick Welfare State. It is living in a Korean boom-day dream.... No politician comes out with the home truth that this country's wide range of welfare services has to be paid for with funds which have to be earned. Demagogy is used as a sedative. The result is that the foreign payments deficit is increasing, internal debt soaring, wage demands accumulating, prices rising, and the Uruguayan peso rapidly depreciating. Nepotism is rife. Now one in every three citizens in Montevideo, which accounts for a third of the country's 3 million inhabitants, is a public servant, draws a small salary, is supposed to work half a day in a Government office, and more often than not spends the rest of his time doing at least one other job in a private enterprise.... Corruption is by no means absent....

"The foreign payments deficit has been running at a monthly rate of about 5 million pesos. The public servants are asking for a substantial increase in salaries. The meat-packing workers are on strike for higher pay and a 'guaranteed' amount of a daily ration of four pounds of meat well below market price....

"No politician here can hope to get a majority by advocating austerity, harder work, and the sacrifice of even some of the Welfare State features."

I should like to pause here to underline this last paragraph, for it illustrates what is perhaps the most ominous aspect of the welfare state everywhere. This is that once a subsidy, pension, or benefit payment is extended to any group, it is immediately regarded as a "right." No matter what the crisis facing the budget or the currency, it becomes "politically impossible" to discontinue or reduce it. We will find this repeatedly illustrated in Uruguay.

* * *

The next snapshot I present was taken by S. J. Rundt & Associates of New York nearly seven years later, in April, 1963:

"In one of his first statements the new President of the National Council admitted that Uruguay is practically bankrupt.... He made it pretty clear, however, that the country's welfare system of long standing will remain more or less unchanged.

"The 'social laboratory of the Americas,' Uruguay has launched a legislative program which goes much further toward the complete 'welfare state' than any similar plan in this hemisphere.... The government grants family allowances based on the number of children; employees cannot be dismissed without proper indemnification; both men and women vote at the age of 18....

"An elaborate and all-encompassing state pension system was introduced as early as 1919. Financed by payroll deductions of 14 to 17 percent, which must be matched by employers, a pension is available to any Uruguayan at the age of 55 after 30 years of work, or at 60 after ten years. At retirement, the worker draws his highest salary, plus what has been deducted for pensions.... Employees obtain free medical service and are entitled to 20 days of annual vacation with pay. The government takes care of expectant and nursing mothers.

"The overwhelming expenses of a super-welfare state (where nearly one-fifth of the population is dependent on government salaries) and the uncertain income from a predominantly livestock and agricultural economy have left their marks. Today, Uruguay is in severe financial and fiscal stress....

"Inflation is rampant.... Local production has declined sharply. Unemployment has risen. There are many severe strikes. Income from tourism has fallen off markedly....

"So far as exchange controls and import restrictions are concerned, Uruguay has tried them all....

"In an effort to prevent an other buying spree in 1963, the new Administration decreed an import ban for 90 days on a wide array of goods considered nonessential.... All told, the ban applies to about one-third of all Uruguayan importations.... The smuggling of goods, mainly from Brazil and Argentina, has become one of the foremost headaches of Montevideo planners....

"Capital flight during 1963 is estimated at between $40 million and $50 million....

"The budget deficit in 1961 nearly doubled to 210 million pesos. The situation turned from bad to worse in 1962 when the Treasury recorded the largest deficit in 30 years.... Press reports cite a red figure of 807 million pesos. The Treasury is said to owe by now nearly 700 million pesos to the pension funds and roughly a billion pesos to Banco de la Republica. The salaries of public officials are at least one month behind schedule. . . .

"Labor costs in Uruguay, the Western Hemisphere's foremost welfare state, are high. The many contributions toward various social benefits—retirement, family allotments, sickness, maternity, accident, and unemployment insurance—vary from industry to industry, but the general average for industry as a whole is at least 50 percent of the payroll. In some sectors, the percentage is much higher . . . .

"Social unrest is rising. . . . Widespread and costly strikes have become the order of the day. As a rule, they involve demands for pay hikes, sometimes as high as 50 percent."

* * *

Our third snapshot was taken by Sterling G. Slappey in *Nation's Business* magazine four years later, in April, 1967:

"Montevideo—Two hundred imported buses are rusting away on an open dock while Uruguayan government bureaucrats bicker with each other over payment of port charges. The buses have not moved in nearly four years.

"Scores of men listed under false female names receive regular government handouts through Uruguay's socialized hospitals. They are listed as 'wet nurses.'

"At many government offices there are twice as many public servants as there are desks and chairs. The trick is to get to work early so you won't have to stand during the four to six hour work-day that Uruguayan bureaucrats enjoy.

"It is rather common for government workers to retire on full pay at 45. It is equally common to collect on one retirement while holding a second job or to hold a job while collecting unemployment compensation. These are a few of the facts of life in Uruguay—a nation gone wild over the welfare state. . . .

"Between 40 and 45 percent of the 2.6 million people in this once affluent land are now dependent on the government for their total income. These include youthful 'pensioners' who have no great problem getting themselves fired or declared redundant, thereby qualifying for large retirement benefits. . . .

"At any given moment eight to ten strikes are going on, in a nation which until fifteen years ago called itself 'the Switzerland of Latin America' because its people were so industrious, busy, and neat. Montevideo is now one of the world's filthiest cities outside the Orient. The people have so little pride left they litter their streets with paper and dump their nastiest garbage on the curb. . . .

"Besides controlling meat and wool production and supplying meat to Montevideo, the government also entirely operates:

"Fishing; seal catching; alcohol production; life and accident insurance; the PTT—post office, telephone and telegraph; petroleum and kerosene industry; airlines; railroads; tug boats; gambling casinos; lotteries; theaters; most hospitals; television and radio channels; three official banks; the largest transit company. . . .

"In 1950 the Uruguayan peso, South America's most solid coin, was worth 50 cents. During a six day period last February, the value of the peso slumped from 72 to the $1 to 77.

"Cost of living went up 88 percent in 1965. During 1966 the increase was something like 40 to 50 percent.

"To keep pace the government has increased its spending, ground out more paper money and lavishly passed out huge pay raises—some as high as 60 percent a year. . . .

"One fiscal expert diagnoses Uruguay's troubles as 'English sickness' which, he says, means trying to get as much as possible out of the community while contributing as little as possible towards it.

"Until President Gestido took over, Uruguay had been ruled for fifteen years by a nine-member council in a collegiate system of government. It was idealistic, unworkable, and rather silly from the start. It quickly fragmented, making the government a coalition of seven different groups. Every year a different member of the council took over as president, or council chief.

"The collegiate system was a Tammany Hall patronage-type of group. Instead of each party watching the opposition, all took care of their friends and got their cousins government sinecures.

"The western world has rarely seen such patronage, nepotism, favoritism."

* * *

The return to a Presidential system brought hopes that Uruguay's extreme welfarism could now be mitigated. But here is our fourth snapshot, taken by C. L. Sulzberger for *The New York Times* of October 11, 1967:

"Montevideo—Contemporary England or Scandinavia might well take a long southwesterly look at Uruguay while murmuring: 'There but for the grace of God go I.' For Uruguay is the welfare state gone wild, and this fact, at last acknowledged by the government, brought about today's political crisis and the declaration of a state of emergency.

"This is the only country in the Western Hemisphere where the kind of democratic socialism practiced in Norway, Labor Britain, or New Zealand has been attempted. Alas, thanks to warped conceptions and biased application, the entire social and economic structure has been set askew. Here charity begins at home. One out of three adults receives some kind of pension. Forty percent of the labor force is employed by the state. Political parties compete to expand a ridiculously swollen bureaucracy which only works a thirty-hour week....

"The cost of living has multiplied 32 times in the past decade. Gross national production has actually declined 9 percent and this year will take a nose dive....

"Instead of having one President, like the Swiss they elected a committee and, not being Swiss, the Uruguayans saw to it the committee couldn't run the country. The result was a system of self-paralysis.

"Anyone can retire on full salary after thirty years on the job, but with full salary worth one thirty-second of its worth ten years ago, the pension isn't very helpful. To compound the confusion, trade unions make a habit of striking. Right now the bank employes refuse to handle government checks so neither wage-earners nor pension-receivers get paid ....

"This was a needless tragedy. Uruguay has proportionately more literacy and more doctors than the United States. It is underpopulated and has a well-developed middle class....

"Uruguay should serve as a warning to other welfare states."

* * *

Our fifth snapshot was taken by S. J. Rundt & Associates on August 6, 1968:

"The mess continues ... and seems to perpetuate itself.... The government is getting tougher and Uruguayans more obstreperous.

The powerful and sharply leftist, communist-led 400,000 member CNT (National Workers Convention) is on and off 24-hour work stoppages in protest against the lid clamped on pay boosts by the price, wage, and dividend freeze decreed on June 28. . . . The currently severe six-month drought has brought a gloomy brownout, after a 50 percent reduction in electric power use was decreed. . . . The near-darkness helps sporadic anti-goverment rioting and terrorist activities. A leading pro-government radio transmitter was destroyed by bombs. . . . Train service has been severely curtailed and at times no newspapers are published. . . . Last year there were 500 strikes; the dismal record will surely be broken in 1968. . . .

"Of a population of around 2.6 million, the number of gainfully active Uruguayans is at the most 900,000. Pensioners number in excess of 300,000. Months ago the unemployed came to 250,000, or almost 28 percent of the work force, and the figure must now be higher. . . .

"The government closed at least three supermarkets and many stores for having upped prices. as well as such institutions as private hospitals that had violated the wage-price freeze decree. But despite rigid press censorship and Draconian anti-riot and anti-strike ukases, threatening punishment by military tribunals, calm fails to return."

* * *

Our sixth and final snapshot of a continuing crisis is from a *New York Times* dispatch of January 21, 1969:

"Striking Government employees rioted in downtown Montevideo today, smashing windows, setting up flaming barricades and sending tourists fleeing in panic. The police reported that one person had been killed and 32 injured.

"The demonstrators acted in groups of 30 to 50, in racing through a 30-block area, snarling traffic with their barricades, and attacking buses and automobiles. The police fought back with tear gas, high-pressure water hoses and clubs. . . .

"The striking civil servants were demanding payment of monthly salary bonuses of $24, which they say are two months overdue."

* * *

These six snapshots, taken at different intervals over a period of twelve years, involve considerable repetition: but the repetition is part of the point. The obvious reforms were never made.

Here are a few salient statistics to show what was happening between the snapshots:

In 1965 consumer prices increased 88 percent over those in the preceding year. In 1966 they increased 49 percent over 1965. In 1967 they increased 136 percent over 1966. By August, 1968 they had increased 61 percent over 1967.

The average annual commercial rate of interest was 36 percent in 1965. In 1966, 1967, and August 1968 it ranged between 32 and 50 percent.

The volume of money increased from 2,924 million pesos in 1961 to 10,509 in 1965, 13,458 in 1966, and 27,490 in 1967.

In 1961 there were 11 pesos to the American dollar. In 1965 there were 60; in 1966, there were 70; in early 1967 there were 86; at the end of 1967 there were 200, and after April 1968 there were 250.

Uruguay's warning to the United States, and to the world, is that governmental welfarism, with its ever-increasing army of pensioners and other beneficiaries, is fatally easy to launch and fatally easy to extend, but almost impossible to bring to a halt—and quite impossible politically to reverse, no matter how obvious and catastrophic its consequences become. It leads to runaway inflation, to state bankruptcy, to political disorder and disintegration, and finally to suppressive dictatorship. Yet no country ever seems to learn from the example of another.

31

Foreign Investment vs. Foreign Aid

At the beginning of Chapter III of his *History of England,* Thomas Babington Macaulay wrote:

"In every experimental science there is a tendency toward perfection. In every human being there is a wish to ameliorate his own condition. These two principles have often sufficed, even when counteracted by great public calamities and by bad institutions, to carry civilization rapidly forward. No ordinary misfortune, no ordinary misgovernment, will do so much to make a nation wretched as the constant effort of every man to better himself will do to make a nation prosperous. It has often been found that profuse expenditures, heavy taxation, absurd commercial restrictions, corrupt tribunals, disastrous wars, seditions, persecutions, conflagrations, inundations, have not been able to destroy capital so fast as the exertions of private citizens have been able to create it. It can easily be proved that, in our own land, the national wealth has, during at least six centuries, been almost uninterruptedly increasing. . . . This progress, having continued during many ages, became at length, about the middle of the eighteenth century, portentously rapid, and has proceeded, during the nineteenth, with accelerated velocity."

We too often forget this basic truth. Would-be humanitarians speak constantly today of "the vicious circle of poverty." Poverty, they tell us, produces malnutrition and disease, which produce apathy and idleness, which perpetuate poverty; and no progess is possible without help from outside. This theory is today propounded unceasingly, as if it were axiomatic. Yet the history of nations and individuals shows it to be false.

It is not only "the natural effort which every man is continually making to better his own condition" (as Adam Smith put it even before Macaulay) that we need to consider, but the constant effort of most families to give their children a "better start" than they enjoyed themselves. The poorest people under the most primitive conditions work first of all for food, then for clothing and shelter. Once they have

From the October 1970 issue of *The Freeman*.

provided a rudimentary shelter, more of their energies are released for increasing the quantity or improving the quality of their food and clothing and shelter. And for providing tools. Once they have acquired a few tools, part of their time and energies can be released for making more and better tools. And so, as Macaulay emphasized, economic progress can become accelerative.

One reason it took so many centuries before this acceleration actually began, is that as men increased their production of the means of subsistence, more of their children survived. This meant that their increased production was in fact mainly used to support an increasing population. Aggregate production, population, and consumption all increased; but per capita production and consumption barely increased at all. Not until the Industrial Revolution began in the late eighteenth century did the rate of production begin to increase by so much that, in spite of leading to an unprecedented increase in population, it led also to an increase in per capita production. In the Western world this increase has continued ever since.

So a country can, in fact, starting from the most primitive conditions, lift itself from poverty to abundance. If this were not so, the world could never have arrived at its present state of wealth. Every country started poor. As a matter of historic fact, most nations raised themselves from "hopeless" poverty to at least a less wretched poverty purely by their own efforts.

Specialization and Trade

One of the ways by which each nation or region did this was by division of labor within its own territory and by the mutual exchange of services and products. Each man enormously increased his output by eventually specializing in a single activity—by becoming a farmer, butcher, baker, mason, bricklayer, or tailor—and exchanging his product with his neighbors. In time this process extended beyond national boundaries, enabling each nation to specialize more than before in the products or services that it was able to supply more plentifully or cheaply than others, and by exchange and trade to supply itself with goods and services from others more plentifully or cheaply than it could supply them for itself.

But this was only one way in which foreign trade accelerated the mutual enrichment of nations. In addition to being able to supply itself with more goods and cheaper goods as a result of foreign trade, each nation supplied itself with goods and services that it could otherwise not produce at all, and of which it would perhaps not even have known the existence.

Thus foreign trade *educates* each nation that participates in it, and not only through such obvious means as the exchange of books and periodicals. This educational effect is particularly important when hitherto backward countries open their doors to industrially advanced countries. One of the most dramatic examples of this occurred in 1854, when Commodore Perry at the head of a U. S. naval force "persuaded" the Japanese, after 250 years of isolation, to open their doors to trade and communication with the U.S. and the rest of the world. Part of Perry's success, significantly, was the result of bringing and showing the Japanese such things as a modern telescope, a model telegraph, and a model railway, which delighted and amazed them.

Some Steps May Be Skipped

Western reformers today, praising some hitherto backward country, in Africa or Asia, will explain how much smarter its natives are than we of the West because they have "leaped in a single decade from the seventeenth into the twentieth century." But the leap, while praiseworthy, is not so surprising when one recalls that what the natives mainly did was to import the machines, instruments, technology, and know-how that had been developed during those three centuries by the scientists and technicians of the West. The backward countries were able to bypass home coal furnaces, gaslight, the street car, and even, in most cases, the railroad, and to import Western automobiles, Western knowledge of road-building, Western airplanes and airliners, telephones, central oil heaters, electric light, radio and television, refrigerators and air conditioning, electric heaters, stoves, dishwashers and clothes washers, machine tools, factories, plants, and Western technicians, and then to send some of their youth to Western colleges and universities to become technicians, engineers, and scientists. The backward countries imported, in brief, their "great leap forward."

In fact, not merely the recently backward countries of Asia and Africa, but every great industrialized Western nation, not excluding the United States, owes a very great part—indeed, the major part—of its present technological knowledge and productivity to discoveries, inventions, and improvements imported from other nations. Notwithstanding the elegant elucidations by the classical economists, very few of us today appreciate all that the world and each nation owes to foreign trade, not only in services and products, but even more in knowledge, ideas, and ideals.

International Investment

Historically, international trade gradually led to international investment. Among independent nations, international investment developed inevitably when the exporters of one nation, in order to increase their sales, sold on short-term credit, and later on longer-term credit, to the importers of another. It developed also because capital was scarcer in the less developed nation, and interest rates were higher. It developed on a larger scale when men emigrated from one country to another, starting businesses in the new country, taking their capital as well as their skills with them.

In fact, what is now known as "portfolio" investment—the purchase by the nationals of one country of the stocks or bonds of the companies of another—has usually been less important quantitatively than this "direct" investment. In 1967 U. S. private investments abroad were estimated to total $93 billion, of which $12 billion were short-term assets and claims, and $81 billion long-term. Of American long-term private investments abroad, $22 billion were portfolio investments and $59 billion direct investments.

The export of private capital for private investment has on the whole been extremely profitable for the capital-exporting countries. In every one of the twenty years from 1945 to 1964 inclusive, for example, the income from old direct foreign investments by U. S. companies exceeded the outflow of new direct investments. In that twenty-year period new outflows of direct investments totaled $22.8 billion, but income from old direct investments came to $37.1 billion, plus $4.6 billion from royalties and fees, leaving an excess inflow of $18.9 billion. In fact, with the exception of 1928, 1929, and 1931, U. S. income from direct foreign investments exceeded new capital outlays in every year since 1919.[1]

Our direct foreign investments also greatly stimulated our merchandise exports. The U. S. Department of Commerce found that in 1964, for example, $6.3 billion, or 25 percent of our total exports in that year, went to affiliates of American companies overseas.

It is one of the ironies of our time, however, that the U. S. Government decided to put the entire blame for the recent "balance-of-payments deficit" on American investments abroad; and beginning in mid-1963, started to penalize and restrict such investment.

The advantages of international investment to the capital-importing country should be even more obvious. In any backward country there are almost unlimited potential ventures, or "investment opportunities," that are not undertaken chiefly because the capital to start them does not exist. It is the domestic lack of capital that makes it so difficult for the "underdeveloped" country to climb out of its wretched condition. Outside capital can enormously accelerate its rate of improvement.

Investment from abroad, like domestic investment, can be of two kinds: the first is in the form of fixed interest-bearing loans, the second in the form of direct equity investment in which the foreign investor takes both the risks and the profits. The politicians of the capital-importing country usually prefer the first. They see their nationals, say, making 15 or 30 percent annual gross profit on a venture, paying off the foreign lender at a rate of only 6 percent, and keeping the difference as net profit. If the foreign investor makes a similar assessment of the situation, however, he naturally prefers to make the direct equity investment himself.

But the foreigner's preference in this regard does not necessarily mean that the capital-importing country is injured. It is to its own advantage if its government puts no vexatious restrictions on the form or conditions of the private foreign investment. For if the foreign investor imports, in addition to his capital, his own (usually) superior management, experience, and technical know-how his enterprise may be more likely to succeed. He cannot help but give employment to labor in the capital-importing country, even if he is allowed to bring in labor freely from his own. Self-interest and wage-rate differentials will probably soon lead him to displace most of whatever common or even skilled labor he originally brings in from his own country with the labor of the host country. He will usually supply the capital-importing country itself with some article or amenity it did not have before. He will raise the average marginal productivity of labor in the country in which he has built his plant or made his investment, and his enterprise will tend to raise wages there. And if his investment proves particularly profitable, he will probably keep reinvesting most of his profits in it as long as the market seems to justify the reinvestment.

There is still another benefit to the capital-importing country from private foreign investment. The foreign investors will naturally seek out first the most profiitable investment opportunities. If they choose wisely, these will also be the investments that produce the greatest surplus of market value over costs and are therefore economically most productive. When the originally most productive investment opportunities have been exploited to a point where the comparative rate of return begins to diminish, the foreign investors will look for the next most productive investment opportunities, originally passed over. And so on. Private foreign investment will therefore tend to promote the most rapid rate of economic improvements.

Foreigners Are Suspect

It is unfortunate, however, that just as the government of the private-capital-exporting country today tends to regard its capital exports with alarm as a threat to its "balance of payments," the government of the private-capital-importing country today tends to regard its capital imports at least with suspicion if not with even greater alarm. Doesn't the private capital-exporting country make a profit on this capital? And if so, mustn't this profit necessarily be at the expense of the capital-importing country? Mustn't the latter country somehow be giving away its patrimony? It seems impossible for the anticapitalist mentality (which prevails among the politicians of the world, particularly in the underdeveloped countries) to recognize that both sides normally benefit from any voluntary economic transaction, whether a purchase-sale or a loan-investment, domestic or international.

Chief among the many fears of the politicians of the capital-importing country is that foreign investors "take the money out of the country." To the extent that this is true, it is true also of domestic investment. If a homeowner in Philadelphia gets a mortgage from an investor in New York, he may point out that his interest and amortization payments are going out of Philadelphia and even out of Pennsylvania. But he can do this with a straight face only by forgetting that he originally borrowed the money from the New York lender either because he could not raise it at all in his home city or because he got better terms than he could get in his home city. If the New Yorker makes an equity investment in Pennsylvania, he may take out all the net profits; but he probably employs Pennsylvania labor to build his factory and operate it. And he probably pays out $85 to $90 annually for labor, supplies, rent, etc., mainly in Pennsylvania, for every $10 he takes back to New York. (In 1969, American manufacturing corporations showed a net profit after taxes of only 5.4 percent on total value of sales.) "They take the money out of the country" is an objection against foreign investors resulting even more from xenophobia than from anticapitalism.

Fear of Foreign Control

Another objection to foreign investment by politicians of the capital-importing country is that the foreign investors may "dominate" the borrowing country's economy. The implication (made in 1965 by the de Gaulle government of France, for example) is that American-owned companies might come to have too much to say about the economic decisions of the government of the countries in which they are located. The real danger, however, is the other way round. The foreign-owned company puts itself at the mercy of the government of the host country. Its capital in the form of buildings, equipment, drilled wells and refineries, developed mines, and even bank deposits, may be trapped. In the last twenty-five years, particularly in Latin America and the Middle East, as American oil companies and others have found to their sorrow, the dangers of discriminatory labor legislation, onerous taxation, harassment, or even expropriation, are very real.

Yet the anticapitalistic, xenophobic, and other prejudices against private foreign investment have been so widespread, in both the countries that would gain from importing capital and the countries that would profit from exporting it, that the governments in both sets of countries have imposed taxes, laws and regulations, red tape, and other obstacles to discourage it.

At the same time, paradoxically, there has grown up in the last quarter-century powerful political pressures in both sets of countries in favor of the richer countries *giving capital away* to the poorer in the form of government-to-government "aid."

The Marshall Plan

This present curious giveaway mania (it can only be called that on the part of the countries making the grants) got started as the result of an historical accident. During World War II, the United States had been pouring supplies—munitions, industrial equipment, foodstuffs—into the countries of its allies and co-belligerents. These were all nominally "loans." American Lend-Lease to Great Britain, for example, came to some $30 billion and to Soviet Russia to $11 billion.

But when the war ended, Americans were informed not only that the Lend-Lease recipients could not repay and had no intention of repaying, but that the countries receiving these loans in wartime had become dependent upon them and were still in desperate straits, and that further credits were necessary to stave off disaster.

This was the origin of the Marshall Plan.

On June 5, 1947, General George C. Marshall, then American Secretary of State, made at Harvard the world's most expensive commencement address, in which he said: "The truth of the matter is that Europe's requirements, for the next three or four years, of foreign food and other essential products—principally from America—are so much greater than her present ability to pay that she must have substantial additional help, or face economic, social, and political deterioration of a very grave character."

Whereupon Congress authorized the spending in the following three-and-a-half years of some $12 billion in aid.

This aid was widely credited with restoring economic health to "free" Europe and halting the march of communism in the recipient countries. It is true that Europe did finally recover from the ravages of World War II—as it had recovered from the ravages of World War I. And it is true that, apart from Yugoslavia, the countries not occupied by Soviet Russia did not go communist. But whether the Marshall Plan accelerated or retarded this recovery, or substantially affected the extent of communist penetration in Europe, can never be proved. What can be said is that the plight of Europe in 1947 was at least as much the result of misguided European governmental economic policies as of physical devastation caused by the war. Europe's recovery was far slower than it could have been, with or without the Marshall Plan.

This was dramatically demonstrated in West Germany in 1948 when the actions between June 20 and July 8 of Economic Minister Ludwig Erhard in simultaneously halting inflation, introducing a thoroughgoing currency reform, and removing the strangling network of price controls, brought the German "miracle" of recovery.

As Dr. Erhard himself described his action: "We decided upon and re-introduced the old rules of a free economy, the rules of *laissez faire*. We abolished practically all controls over allocation, prices and wages, and replaced them with a price mechanism controlled predominantly by money."

The result was that German industrial production in the second half of 1948 rose from 45 percent to nearly 75 percent of the 1936 level, while steel production doubled that year.

It is sometimes claimed that it was Germany's share of Marshall aid that brought on the recovery. But nothing similar occurred in Great Britain, for example, which received more than twice as much Marshall aid. The German per capita gross national product, measured in constant prices, increased 64 percent between 1950 and 1958, whereas the per capita increase in Great Britain, similarly measured, rose only 15 percent.

Once American politicians got the idea that the American taxpayer owed other countries a living, it followed logically that his duty could not be limited to just a few. Surely that duty was to see that poverty was abolished everywhere in the world. And so in his inaugural address of January 20, 1949, President Truman called for "a bold new program" to make "the benefits of our scientific advances and industrial progress available for the improvement and growth of underdeveloped areas.... This program can greatly increase the industrial activity in other nations and can raise substantially their standards of living."

Because it was so labeled in the Truman address, this program became known as "Point Four." Under it the "emergency" foreign aid of the Marshall Plan, which was originally to run for three or four years at most, was universalized, and has now been running for more than twenty years. So far as its advocates and built-in bureaucracy are concerned, it is to last until foreign poverty has been abolished from the face of the earth, or until the per capita "gap" between incomes in the backward countries and the advanced countries has been closed—even if that takes forever.

The cost of the program already is appalling. Total disbursements to foreign nations, in the fiscal years 1946 through 1970, came to $131 billion. The total net interest paid on what the U. S. borrowed to give away these funds amounted in the same period to $68 billion, bringing the grand total through the 25-year period to $199 billion.[2]

This money went altogether to some 130 nations. Even in the fiscal year 1970, the aid program was still operating in 99 nations and five territories of the world, with 51,000 persons on the payroll, including U. S. and foreign personnel. Congressman Otto E. Passman, chairman of the Foreign Operations Subcommittee on Appropriations, declared on July 1, 1969: "Of the three-and-a-half billion people of the world, all but 36 million have received aid from the U. S."

Domestic Repercussions

Even the colossal totals just cited do not measure the total loss that the foreign giveaway program has imposed on the American economy. Foreign aid has had the most serious economic side-effects. It has led to grave distortions in our economy. It has undermined our currency, and contributed toward driving us off the gold standard. It has accelerated our inflation. It was sufficient in itself to account for the total of our Federal deficits in the 1946–70 period. The $199 billion foreign aid total exceeds by $116 billion even the $83 billion increase in our gross national debt during the same years. Foreign aid has also been sufficient in itself to account for all our balance-of-payments deficits (which our government's policies blame on private foreign investment).

The advocates of foreign aid may choose to argue that though our chronic Federal budget deficits in the last 25 years *could* be imputed to foreign aid, we could alternatively impute those deficits to other expenditures, and assume that the foreign aid was paid for entirely by raising additional taxes. But such an assumption would hardly improve the case for foreign aid. It would mean that taxes during this quarter-century averaged at least $5 billion higher each year than they would have otherwise. It would be difficult to exaggerate the setbacks to personal working incentives, to new ventures, to profits, to capital investment, to employment, to wages, to living standards, that an annual burden of $5 billion in additional taxation can cause.

If, finally, we make the "neutral" assumption that our $131 or $199 billion in foreign aid (whichever way we choose to calculate the sum) was financed in exact proportion to our actual deficit and tax totals in the 25-year period, we merely make it responsible for part of both sets of evils.

In sum, the foreign aid program has immensely set back our own potential capital development. It ought to be obvious that a foreign giveaway program can raise the standards of living of the so-called "underdeveloped areas" of the world only by lowering our own living standards compared with what they could otherwise be. If our taxpayers are forced to contribute millions of dollars for hydroelectric plants in Africa or Asia, they obviously have that much less for productive investment in the U. S. If they contribute $10 million dollars for a housing project in Uruguay, they have just that much less for their own housing, or any other cost equivalent, at home. Even our own socialist and statist do-gooders would be shaken if it occurred to them to consider how much might have been done with that $131 or $199 billion of foreign aid to mitigate pollution at home, build subsidized housing, and relieve "the plight of our cities." Free enterprisers, of course, will lament the foreign giveaway on the far more realistic calculation of how enormously the production, and the wealth and welfare of every class of our population, could have been increased by $131 to $199 billion in more private investment in new and better tools and cost-reducing equipment, and in higher living standards, and in more and better homes, hospitals, schools, and universities.

The Political Arguments

What have been the economic or political compensations to the United States for the staggering cost of its foreign aid program? Most of them have been illusory.

When our successive Presidents and foreign aid officials make inspirational speeches in favor of foreign aid, they dwell chiefly on its alleged humanitarian virtues, on the need for American generosity and compassion, on our duty to relieve the suffering and share the burdens of all mankind. But when they are trying to get the necessary appropriations out of Congress, they recognize the advisability of additional arguments. So they appeal to the American taxpayer's material self-interest. It will redound to his benefit, they argue, in three ways: (1) It will increase our foreign trade, and consequently the profits from it. (2) It will keep the underdeveloped countries from going communist.

(3) It will turn the recipients of our grants into our eternally grateful friends.

The answers to these arguments are clear:

1. Particular exporters may profit on net balance from the foreign aid program, but they necessarily do so at the expense of the American taxpayer. It makes little difference in the end whether we give other countries the dollars to pay for our goods, or whether we directly give them the goods. We cannot grow rich by giving our goods or our dollars away. We can only grow poorer. (I would be ashamed of stating this truism if our foreign aid advocates did not so systematically ignore it.)

2. There is no convincing evidence that our foreign aid played any role whatever in reversing, halting, or even slowing down any drift toward communism. Our aid to Cuba in the early years of the program, and even our special favoritism toward it in assigning sugar quotas and the like, did not prevent it from going communist in 1958. Our $769 million of aid to the United Arab Republic did not prevent it from coming under Russian domination. Our $460 million aid to Peru did not prevent it from seizing American private properties there. Neither our $7,715 million aid to India, nor our $3,637 million aid to Pakistan, prevented either country from moving deeper and deeper into socialism and despotic economic controls. Our aid, in fact, subsidized these very programs, or made them possible. And so its goes, country after country.

3. Instead of turning the recipients into grateful friends, there is ever-fresh evidence that our foreign aid program has had precisely the opposite effect. It is pre-eminently the American embassies and the offlcial American libraries that are mobbed and stoned, the American flag that is burned, the Yanks that are told to go home. And the head of almost every government that accepts American aid finds it necessary to denounce and insult the United States at regular intervals in order to prove to his own people that he is not subservient and no puppet.

So foreign aid hurts both the economic and political interest of the country that extends it.

The Unseen Costs of Utopian Programs

But all this might be overlooked, in a broad humanitarian view, if foreign aid accomplished its main ostensible purpose of raising the living levels of the countries that received it. Yet both reason and experience make it clear that in the long run it has precisely the opposite effect.

Of course, a country cannot give away $131 billion without its doing *something* abroad (though we must always keep in mind the reservation—instead of something *else* at home). If the money is spent on a public housing project, on a hydroelectric dam, on a steel mill (no matter how uneconomic or ill-advised), the housing or the dam or the mill is brought into existence. It is visible and undeniable. But to point to that is to point only to the visible gross gain while ignoring the costs and the offsets. In all sorts of ways—economic, political, spiritual—the aid in the long run hurts the recipient country. It becomes dependent on the aid. It loses self-respect and self-reliance. The poor country becomes a pauperized country, a beggar country.

There is a profound contrast between the effects of foreign aid and of voluntary private investment. Foreign aid goes from government to government. It is therefore almost inevitably statist and socialistic. A good part of it goes into providing more goods for immediate consumption, which may do nothing to increase the country's productive capacity. The rest goes into government projects, government five-year plans, government airlines, government hydroelectric plants and dams, or government steel mills, erected principally for prestige reasons, and for looking impressive in colored photographs, regardless of whether the projects are economically justified or self-supporting. As a result, real economic improvement is retarded.

The Insoluble Dilemma

From the very beginning, foreign aid has faced an insoluble dilemma. I called attention to this in a book published in 1947, *Will Dollars Save the World?,* when the Marshall Plan was proposed but not yet enacted:

> Intergovernmental loans [they have since become mainly gifts, which only intensifies the problem] are on the horns of this dilemma. If on the one hand they are made without conditions, the funds are squandered and dissipated and fail to accomplish their purpose. They may even be used for the precise opposite of the purpose that the lender had in mind. But if the

> lending government attempts to impose conditions, its attempt causes immediate resentment. It is called "dollar diplomacy"; or "American imperialism"; or "interfering in the internal affairs" of the borrowing nation. The resentment is quickly exploited by the Communists in that nation.

In the 23 years since the foreign-aid program was launched, the administrators have not only failed to find their way out of this dilemma; they have refused even to acknowledge its existence. They have zigzagged from one course to the other, and ended by following the worst course of all: they have insisted that the recipient governments adopt "growth policies"—which mean, in practice, government "planning," controls, inflation, ambitious nationalized projects—in brief, socialism.

If the foreign aid were not offered in the first place, the recipient government would find it advisable to try to attract foreign private investment. To do this it would have to abandon its socialistic and inflationary policies, its exchange controls, its laws against taking money out of the country. It would have to abandon harassment of private business, restrictive labor laws, and discriminatory taxation. It would have to give assurances against nationalization, expropriation, and seizure.

Specifically, if the nationals of a poor country wanted to borrow foreign capital for a private project, and had to pay a going rate of, say, 7 percent interest for the loan, their project would have to be one that promised to yield at least 7 percent before the foreign investors would be interested. If the government of the poor country, on the other hand, can get the money from a foreign government without having to pay interest at all, it need not trouble to ask itself whether the proposed project is likely to prove economic and self-liquidating or not. The essential market guide to comparative need and utility is then completely removed. What decides priorities is the grandiose dreams of the government planners, unembarrassed by bothersome calculations of comparative costs and usefulness.

The Conditions for Progress

Where foreign government aid is not freely offered, however, a poor country, to attract private foreign investment, must establish an actual record of respecting private property and maintaining free markets. Such a free-enterprise policy by itself, even if it did not at first attract a single dollar of foreign investment, would give enormous stimulus to the economy of the country that adopted it. It would first of all stop the flight of capital on the part of its own nationals and stimulate *domestic* investment. It is constantly forgotten that both domestic and foreign capital investment are encouraged (or discouraged) by the same means.

It is not true, to repeat, that the poor countries are necessarily caught in a "vicious circle of poverty," from which they cannot escape without massive handouts from abroad. It is not true that "the rich countries are getting richer while the poor countries are getting poorer." It is not true that the "gap" between the living standards of the poor countries and the rich countries is growing ever wider. Certainly that is not true in any proportionate sense. From 1945 to 1955, for example, the average rate of growth of Latin American countries in national income was 4.5 percent per annum, and in output per head 2.4 percent—both rates appreciably higher than the corresponding figure for the United States.[3]

Intervention Breeds Waste

The foreign aid ideology is merely the relief ideology, the guaranteed-income ideology, applied on an international scale. Its remedy, like the domestic relief remedy, is to "abolish poverty" by seizing from the rich to give to the poor. Both proposals systematically ignore the reasons for the poverty they seek to cure. Neither draws any distinction between the poverty caused by misfortune and the poverty brought on by shiftlessness and folly. The advocates of both proposals forget that their chief attention should be directed to restoring the incentives, self-reliance, and *production* of the poor family or the poor country, and that the principal means of doing this is through the free market.

In sum, government-to-government foreign aid promotes statism, centralized planning, socialism, dependence, pauperization, inefficiency, and waste. It prolongs the poverty it is designed to cure. Voluntary private investment in private enterprise, on the other hand, promotes capitalism, production, independence, and self-reliance. It is by attracting foreign private investment that the great industrial nations of the world were once helped. It is so that America itself was helped by British capital, in the nineteenth century, in building its railroads and exploiting its great national resources. It is so that the still "underdeveloped areas" of the world can most effectively be helped today to develop their own great potentialities and to raise the living standards of their masses.

---

1. See *The United States Balance of Payments* (Washington: International Economic Policy Association, 1966), pp. 21 and 22.

2. Source: Foreign Operations Subcommittee on Appropriations, House of Representatives, July 1, 1970.

3. Cf."Some Observations on 'Gapology,'" by P. T. Bauer and John B. Wood in *Economic Age* (London), November-December 1969. Professor Bauer is one of the few academic economists who have seriously analyzed the fallacies of foreign aid. See also his Yale lecture on foreign aid published by The Institute of Economic Affairs (London), 1966, and his article on "Development Economics" in *Roads to Freedom: Essays in Honour of Friedrich A. von Hayek* (London: Routledge & Kegan Paul, 1969). I may also refer the reader to my own book, *Will Dollars Save the World?* (Appleton, 1947), to my pamphlet, *Illusions of Point Four* (Irvington-on-Hudson, N.Y.: Foundation for Economic Education, 1950), and to my chapter on "The Fallacy of Foreign Aid" in my *Man vs. the Welfare State* (Arlington House, 1969).

OF TRUTH AND VIGILANCE

32

Why Anticapitalism Grows

A correspondent who describes himself as "a 26-year old college graduate who strongly supports a system of free enterprise," recently wrote me to say that he is "continuously confronted with questions that are most difficult to answer." He appended a list of 10 of them, and asked for my comments.

I offer my answer here. To save space, I have not repeated his questions, assuming they can be clearly guessed from my replies.

* * *

Dear Mr.________________:

The number of faults that have been alleged against capitalism are without limit. Few of the allegations have any merit, and when they do the reason will usually be found to lie deep in the weaknesses of human nature itself. Practically all the criticisms tacitly assume that the imputed faults could be easily cured by some form of socialism or communism, or some ad hoc government intervention that would, in fact, usually make the complained-about condition much worse.

With these preliminary remarks, let me try to give brief answers to your ten questions.

1. Capitalism does depend upon the consumption of natural resources, and some of these could eventually be depleted. But this must happen under any conceivable system of production when the population becomes large enough in comparison with the resources. But capitalism has proved resourceful in finding substitutes or for providing for renewal of resources (as in scientific forestry, for example).

2. There will probably always be some efforts toward collusion and private price-fixing. Encouraging private competition is probably the best cure for this, plus appropriate laws against clearly harmful collusion.

3. Not only do utilities often give lower rates to those who use more power; nearly all sellers give lower rates to bigger consumers

From the July 1983 issue of *The Freeman*.

because they can be supplied with the commodity at a lower cost. If big automobile companies consume more steel than a small hardware manufacturer, this does not necessarily mean that big companies are using steel more wastefully.

4. Private capitalism means free competition. Capitalism has far less tendency toward concentration than does socialism, and well-drafted laws can prevent coercive methods of concentration. True, big companies can sometimes lower prices excessively to try to drive out small competitors, but they can do this only at a serious cost to themselves. It is more often alleged than proved that such practices happen with any real frequency.

5. True, adequate capital is sometimes difficult for small producers to obtain. But it can be obtained by savings, by previous profits from small-scale operations, or by borrowing. The borrowing can be done if a would-be enterpriser can convince a friend or a bank that he is likely to be successful. For a government agency to supply capital to individuals to become producers would only breed favoritism, corruption, and scandalous waste.

6. True, officers or directors of big corporations can sometimes try to use the capital and management of their company primarily to enrich themselves. Such practices can be minimized by watchful stockholders and appropriate corporate laws and law enforcement. But companies in which the practices occur extensively will soon go broke and be eliminated in favor of honestly-run companies.

7. There is no scientific way of measuring "productivity" in a service-oriented economy. Most of the current attempts to measure it rest on fallacious assumptions. The total value of output is essentially subjective, and not objectively measurable. The official GNP calculations are largely fraudulent. A short crop of wheat or corn, for example, usually sells for a greater money total than an above-normal crop. If we could produce everything anybody wanted, the national income would be zero. As nothing would be scarce, nothing could command a price.

8. It is sometimes difficult to know what injuries on the job are the fault of the individual worker and what of bad working conditions supplied by the employer. In any case, almost everywhere today the employer is legally obliged to pay "workmen's compensation" for most such injuries.

9. True, capitalism does not supply "equal" housing or "equal"

pay. If we tried to do the latter, regardless of the difference between the skills and industry of different workers or even whether a man did not work at all, we would soon destroy all incentives to production and have little creation of housing or anything else.

10. There is nothing "inhuman" about capitalism itself. It does not legally compel compassion or charity on the part of private individuals, but neither does it stand in the way. Socialism assumes that nobody will help the poor unless the politicians compel him to. Capitalism is, in fact, the most "human" of all systems. It provides the greatest amount of material goods and services, both necessities and luxuries, for humanity. It supports the greatest number of human beings, and provides the more successful with a surplus above their needs capable of being turned over to the less successful, voluntarily or through taxation. Without capitalism, in short, most of its present detractors wouldn't be around today to denounce it.

A Flawed System

One final word. Your questions tacitly assume that capitalism is the system we are now in fact living under. We are not. We are living under what the late Ludwig von Mises called "sabotaged" capitalism. We are living under a network of government interventions that discourage or prevent capitalism from doing its work. With the "progressive" income tax, the government expropriates a crucial part of precisely the funds that would otherwise be invested in increased production and employment. By imposing minimum wage laws, encouraging coercive unionism, and subsidizing unemployment, government has brought about excessive American wage rates in many lines—making our automobile and steel industries at the moment unable to compete against foreign imports, and bringing about chronic unemployment. Having done this, the politicians denounce our domestic manufacturers for no longer being "competitive," "aggressive," or "innovative," and propose still more interventions to force them to be so. Thus anticapitalism begets still more anticapitalism.

33

Can We Keep Free Enterprise?

Nine-tenths of what is written today on economic questions is either an implied or explicit attack on capitalism. The attacks are occasionally answered. But none of the answers, even when they are heard, are ever accepted as conclusive. The attacks keep coming, keep multiplying. You cannot pick up your daily newspaper without encountering half a dozen. The sporadic answers are lost in the torrent of accusation. The charges or implied charges outnumber the rebuttals ten to one.

What is wrong? Does capitalism, after all, have an indefensible case? Have its champions been not only hopelessly outnumbered but hopelessly outargued? We can hardly think so if we recall only a few of the great minds that have undertaken the task of defense, directly or indirectly, in the past—Hume, Adam Smith, Ricardo, Malthus, Bastiat, Senior, Böhm-Bawerk, John Bates Clark; or of the fine minds that have undertaken it in our day—Ludwig von Mises, F. A. Hayek, Milton Friedman, Murray Rothbard, Hans Sennholz, Israel Kirzner, David McCord Wright, and so many others.

What, then, is wrong? I venture to suggest that no defense of capitalism, no matter how brilliant or thorough, will ever be generally accepted as definitive. The attacks on capitalism stem from at least five main impulses or propensities, all of which will probably be with us permanently, because they seem to be inherent in our nature. They are: (1) genuine compassion at the sight of individual misfortune; (2) impatience for a cure; (3) envy; (4) the propensity to think only of the intended or immediate results of any proposed government intervention and to overlook the secondary or long-term results; and (5) the propensity to compare any actual state of affairs, and its inevitable defects, with some hypothetical ideal.

These five drives or tendencies blend and overlap. Let us look at them in order, beginning with compassion. Most of us, at the sight of extreme poverty, are moved to want to do something to relieve it—or to get others to relieve it. And we are so impatient to see the poverty relieved as soon as possible that, no matter how forbidding the dimen-

From the June 1973 issue of *The Freeman*.

sions of the problem, we are tempted to think it will yield to some simple, direct, and easy solution.

The Role of Envy

Let us look now at the role of envy. Few of us are completely free from it. It seems to be part of man's nature never to be satisfied as long as he sees other people better off than himself. Few of us, moreover, are willing to accept the better fortune of others as the result of greater effort or gifts on their part. We are more likely to attribute it at best to "luck" if not to "the system." In any case, the pressure to pull down the rich seems stronger and more persistent in most democracies than the prompting to raise the poor.

Envy reveals itself daily in political speeches and in our laws. It plays a definite role in the popularity of the graduated income tax, which is firmly established in nearly every country today, though it violates every canon of equity. As J. R. McCulloch put it in the 1830s: "The moment you abandon the cardinal principle of exacting from all individuals the *same proportion of their income* or *of their property*, you are at sea without rudder or compass, and there is no amount of injustice or folly you may not commit."

McCulloch's prediction has been borne out by events. Historically almost every time there has been a revision of income-tax rates the progression has become steeper. When the graduated income tax was first adopted in the United States in 1913, the top rate was 7 percent. Some thirty years later it had risen to 91 percent. In Great Britain the top rate went from 8¼ to 97½ percent in a similar period. It has been repeatedly demonstrated that these confiscatory rates yield negligible revenues. The reduction of real income that they cause is certainly greater than the revenue they yield. In brief, they have hurt even the taxpayers in the lower brackets.

Yet envy has played a crucial role in keeping the progressive income tax. The bulk of the taxpayers accept far higher rates of taxation than they would if the rates were uniform; for the taxpayers in each tax bracket console themselves with the thought that their wealthier neighbors must be paying a far higher rate. Thus though about two-thirds (65.5 percent) of the income tax is paid (1969) by those with adjusted gross incomes of $20,000 or less, there is an almost universal illusion that the real burden of the tax is falling on the very rich.

But perhaps the greatest reason why governments again and again abandon the principles of free enterprise is mere short-sightedness. They attempt to cure some supposed economic evil directly by some simple measure, and completely fail to foresee or even to ask what the secondary or long-term consequences of that measure will be.

Tampering with Money

From time immemorial, whenever governments have felt that their country was insufficiently wealthy, or when trade was stagnant or unemployment rife, the theory has arisen that the fundamental trouble was a "shortage of money." After the invention of the printing press, when a government could stamp a slip of paper with any denomination or issue notes without limit, any imaginable increase in the money supply became possible.

What was not understood was that any stimulative effect was temporary, and purchased at excessive cost. If the boom was obtained by an overexpansion of bank credit, it was bound to be followed by a recession or crisis when the new credit was paid off. If the boom was obtained by printing more government fiat money, it temporarily made some people richer only at the cost of making other people (in real terms) poorer.

When the supply of money is increased, the purchasing power of each unit must correspondingly fall. In the long run, nothing whatever is gained by increasing the issuance of paper money. Prices of goods tend, other things equal, to rise proportionately with the increase in money supply. If the stock of money is doubled, it can in the long run purchase no more goods and services than the smaller stock of money would have done.

And yet the government of nearly every country in the world today is busily increasing the issuance of paper money, partly if not entirely because of its belief that it is "relieving the shortage of money" and "promoting faster economic growth." This illusion is intensified by the habit of counting the currency unit as if its purchasing power were constant. In 1971 there was a great outburst of hurrahs because the GNP (gross national product) had at last surpassed the magic figure of a trillion dollars. (It reached $1,046 billion.) It was forgotten that if the putative GNP of 1971 had been stated in terms of dollars at their purchasing power in 1958 this 1971 GNP would have come to only

$740 billion, and if stated in terms of the dollar's purchasing power in 1939 would have come to only $320 billion.

Yet monetary expansion is everywhere today—in every country and in the International Monetary Fund with its SDR's—the offlcial policy. Its inevitable effect is rising prices. But rising prices are not popular. Therefore governments forbid prices to rise.

And this price control has the enormous political advantage of deflecting attention away from the government's own responsibility for creating inflation, and by implication puts the blame for rising prices on the greed of producers and sellers.

Price Control

The record of price controls goes as far back as human history. They were imposed by the Pharaohs of ancient Egypt. They were decreed by Hammurabi, king of Babylon, in the eighteenth century B. C. They were tried in ancient Athens.

In 301 A. D., the Roman Emperor Diocletian issued his famous edict fixing prices for nearly 800 different items, and punishing violation with death. Out of fear, nothing was offered for sale and the scarcity grew far worse. After a dozen years and many executions, the law was repealed.

In Britain, Henry III tried to regulate the price of wheat and bread in 1202. Antwerp enacted price-fixing in 1585, a measure which some historians believe brought about its downfall. Price-fixing laws enforced by the guillotine were also imposed during the French Revolution, though the soaring prices were caused by the revolutionary government's own policy in issuing enormous amounts of paper currency.

Yet from all this dismal history the governments of today have learned absolutely nothing. They continue to overissue paper money to stimulate employment and "economic growth"; and then they vainly try to prevent the inevitable soaring prices with ukases ordering everybody to hold prices down.

Harmful Intervention

But though price-fixing laws are always futile, this does not mean that they are harmless. They can do immensely more economic damage than the inflation itself. They are harmful in proportion as the legal price-ceilings are below what unhampered market prices would be, in proportion to the length of time the price controls remain in effect, and in proportion to the strictness with which they are enforced.

For if the legal price for any commodity, whether it is bread or shoes, is held by edict substantially below what the free market price would be, the low fixed price must overencourage the demand for it, discourage its production, and bring about a shortage. The profit margin in making or selling it will be too small as compared with the profit margin in producing or selling something else.

In addition to causing scarcities of some commodities, and bottlenecks in output, price-control must eventually distort and unbalance the whole structure of production. For not only the absolute quantities, but the proportions in which the tens of thousands of different goods and services are produced, are determined in a free market by the relative supply and demand, the relative money prices, and the relative costs of production of commodities A, B, C, and N. Market prices have work to do. They are signals to both producers and consumers. They tell where the shortages and surpluses are. They tell which commodities are going to be more profitable to produce and which less. To remove or destroy or forbid these signals must discoordinate and discourage production.

Selective Controls—No Stopping Place

General price controls are comparatively rare. Governments more often prefer to put a ceiling on one particular price. A favorite scapegoat since World War I has been the rent of apartments and houses.

Rent controls, once imposed, are sometimes continued for a generation or more. When they are imposed, as they nearly always are, in a period of inflation, the frozen rents year by year become less and less realistic. The long-term effect is that the landlords have neither the incentive nor the funds to keep the rental apartments or houses in decent repair, let alone to improve them. Losses often force owners to abandon their properties entirely. Private builders, fearing the same fate, hesitate to erect new rental housing. Slums proliferate, a shortage of housing develops, and the majority of tenants, in whose supposed interest the rent control was imposed in the first place, become worse off than ever.

Perhaps the oldest and most widespread form of price control in the world is control of interest rates. In ancient China, India, and Rome, and nearly everywhere throughout the Middle Ages, all interest was called "usury," and prohibited altogether. This made economic progress all but impossible. Later, the taking of interest was permitted, but fixed legal ceilings were imposed. These held back economic progress but did not, like total prohibition, prevent it entirely.

Yet political hostility to higher-than-customary interest rates never ceases. Today, bureaucrats combat such "exorbitant" rates more often by denunciation than by edict. The favorite government method today for keeping interest rates down is to have the monetary managers flood the market with new loanable funds. This may succeed for a time, but the long-run effect of overissuance of money and credit is to arouse fears among businessmen that inflation and rising prices will continue. So lenders, to protect themselves against an expected fall in the future purchasing power of their dollars, add a "price premium." This makes the gross market rate of interest higher than ever.

The propensity of politicians to learn nothing about economics is illustrated once again in the laws governing foreign trade. The classical economists of the eighteenth century utterly demolished the arguments for protectionism. They showed that the long-run effect of protective tariffs and other barriers could only be to make production more inefficient, to make consumers pay more and to slow down economic progress. Yet protectionism is nearly as rampant as it was before 1776, when *The Wealth of Nations* was published.

The Conquest of Poverty

In the same way, all the popular political measures to reduce or relieve poverty are more distinguished for their age than for their effectiveness.

The major effect of minimum wage laws is to create unemployment, chiefly among the unskilled workers that the law is designed to help. We cannot make a worker's services worth a given amount by making it illegal for anyone to offer him less. We merely deprive him of the right to earn the amount that his abilities and opportunities would permit him to earn, while we deprive the community of the moderate services he is capable of rendering. We drive him on relief.

And by driving more people on relief by minimum-wage laws on the one hand, while on the other hand enticing more and more people to get on relief by constantly increasing the amounts we offer them, we encourage the runaway growth of relief rolls. Now, as a way to "cure" this growth, reformers come forward to propose a guaranteed annual income or a "negative income tax." The distinguishing feature of these handouts is that they are to be given automatically, without a means test, and regardless of whether or not the recipient chooses to work. The result could only be enormously to increase the number of idle, and correspondingly to increase the tax burden on those who work. We can always have as much unemployment as we are willing to pay for.

At bottom, almost every government "antipoverty" measure in history has consisted of seizing part of the earnings or savings of Peter to support Paul. Its inevitable long-run result is to undermine the incentives of both Peter and Paul to work or to save.

What is overlooked in all these government interventions is the miracle of the market—the amazing way in which free enterprise maximizes the incentives to production, to work, innovation, efficiency, saving, and investment, and graduates both its penalties and rewards with such accuracy as to tend to bring about the production of the tens of thousands of wanted goods and services in the proportions in which they are most demanded by consumers. Only free private enterprise, in fact, can solve what economists call this problem of economic calculation.

The Problem of Calculation

Socialism is incapable of solving the problem. The bureaucratic managers of nationalized industries may be conscientious, God-fearing men; but as they have no fear of suffering personal losses through error or inefficiency, and no hope of gaining personal profits through cost-cutting or daring innovation, they are bound, at best, to become safe routineers, and to tolerate a torpid inefficiency.

But this is the smallest part of the problem. For a complete socialism would be without the guide of the market, without the guide of money prices or of costs in terms of money. The bureaucratic managers of the socialist economy would not know which items they were producing at a social profit and which at a social loss. Nor would they know how much to try to produce of each item or service, or how to make sure that the production of tens of thousands of different commodities was synchronized or coordinated. They could, of course (as they sometimes have), assign arbitrary prices to raw materials and to the various finished items. But they would still not know how much or whether the bookkeeping profits or losses shown reflected real profits or losses. In short, they would be unable to solve the problem of economic calculation. They would be working in the dark.

The directors of a socialist economy would have to fix wages arbitrarily, and if these did not draw the right number of competent workers into making the various things the directors wanted produced, and in the quantities they wanted them to be produced, they would have to use coercion, forcibly assign workers to particular jobs, and direct the economy from the center, in a military kind of organization. This militarization and regimentation of work is what, in fact, Cuba, Russia, and Red China have resorted to.

Rising Expectations

We come finally to the fifth reason that I offered at the beginning for the chronic hostility to free enterprise. This is the tendency to compare any actual state of affairs, and its inevitable defects, with some hypothetical ideal; to compare whatever is with some imagined paradise that might be. In spite of the prodigious and accelerative advances that a dominantly private enterprise economy has made in the last two centuries, and even in the last two decades, these advances can always be shown to have fallen short of some imaginable state of affairs that might be even better.

It may be true, for example, that money wages in the United States have increased fivefold, and even after all allowance has been made for rising living costs, that real wages have more than doubled in the last generation. But why haven't they tripled? It may be true that the number of the "poor," by the Federal bureaucrats' yardstick, fell from 20 percent of the population in 1962 (when the estimate was first made) to 13 percent in 1970. But why should there be any poor people left at all? It may be true that the employees of the corporations already get seven-eighths of the entire sum available for distribution between them and the stockholders. But why don't the workers get the whole of it? And so on and so on.

The very success of the system has encouraged constantly rising expectations and demands—expectations and demands that keep racing ahead of what even the best imaginable system could achieve.

The struggle to secure what we now know as capitalism—i.e, unhampered markets and private ownership of the means of production—was long and arduous. It has proved an inestimable boon to mankind. Yet if this system is to be saved from willful destruction, the task of the incredibly few who seem to understand how and why it works is endless. They cannot afford to rest their case on any defense of free enterprise, or any exposure of socialism or other false remedies, that they or their predecessors may have made in the past. There have been some magnificent defenses over the past two centuries, from Adam Smith to Bastiat, and from Böhm-Bawerk to Mises and Hayek. But they are not enough. Every day capitalism faces some new accusation, or one that parades as new.

Eternal Vigilance—Truth Needs Repeating

In brief, ignorance, shortsightedness, envy, impatience, good intentions, and a utopian idealism combine to engender an endless barrage of charges against "the system"—which means against free enterprise. And so the return fire, if free enterprise is to be preserved, must also be endless.

I find I have only been applying to one particular field an exhortation that Goethe once applied to all fields of knowledge. In 1828 he wrote in a letter to Eckermann: "The truth must be repeated again and again, because error is constantly being preached round about us. And not only by isolated individuals, but by the majority. In the newspapers and encyclopedias, in the schools and universities, everywhere error is dominant, securely and comfortably ensconced in public opinion which is on its side."

Yet above all in political and economic thought today, the need to keep repeating the truth has assumed an unprecedented urgency. What is under constant and mounting attack is capitalism—which means free enterprise—which means economic freedom—which means, in fact, the whole of human freedom. For as Alexander Hamilton warned: "Power over a man's subsistence is power over his will."

What is threatened, in fact, is no less than our present civilization itself; for it is capitalism that has made possible the enormous advances not only in providing the necessities and amenities of life, but in science, technology, and knowledge of all kinds, upon which that civilization rests.

All those who understand this have the duty to explain and defend the system. And to do so, if necessary, over and over again.

This duty does not fall exclusively on professional economists. It falls on each of us who realizes the untold benefits of free enterprise and the present threat of its destruction to expound his convictions within the sphere of his own influence, as well as to support others who are expounding like convictions. Each of us is as free to practice what he preaches as to preach what he practices. The opportunity is as great as the challenge.

34

The Task Confronting Libertarians

From time to time over the last thirty years, after I have talked or written about some new restriction on human liberty in the economic field, some new attack on private enterprise, I have been asked in person or received a letter asking, "What can I do" —to fight the inflationist or socialist trend? Other writers or lecturers, I find, are often asked the same question.

The answer is seldom an easy one. For it depends on the circumstances and ability of the questioner—who may be a businessman, a housewife, a student, informed or not, intelligent or not, articulate or not. And the answer must vary with these presumed circumstances.

The general answer is easier than the particular answer. So here I want to write about the task now confronting all libertarians considered collectively.

This task has become tremendous, and seems to grow greater every day. A few nations that have already gone completely communist, like Soviet Russia and its satellites, try, as a result of sad experience, to draw back a little from complete centralization, and experiment with one or two quasi-capitalistic techniques; but the world's prevailing drift—in more than 100 out of the 107 nations and mini-nations that are now members of the International Monetary Fund—is in the direction of increasing socialism and controls.

The task of the tiny minority that is trying to combat this socialistic drift seems nearly hopeless. The war must be fought on a thousand fronts, and the true libertarians are grossly outnumbered on practically all these fronts.

In a thousand fields the welfarists, statists, socialists, and interventionists are daily driving for more restrictions on individual liberty; and the libertarians must combat them. But few of us individually have the time, energy, and special knowledge to be able to do this in more than a handful of subjects.

One of our gravest problems is that we find ourselves confronting

---

From the March 1968 issue of *The Freeman*.

armies of bureaucrats already controlling us, and with a vested interest in keeping and expanding the controls they were hired to enforce.

A Growing Bureaucracy

Let me try to give you some idea of the size and extent of this bureaucracy in the United States. The Hoover Commission found in 1954 that the Federal government embraced no fewer than 2,133 different functioning agencies, bureaus, departments, and divisions. I do not know what the exact count would be today, but the known multiplicity of Great Society agencies would justify our rounding out that figure at least to 2,200.

We do know that the full-time permanent employees in the Federal government now number about 2,615,000.

And we know, to take a few specific examples, that of these bureaucrats 15,400 administer the programs of the Department of Housing and Urban Development, 100,000 the programs (including Social Security) of the Department of Health, Education, and Welfare, and 154,000 the programs of the Veterans Administration.

If we want to look at the rate at which parts of this bureaucracy have been growing, let us take the Department of Agriculture. In 1929, before the U. S. government started crop controls and price supports on an extensive scale, there were 24,000 employees in that Department. Today, counting part-time workers, there are 120,000, five times as many, all of them with a vital economic interest—to wit, their own jobs—in proving that the particular controls they were hired to formulate and enforce should be continued and expanded.

What chance does the individual businessman, the occasional disinterested professor of economics, or columnist or editorial writer, have in arguing against the policies and actions of this 120,000-man army, even if he has had time to learn the detailed facts of a particular issue? His criticisms are either ignored or drowned out in the organized counterstatements.

This is only one example out of scores. A few of us may suspect that there is much unjustified or foolish expenditure in the U. S. Social Security program, or that the unfunded liabilities already undertaken by the program (one authoritative estimate of these exceeds a *trillion* dollars) may prove to be unpayable without a gross monetary inflation. A handful of us may suspect that the whole principle of compulsory government old-age and survivor's insurance is open to question. But there are nearly 100,000 full-time permanent employees in the Department of Health, Education, and Welfare to dismiss all such fears as foolish, and to insist that we are still not doing nearly enough for our older citizens, our sick, and our widows and orphans.

And then there are the millions of those who are already on the receiving end of these payments, who have come to consider them as an earned right, who of course find them inadequate, and who are outraged at the slightest suggestion of a critical reexamination of the subject. The political pressure for constant extension and increase of these benefits is almost irresistible.

And even if there weren't whole armies of government economists, statisticians, and administrators to answer him, the lone disinterested critic, who hopes to have his criticism heard and respected by other disinterested and thoughtful people, finds himself compelled to keep up with appalling mountains of detail.

Too Many Cases to Follow

The National Labor Relations Board, for example, hands down hundreds of decisions every year in passing on "unfair" labor practices. In the fiscal year 1967 it passed on 803 cases "contested as to the law and the facts." Most of these decisions are strongly biased in favor of the labor unions; many of them pervert the intention of the Taft-Hartley Act that they ostensibly enforce; and in some of them the board arrogates to itself powers that go far beyond those granted by the act. The texts of many of these decisions are very long in their statement of facts or alleged facts and of the Board's conclusions. Yet how is the individual economist or editor to keep abreast of the decisions and to comment informedly and intelligently on those that involve an important principle or public interest?

Or take again such major agencies as the Federal Trade Commission, the Securities and Exchange Commission, the Internal Revenue Service, the Interstate Commerce Commission, the Food and Drug Administration, the Federal Communications Commission. All these agencies engage in quasi-legislative, quasi-judicial, and administrative functions. They issue rules and regulations, grant licenses, issue cease-and-desist orders, award damages, and compel individuals and corporations to do or refrain from many things. They often combine the functions of legislators, prosecutors, judges, juries, and bureaucrats. Their decisions are not always based solely on existing law and yet when they inflict injury on corporations or individuals, or deprive them of constitutional liberties and legal rights, appeal to the courts is often difficult, costly, or impossible.

Once again, how can the individual economist, student of government, journalist, or anyone interested in defending or preserving liberty, hope to keep abreast of this Niagara of decisions, regulations, and administrative laws? He may sometimes consider himself lucky to be able to master in many months the facts concerning even one of these decisions.

Professor Sylvester Petro of New York University has written a full book on the Kohler strike and another full book on the Kingsport strike, and the public lessons to be learned from them. Professor Martin Anderson has specialized in the follies of urban renewal programs. But how many are there among us libertarians who are willing to—or have the time to—do this specialized and microscopic but indispensa zble research?

In July 1967, the Federal Communications Commission handed down an extremely harmful decision ordering the American Telephone & Telegraph Company to lower its interstate rates—which were already 20 percent lower than in 1940, though the general price level since that time had gone up 163 percent. In order to write a single editorial or column on this (and to feel confident he had his facts straight), a conscientious journalist had to study, among other material, the text of the decision. That decision consisted of 114 single-spaced typewritten pages.

. . . and Schemes for Reform

We libertarians have our work cut out for us.

In order to indicate further the dimensions of this work, it is not merely the organized bureaucracy that the libertarian has to answer; it is the individual private zealots. A day never passes without some ardent reformer or group of reformers suggesting some new government intervention, some new statist scheme to fill some alleged "need" or relieve some alleged distress. They accompany their scheme by citing statistics that supposedly prove the need or the distress that they want the taxpayers to relieve. So it comes about that the reputed "experts" on relief, unemployment insurance, social security, medicare, subsidized housing, foreign aid, and the like are precisely the people who are advocating more relief, unemployment insurance, social security, medicare, subsidized housing, foreign aid, and all the rest.

Let us come to some of the lessons we must draw from all this.

Specialists for the Defense

We libertarians cannot content ourselves merely with repeating pious generalities about liberty, free enterprise, and limited government. To assert and repeat these general principles is absolutely necessary, of course, either as prologue or conclusion. But if we hope to be individually or collectively effective, we must individually master a great deal of detailed knowledge, and make ourselves specialists in one or two lines, so that we can show how our libertarian principles apply in special fields, and so that we can convincingly dispute the proponents of statist schemes for public housing, farm subsidies, increased relief, bigger social security benefits, bigger medicare, guaranteed incomes, bigger government spending, bigger taxation, especially more progressive income taxation, higher tariffs or import quotas, restrictions or penalties on foreign investment and foreign travel, price controls, wage controls, rent controls, interest rate controls, more laws for so-called "consumer protection," and still tighter regulations and restrictions on business everywhere.

This means, among other things, that libertarians must form and maintain organizations not only to promote their broad principles—as does, for example, The Foundation for Economic Education—but to promote these principles in special fields. I am thinking, for example, of such excellent existing specialized organizations as the Citizens Foreign Aid Committee, the Economists' National Committee on Monetary Policy, the Tax Foundation, and so on. I am happy to report the very recent formation of Americans for Effective Law Enforcement.

We need not fear that too many of these specialized organizations will be formed. The real danger is the opposite. The private libertarian organizations in the United States are probably outnumbered ten to one by communist, socialist, statist, and other left-wing organizations that have shown themselves to be only too effective.

And I am sorry to report that almost none of the old-line business associations that I am acquainted with are as effective as they could be.

It is not merely that they have been timorous or silent where they should have spoken out, or even that they have unwisely compromised. Recently, for fear of being called ultraconservative or reactionary, they have been supporting measures harmful to the very interests they were formed to protect. Several of them, for example, have come out in favor of the Administration's proposed tax increase on corporations, because they were afraid to say that the Administration ought rather to slash its profligate welfare spending.

The sad fact is that today most of the heads of big businesses in America have become so confused or intimidated that, so far from carrying the argument to the enemy, they fail to defend themselves adequately even when attacked. The pharmaceutical industry, subjected since 1962 to a discriminatory law that applies questionable and dangerous legal principles that the government has not yet dared to apply in other fields, has been too timid to state its own case effectively. And the automobile makers, attacked by a single zealot for turning out cars "Unsafe at Any Speed," handled the matter with an incredible combination of neglect and ineptitude that brought down on their heads legislation harmful not only to the industry but to the driving public.

The Timidity of Businessmen

It is impossible to tell today where the growing anti-business sentiment in Washington, plus the itch for more government control, is going to strike next. Only within the last few months Congress, with little debate, allowed itself to be stampeded into a dubious extension of Federal power over intrastate meat sales. When this article appears, or shortly after, Congress may have passed a Federal "truth-in-lending" law, forcing lenders to calculate and state interest rates the way Federal bureaucrats want them calculated and stated. There is also pending an Administration bill in which government bureaucrats are to prescribe "standards" telling just how surgical devices like bone pins and catheters and even artificial eyes are to be made.

And a few weeks ago the President suddenly announced that he was prohibiting American business from making further direct investments in Europe, that he was restricting them elsewhere, and that he would ask Congress to pass some law restricting Americans from traveling to Europe. Instead of raising a storm of protest against these unprecedented invasions of our liberties, most newspapers and businessmen deplored their "necessity" and hoped they would be only "temporary."

The very existence of the business timidity that allows these things to happen is evidence that government controls and power are already excessive.

Why are the heads of big business in America so timid? That is a long story, but I will suggest a few reasons: (1) They may be entirely or largely dependent on government war contracts. (2) They never know when or on what grounds they will be held guilty of violating the antitrust laws. (3) They never know when or on what grounds the National Labor Relations Board will hold them guilty of unfair labor practices. (4) They never know when their personal income tax returns will be hostilely examined, and they are certainly not confident that such an examination, and its findings, will be entirely independent of whether they have been personally friendly or hostile to the Administration in power.

It will be noticed that the governmental actions or laws of which businessmen stand in fear are actions or laws that leave a great deal to administrative discretion. Discretionary administrative law should be reduced to a minimum; it breeds bribery and corruption, and is always potentially blackmail or blackjack law.

A Confusion of Interests

Libertarians are learning to their sorrow that big businessmen cannot necessarily be relied upon to be their allies in the battle against extension of governmental encroachments. The reasons are many. Sometimes businessmen will advocate tariffs, import quotas, subsidies, and restrictions of competition, because they think, rightly or wrongly, that these government interventions will be in their personal interest, or in the interest of their companies, and are not concerned whether or not they may be at the expense of the general public. More often, I think, businessmen advocate these interventions because they are honestly confused, because they just don't realize what the actual consequences will be of the particular measures they propose, or perceive the cumulative debilitating effects of growing restrictions of human liberty.

Perhaps most often of all, however, businessmen today acquiesce in new government controls out of sheer timidity.

A generation ago, in his pessimistic book, *Capitalism, Socialism and Democracy* (1942), the late Joseph A. Schumpeter maintained the thesis that "in the capitalistic system there is a tendency toward self-destruction." And as one evidence of this he cited the "cowardice" of big businessmen when facing direct attack:

> They talk and plead—or hire people to do it for them; they snatch at every chance of compromise; they are ever ready to give in; they never put up a fight under the flag of their own ideals and interests—in this country there was no real resistance anywhere against the imposition of crushing financial burdens during the last decade or against labor legislation incompatible with the effective management of industry.

So much for the formidable problems facing dedicated libertarians. They find it extremely difficult to defend particular firms and industries from harassment or persecution when those industries will not adequately or competently defend themselves. Yet division of labor is both possible and desirable in the defense of liberty as it is in other fields. And many of us, who have neither the time nor the specialized knowledge to analyze particular industries or special complex problems, can be nonetheless effective in the libertarian cause by hammering incessantly on some single principle or point until it is driven home.

Basic Principles upon Which Libertarians May Rely

Is there any single principle or point on which libertarians could most effectively concentrate? Let us look, and we may end by finding several.

One simple truth that could be endlessly reiterated, and effectively applied to nine-tenths of the statist proposals now being put forward or enacted in such profusion, is that the government has nothing to give to anybody that it doesn't first take from somebody else. In other words, all its relief and subsidy schemes are merely ways of robbing Peter to support Paul.

Thus, it can be pointed out that the modern welfare state is merely a complicated arrangement by which nobody pays for the education of his own children, but everybody pays for the education of everybody else's children; by which nobody pays his own medical bills, but everybody pays everybody else's medical bills; by which nobody provides for his own old-age security, but everybody pays for everybody else's old-age security; and so on. Bastiat, with uncanny clairvoyance, exposed the illusive character of all these welfare schemes more than a century ago in his aphorism: "The State is the great fiction by which everybody tries to live at the expense of everybody else."

Another way of showing what is wrong with all the state handout schemes is to keep pointing out that you can't get a quart out of a pint jug. Or, as the state giveaway programs must all be paid for out of taxation, with each new scheme proposed the libertarian can ask, "*Instead of what?*" Thus, if it is proposed to spend another $1 billion on getting a man to the moon or developing a supersonic commercial plane, it may be pointed out that this $1 billion, taken in taxation, will not then be able to meet a million personal needs or wants of the millions of taxpayers from whom it is to be taken.

Of course, some champions of ever-greater governmental power and spending recognize this very well, and like Professor J. K. Galbraith, for instance, they invent the theory that the taxpayers, left to themselves, spend the money they have earned very foolishly, on all sorts of trivialities and rubbish, and that only the bureaucrats, by first seizing it from them, will know how to spend it wisely.

Knowing the Consequences

Another very important principle to which the libertarian can constantly appeal is to ask the statists to consider the secondary and long-run consequences of their proposals as well as merely their intended direct and immediate consequences. The statists will sometimes admit quite freely, for example, that they have nothing to give to anybody that they must not first take from somebody else. They will admit that they must rob Peter to pay Paul. But their argument is that they are seizing only from rich Peter to support poor Paul. As President Johnson once put it quite frankly in a speech on January 15, 1964: "We are going to try to take all of the money that we think is unnecessarily being spent and take it from the 'haves' and give it to the 'have nots' that need it so much."

Those who have the habit of considering long-run consequences will recognize that all these programs for sharing-the-wealth and guaranteeing incomes must reduce incentives at both ends of the economic scale. They must reduce the incentives both of those who are capable of earning a high income, but find it taken away from them, and those who are capable of earning at least a moderate income, but find themselves supplied with the necessities of life without working.

This vital consideration of incentives is almost systematically overlooked in the proposals of agitators for more and bigger government welfare schemes. We should all rightly be concerned with the plight of the poor and unfortunate. But the hard two-part question that any plan for relieving poverty must answer is: How can we mitigate the penalties of failure and misfortune *without undermining the incentives to effort and success*? Most of our would-be reformers and humanitarians simply ignore the second half of this problem. And when those of us who advocate freedom of enterprise are compelled to reject one of these specious "antipoverty" schemes after another on the ground that it will undermine these incentives and in the long run produce more evil than good, we are accused by the demagogues and the thoughtless of being "negative" and stony-hearted obstructionists. But the libertarian must have the strength not to be intimidated by this.

Finally, the libertarian who wishes to hammer in a few general principles can repeatedly appeal to the enormous advantages of liberty as compared with coercion. But he, too, will have influence and perform his duty properly only if he has arrived at his principles through careful study and thought. "The common people of England," once wrote Adam Smith, "are very jealous of their liberty, but like the common people of most other countries have never rightly understood in what it consists." To arrive at the proper concept and definition of liberty is difficult, not easy. But this is a subject too big to be developed further here.

Legal and Political Aspects

So far, I have talked as if the libertarian's study, thought, and argument need be confined solely to the field of economics. But, of course, liberty cannot be enlarged or preserved unless its necessity is understood in many other fields—and most notably in law and in politics.

We have to ask, for example, whether liberty, economic progress, and political stability can be preserved if we continue to allow the people on relief—the people who are mainly or solely supported by the government and who live at the expense of the taxpayers—to exercise the franchise. The great liberals of the nineteenth and early twentieth centuries expressed the most serious misgivings on this point. John Stuart Mill, writing in his *Representative Government* in 1861, did not equivocate: "I regard it as required by first principles that the receipt of parish relief should be a preemptory disqualification for the franchise. He who cannot by his labor suffice for his own support has no claim to the privilege of helping himself to the money of others." And A. V. Dicey, the eminent British jurist, writing in 1914, also raised the question whether it is wise to allow the recipients of poor relief to retain the right to join in the election of a member of Parliament.

An Honest Currency and an End to Inflation

This brings me, finally, to one more single issue on which all those libertarians who lack the time or background for specialized study can effectively concentrate. This is in demanding that the government provide an honest currency, and that it stop inflating.

This issue has the inherent advantage that it can be made clear and simple because fundamentally it is clear and simple. All inflation is government-made. All inflation is the result of increasing the quantity of money and credit; and the cure is simply to halt the increase.

If libertarians lose on the inflation issue, they are threatened with the loss of every other issue.

If libertarians could win the inflation issue, they could come close to winning everything else. If they could succeed in halting the increase in the quantity of money, it would be because they could halt the chronic deficits that force this increase. If they could halt these chronic deficits, it would be because they had halted the rapid increase in welfare spending and all the socialistic schemes that are dependent on welfare spending. If they could halt the constant increase in spending, they could halt the constant increase in government power.

The devaluation of the British pound a few months ago, though it may shake the whole world currency system to its foundations, may as an offset have the longer effect of helping the libertarian cause. It exposes as never before the bankruptcy of the Welfare State. It exposes the fragility and complete undependability of the paper-gold international monetary system under which the world has been operating for the last twenty years. There is hardly one of the hundred or more currencies in the International Monetary Fund, with the exception of the dollar, that has not been devalued at least once since the I.M.F. opened its doors for business. There is not a single currency unit—and there is no exception to this statement—that does not buy less today than when the Fund started.

The dollar, to which practically every other currency is tied in the present system, is now in the gravest peril. If liberty is to be preserved, the world must eventually get back to a full gold standard system in which each major country's currency unit must be convertible into gold on demand, by anybody who holds it, without discrimination. I am aware that some technical defects can be pointed out in the gold standard, but it has one virtue that more than outweighs them all. It is not, like paper money, subject to the day-to-day whims of the politicians; it cannot be printed or otherwise manipulated by the politicians; it frees the individual holder from that form of swindling or expropriation by the politicians; it is an essential safeguard for the preservation, not only of the value of the currency unit itself, but of human liberty. Every libertarian should support it.

I have one last word. In whatever field he specializes, or on whatever principle or issue he elects to take his stand, the libertarian *must* take a stand. He cannot afford to do or say nothing. I have only to remind you of the eloquent call to battle on the final page of Ludwig von Mises's great book on *Socialism* written 35 years ago:

> Everyone carries a part of society on his shoulders; no one is relieved of his share of responsibility by others. And no one can find a safe way out for himself if society is sweeping toward destruction. Therefore everyone, in his own interests, must thrust himself vigorously into the intellectual battle. None can stand aside with unconcern; the interests of everyone hang on the result. Whether he chooses or not, every man is drawn into the real historical struggle, the decisive battle into which our epoch has plunged us.

35

The Literature of Freedom

The Free Man's Library is a descriptive and critical bibliography of works on the philosophy of individualism—"individualism" in a broad sense. The bibliography includes works which explain the workings and advantages of free trade, free enterprise, and free markets; which recognize the evils of excessive state power; and which champion the cause of individual freedom of worship, speech, and thought.

Such a compilation seemed to me to be increasingly urgent because so few writers and speakers on public questions today reveal any idea of the wealth, depth, and breadth of the literature of freedom. What threatens us today is not merely the outright totalitarian philosophies of fascism and communism, but the increasing drift of thought in the totalitarian direction. Many people today who complacently think of themselves as "middle-of the-roaders" have no conception of the extent to which they have already taken over statist, socialist, and collectivist assumptions—assumptions which, if logically followed out, must inevitably carry us further and further down the totalitarian road.

One of the crowning ironies of the present era is that it is precisely the people who flatteringly refer to themselves as "liberals" who have forgotten or repudiated the essence of the true liberal tradition. The typical butts of their ridicule are such writers as Adam Smith, Bastiat, Cobden ("the Manchester School"), and Herbert Spencer. Whatever errors any of these writers may have been guilty of individually, they were among the chief architects of true liberalism. Yet our modern "progressives" now refer to this whole philosophy contemptuously as *laissez faire*.

Many of today's are most eloquent in their arguments for liberty in fact preach philosophies that would destroy it. It seems to be typical of the books of our intelligentsia to praise one kind of liberty inces-

---

This essay, which appeared in the June 1956 issue of *The Freeman,* is taken from Henry Hazlitt's introduction to his book, *The Free Man's Library,* a descriptive listing of more than 540 outstanding contributions to the literature of freedom beginning with the early seventeenth century and carrying through to our own time. Most of the books listed in *The Free Man's Library* and still in print are available from the Foundation for Economic Education. Cf. the 1993 FEE Catalogue.

santly while disparaging or ridiculing another kind. The liberty that they so rightly praise is the liberty of thought and expression. But the liberty that they so foolishly denounce is economic liberty.

Unfortunately the authors who have fallen into this practice include some of the finest minds of our generation. (I think particularly of Bertrand Russell and the late Morris Cohen.) Such writers seem to me to be at least in part reflecting an occupational bias. Being writers and thinkers, they are acutely aware of the importance of liberty of writing and thinking. But they seem to attach scant value to economic liberty because they think of it not as applying to themselves but to businessmen. Such a judgment may be uncharitable; but it is certainly fair to say that they misprize economic liberty because, in spite of their brilliance in some directions, they lack the knowledge or understanding to recognize that when economic liberties are abridged or destroyed, all other liberties are abridged or destroyed with them. "Power over a man's subsistence," as Alexander Hamilton reminded us, "is power over his will." And if we wish a more modern authority, we can quote no less a one than Leon Trotsky, the colleague of Lenin, who in 1937, in a moment of candor, pointed out clearly that: "In a country where the sole employer is the State, opposition means death by slow starvation: The old principle: who does not work shall not eat, has been replaced by a new one: who does not obey shall not eat."

Liberty is a whole, and to deny economic liberty is finally to destroy all liberty. Socialism is irreconcilable with freedom. This is the lesson that most of our modern philosophers and litterateurs have yet to learn.

Historically, the liberals fought against governmental tyranny; against governmental abridgment of freedom of speech and action; against governmental restrictions on agriculture, manufacture, and trade; against constant detailed governmental regulation, interference, and harassment at a hundred points; against (to use the phrases of the Declaration of Independence) "a multitude of new offices" and "swarms of officers"; against concentration of governmental power, particularly in the person of one man; against government by whim and favoritism. Historic liberalism called, on the other hand, for the Rule of Law, and for equality before the law. The older conservatives opposed many or most of these liberal demands because they believed in existing governmental interferences and sweeping governmental powers; or because they wished to retain their own special privileges and prerogatives; or simply because they were temperamentally fearful of altering the status quo, whatever it happened to be.

Those who flatteringly call themselves "liberals" today, and to whom confused opponents allow or even assign the name, are for nearly everything that the old liberals opposed. Most self-styled present-day "liberals," particularly in America, are urging the constant extension of governmental power, of governmental intervention, of governmental "planning." They constantly press for a greater concentration of governmental power, whether in the central government at the expense of the States and localities or in the hands of a one-man executive at the expense of any check, limitation, or even investigation by a legislature. And they look with favor on an ever-growing bureaucracy and on the spread of bureaucratic discretion at the expense of a Rule of Law. Those who oppose this trend toward a new despotism, on the other hand, and plead for the preservation of the ancient freedoms of the individual, are today's conservatives. The intelligent conservative, in brief, is today the true defender of liberty.

This conclusion should not seem too paradoxical. It was always possible to reconcile intelligent conservatism with real liberalism. There is no conflict between wishing to conserve and hold the precious gains that have been achieved in the past, which is the aim of the true conservative, and wishing to carry those achievements even further, which is the aim of the true liberal.

INDEX

About The Foundation for Economic Education

The Foundation for Economic Education (FEE) is a "home" for the friends of freedom everywhere. Its spirit is uplifting, reassuring, contagious: FEE has inspired the creation of numerous similar organizations at home and abroad.

FEE is the oldest conservative research organization dedicated to the presentation of individual freedom and the private-property order. It was established in 1946 by Leonard E. Read, and guided by its adviser, the eminent Austrian economist, Ludwig von Mises. Both served FEE until their deaths in 1983 and 1973, respectively.

Throughout the years the mission of FEE has remained unchanged: to study the moral and intellectual foundation of a free society and share its knowledge with individuals everywhere. It avoids getting embroiled in heated political controversies raging in Washington, D.C. Located in Irvington-on-Hudson, New York, FEE has remained a purely educational organization.

Since 1956, FEE has published *The Freeman,* an award-winning monthly journal with a long and noble lineage. Under the profound editorship of Paul Poirot it rose to great heights, always fighting for the timeless principles of the free society.

The *Freeman Classics* series of books reflects these heights, consisting of topical collections of great essays and articles published throughout the years. The first three volumes in the series are: *The Morality of Capitalism, Private Property and Political Control,* and *Prices and Price Controls.*

—Hans F. Sennholz